C. L. R. JAMES

C. L. R. James
A Critical Introduction

Aldon Lynn Nielsen

UNIVERSITY PRESS OF MISSISSIPPI
Jackson

Copyright © 1997 by the University Press of Mississippi
All rights reserved
Manufactured in the United States of America

The paper in this book meets the guidelines for permanence and durability of the Committee on Production Guidelines for Book Longevity of the Council on Library Resources.

Library of Congress Cataloging-in-Publication Data
Nielsen, Aldon Lynn.
  C.L.R. James : a critical introduction / Aldon Lynn Nielsen.
   p. cm.
  Includes bibliographical references and index.
  ISBN: 978-1-61703-846-4
  1. James, C. L. R. (Cyril Lionel Robert), 1901– —Criticism and interpretation. 2. Politics and literature—Caribbean Area. 3. Caribbean Area—Intellectual life. 4. Caribbean Area—In literature. 5. Trinidad—In literature. 6. Blacks in literature. I. Title.
PR9272.9.J35Z79 1997
818—dc21   96-39332
                                                           CIP

British Library Cataloging-in-Publication data available
Designed by Amanda K. Lucas

for those who gathered
at 629
Hudson Street

CONTENTS

Acknowledgments	IX
Abbreviations	XI
Introduction: The Black Critic as Prisoner and Artist	XIII
CHAPTER ONE: SPHERES OF EXISTENCE: WHAT MAISIE KNEW	3
I. Discovering Literature in Trinidad	3
II. Minty Alley	17
III. Preface to Criticism	35
CHAPTER TWO: AT THE RENDEZVOUS OF VICTORY	51
I. The Philosophy of History and Necessity	51
II. Histories of Pan-African Revolt	61
III. World Revolution	87
CHAPTER THREE: THE FUTURE IN THE PRESENT	101
I. Notes on Dialectics	101
II. Dialectics and the Fate of Humanity	123
CHAPTER FOUR: THE STRUGGLE FOR HAPPINESS	143
I. Popular Arts and Modern Society	143
II. The Art and Practic Part	169
Works Cited	189
Index	195

ACKNOWLEDGMENTS

It was only after I had completed the draft of this study that I had an opportunity to meet and correspond with several individuals who had worked with C. L. R. James during his first extended stay in the United States, a remarkable band of people I had first heard about from James himself nearly two decades previously. I want to thank them here for their welcome, and for the future work they have made possible. Martin Glaberman invited me to his hospital bedside to talk about James, actually read my manuscript, and has continued to provide me with assistance in the months since he returned to work. (Judging from what I saw in the hospital, he had never left work.) Grace Lee Boggs has generously taken time to answer my questions and has provided me with copies of her later writings. She also put me in touch with Freddy Paine, and I particularly want to thank Freddy for meeting with me under trying circumstances and for providing me with a wealth of information, as well as a sampling from her fruit trees. The exceptional personal qualities of these activists, writers, and thinkers made it clear to me why James still spoke so fervently of their work together after so much time and controversy had passed between them. Each of them will recognize the significance of this book's dedication, to which I can only add here, in the words of a favorite song, "Oh, how I wish I could be in that number."

Seetha A-Srinivasan sought me out when she learned of my work on James's legacy, and it is because of her that this book exists. Few editors share her expansive vision, and I am grateful to her for her trust in me. I have been fortunate in my career to have worked with many fine publishing professionals. The staff of the University Press of Mississippi are among the most gracious and helpful I have yet encountered.

While there is already much contention among scholars examining the work and life of C. L. R. James, the field is rapidly gathering force from some of the fine studies that have appeared in recent years. I cannot here name every individual to whom I am indebted, but the following have all, in word or deed, often without knowing it, encouraged me by their example: Robert Hill, Sylvia Winter, Paul Buhle, Selwyn Cudjoe, Paget Henry, Scott McLemee, Kent Worcester, Gregory Rigsby, E. Ethelbert Miller, Anna

Grimshaw, and Grant Farred. This really began with Gregory Rigsby, in his course on Caribbean literature offered at Federal City College. As I expressed my admiration for a passage of *The Black Jacobins* in class one day, Professor Rigsby suggested that I go downstairs and tell it to James himself. Thus, as a fan of his writing style first and foremost, was I introduced to the man who, more than any other person, was responsible for the directions of my subsequent career.

A portion of the research and writing of this book was completed during the course of a summer seminar sponsored by the National Endowment for the Humanities, and I want to thank Sam Weber for allowing me to work with him and with the other members of the seminar. I also wish to thank Eric Sundquist, whose invitation to visit the University of California, Los Angeles, English Department made it possible for me to complete the writing of the manuscript almost on time. The library staff at UCLA have also been most accommodating, and Robert Hill has kindly taken moments from his numerous projects to answer my questions while I have been in Los Angeles. As always, I have deeply appreciated the assistance and patience of my colleagues at San Jose State University.

Anna Everett has once more agreed to debate with me, to read me, even to dance with me, and I remain happily indebted to her for her suggestions and insights.

An earlier version of the introduction appeared in *River City*, and I thank the editors of that journal for offering that preview.

ABBREVIATIONS

Abbreviated titles for published volumes of the writings of C. L. R. James are cited as follows:

AC	*American Civilization*
RV	*At the Rendezvous of Victory*
BB	*Beyond a Boundary*
BJ	*The Black Jacobins*
BL	*C. L. R. James's Eightieth Birthday Lectures*
NQ	*C. L. R. James on the "Negro Question"*
JR	*The C. L. R. James Reader*
RM	*C. L. R. James and Revolutionary Marxism*
C	*Cricket*
EC	*Every Cook Can Govern, and What Is Happening Every Day*
FR	*Facing Reality*
FP	*The Future in the Present*
NR	*A History of Negro Revolt* (also titled *A History of Pan-African Revolt*)
IS	*The Invading Socialist Society*
LO	*Letters on Organization*
LC	*The Life of Captain Cipriani*
MRC	*Mariners, Renegades and Castaways*
MA	*Minty Alley*
MP	*Modern Politics*
ND	*Notes on Dialectics*
NG	*Nkrumah and the Ghana Revolution*
PP	*Party Politics in the West Indies*
SD	*Special Delivery: The Letters of C. L. R. James to Constance Webb, 1939–1948*
SE	*Spheres of Existence*
SC	*State Capitalism and World Revolution*
QP	*Walter Rodney and the Question of Power*
WR	*World Revolution*

Uncollected writings are cited individually and referenced in the Works Cited.

A NOTE ON USAGE

Except when I am quoting other sources, I have generally followed James's own usage. So, for example, I generally refer to "San Domingo," as James does in *The Black Jacobins*. Similarly, though Toussaint Louverture dropped the apostrophe from the spelling of his name, I follow James in retaining the spelling of "L'Ouverture" throughout.

INTRODUCTION

The Black Critic as Prisoner and Artist

Here, then, is the untimely, timely end;—Life's last chapter well stitched into the middle! Nor book, nor author of the book, hath any sequel, though each hath its last lettering!— It is ambiguous still.

Herman Melville, *Pierre, or The Ambiguities*

France was a place where they were starving me
To death, because a black man had a brain.

Edwin Arlington Robinson, "Toussaint L'Ouverture"

My first lessons in the Socratic method as it was employed by C. L. R. James came in the first minutes of a history course at what was then Federal City College in Washington, D.C. Waving his open hand at the class in what I later recognized as a characteristic gesture, James asked, "Where did William Faulkner come from?" As the new kid in class I waited to see where a history professor was going with a question about the origins of American novelists. "Mississippi . . . ?" ventured a young woman to my right in the tentative voice of the American undergraduate who lives in perpetual fear of "getting it wrong." "And where did Richard Wright come from?" James asked, with more assertive hand waving. There was a very long pause, which, as the lone literature major, I felt compelled to fill. "Mississippi," I answered. James looked gleefully my way and practically shouted out his follow-up question: "And where did George Jackson come from?" I fell into the trap. "Mississippi . . . ?" I ventured as tentatively as had the young woman to my right. Pointing his very long and seemingly inescapable index finger directly at me, James thundered: "No! He came from jail!"

I learned a great deal that day, about rhetoric, about my own ego, about C. L. R. James, and, most important for me at that time, about American reading and writing practices as social acts, as frequently criminalized social acts. This took place shortly before the appearance of H. Bruce Franklin's landmark study of the literature of the American prison, and much that seems obvious to readers today was only then coming to the attention of American English departments as they began to brush the tenacious dust of the New Criticism from their eyes. Our subsequent rereadings of American literature have retrieved and circulated knowledges that were always in evidence, always in plain view within American writings, but that, like Poe's purloined letter, had gone unremarked by those intent upon enforcing certain other forms of knowledge about American character and history. It should no longer be possible to read the mythos of the free-ranging, self-constituting American innocent without reading, at the same time and within the same texts, the tropes of confinement and bondage that are the enabling and empowering ground of that innocence. We can no longer revisit the office of *The Scarlet Letter* without remarking, as Melvin B. Tolson does in his *Libretto for the Republic of Liberia,* Hawthorne's prophetic figure of the black flower of civilized society, the prison. We cannot read *Huckleberry Finn* without reading the Africanity of American culture, nor can we read Twain's text without attending to the multitudinous ways in which it figuratively imprisons blackness even as it narrates an emancipation. Nor should we read Alice Walker and refuse to read George Jackson.

The texts of C. L. R. James are haunted by prophetic figures of imprisonment that seem attendant upon his narratives of emancipation. His major reading of Melville's novels, *Mariners, Renegades and Castaways: The Story of Herman Melville and the World We Live In,* is inhabited by specters of imprisonment, is narrated in confinement, and is written to serve as an instrument for bringing James out of jail and into the American body politic. From the outset of James's historical studies he had an understanding of the relationship between the aspiration for freedom and the criminalization of the writing of that aspiration. He recalls in *Beyond a Boundary* how, when he was a lecturer at the Teachers' Training College, he began to study the history of the Caribbean islands and to speak to others his forming thoughts about independence. He remembers: "My hitherto vague ideas of freedom crystallized around a political conviction: we should be free to govern ourselves. I said nothing to anyone. After all, I was working for the government. When I told my brother some of my ideas his only comment was: 'You will end up in gaol' " (BB 115). James's brother clearly discerned the future in the present. Precisely because of his practices as a reader, writer, and speaker C. L. R. James was imprisoned on Ellis Island by the United States government, and it was there that he wrote his study of another who had been a habitué of island jails, Herman Melville. Subsequently, and for much the same reasons, James's former colleague Eric Williams placed him under house arrest in Trinidad. Williams also "arrested" James's texts themselves, impounding the press run of the book *Modern Politics,* a more than usually direct form of reader response criticism. When Williams eventually relented and allowed the books a reprieve, it was so that the whole lot could be taken out of Trinidad by a New York book dealer. Thus C. L. R. James, who had been deported from the United States largely on the evidence of his published books, saw his books deported for political reasons from Trinidad and circulated by a sort of literary commodities futures trader in the United States. James, an enormous appreciator of ironies, may have remembered in this moment Melville's prophecy in *Pierre:* "another and more comprehensive equivocalness, . . . shall absorb all minor ones in itself: and so make one pervading ambiguity the only possible explanation for all the ambiguous details" (224).

James's studies of history had brought him to confront many such ambiguities in the past. What more tragic ironies can be found in history than the response of revolutionary France to the revolt for freedom by the Africans of San Domingo? In *The Black Jacobins* James argues that "the logical development of the revolution in France had brought to the front of the stage masses who, when they said abolition, meant it in theory and in practice" (120). But the forces of counterrevolution arise to contain that staging by the masses of their own drama of emancipation. James views this history, as he so often does, in literary terms, describing the apotheosis of Toussaint L'Ouverture as the tragically fated consummation of a democratic narrative: "not Shakespeare himself could have found such a dramatic embodiment of fate as Toussaint struggled against, Bonaparte himself; nor could the furthest imagination have envisaged the entry of the chorus, of the ex-slaves themselves, as the arbiters of their own fate. Toussaint's certainty of this as the ultimate and irresistible resolution of the problem to which he refused to limit himself, that explains his mistakes and atones for them" (BJ 292). This is a typically Jamesian moment: the dramatic characters of Toussaint and Bonaparte, like Ishmael and Ahab, standing forth upon the ground formed and made ready by the masses. As James puts it in his frequently cited preface to *The Black Jacobins,* "Great men make history, but only such history as it is possible for them to make" (BJ x). As the storming of the Bastille and the freeing of its few prisoners marks the taking to the stage of the masses in the French Revolution, Bonaparte's imprisoning of Toussaint L'Ouverture marks the limit point of one revolution and the long march toward another.

The American poet Edwin Arlington Robinson, in one of his most powerful dramatic monologues, imagines Toussaint of Breda imagining his own end in the Fortress de-Joux in the Jura mountains. Toussaint, starving and cold, conceives himself carried "out of this cold and darkness / To a place where black and white are dark together" (232). Here is the tragic vision of Melville, who writes in *Pierre* that "one is apt to look black while writing Infernoes" (317). C. L. R. James spends a good portion of *Mariners, Renegades and Castaways* contemplating Melville's ambiguous creation. Pierre, too, is a writer imprisoned, but one whose example is difficult to gloss. Somehow in the death cells of Toussaint L'Ouverture and Pierre Glendinning, James glimpses both the tragic confinements of New World history and the possibilities of emancipation to be read out of that history. At *Pierre's* end, Isabel, whose ebony hair arbors the dead Glendinning, emits the ambiguous novel's ambiguous last words: " 'All's o'er, and ye know him not!' came gasping from the wall" (362). Melville writes this as if Isabel were of a piece with the prison that confines both her and Pierre, as if the ebon vines of her hair grew forth from the speaking wall of her prison. That this is somehow inscribed in both incestuous sin and colonial conquest is undeniable. That same Isabel who declares our lack of knowledge of Pierre uses a colonialist trope to describe her own mystification by the world around her. "The world seems all one unknown India to me" (189), she cautions Pierre.

In the dark fastness of the Fort de-Joux we find a premonitory echo of this scene. Isabel's earliest memories, as she relates them to Pierre, include a period of confinement in a gothic house of bedlam, a place where, as Isabel puts it, "Some harangued the wall" (121). How near this was to the place where Toussaint spoke into the damp and darkness to which Bonaparte had consigned him may be judged from a set of spectral facts inscribed in the margins of L'Ouverture's biography. There is, of course, no direct route from Pierre Glendinning's cell to that of Toussaint L'Ouverture, but, as Melville advises us, "Let the ambiguous procession of events reveal their own ambiguousness" (*Pierre* 181); for in the intertextual echoes gasping from the walls of these two prisons separated by an ocean we can make out dimly the very founding tropes of James's critical readings of the Americas.

Toussaint L'Ouverture's narrative links the old worlds and the new along the navigational paths of the triangle trade. His life marks Middle Passage and revolutionary rupture. Having staged, as James describes it, the logical outcome of the French Revolution in the West Indies, Toussaint's text is transported in two directions simultaneously. The narrative of the uprisings in San Domingo resounds in North America where it echoes in the rebellion of Nat Turner, in the national consciousness of a terrified citizenry who chose to constitute themselves as white, and in the novels of that Mississippi writer who so fascinated C. L. R. James, William Faulkner. The body and writings of Toussaint L'Ouverture were spirited away to the East, locked in a fortress where they became part of the very stuff of French might and repression. Following the death of Toussaint L'Ouverture his body was placed in a vault in the chapel of Saint Pierre, adjoining the fort. More than seventy years later the chapel was demolished and new fortifications were built. But nothing was wasted. The parsimonious French builders used the rubble of the old fortress and chapel to build the new. Scattered within the floors and walls of the Chateau du Joux are the mortal remains of Toussaint L'Ouverture, mixed with the bones of other prisoners, an eloquent if seldom remarked monument to imperial oppression and to the revolutionary instinct for freedom. Toussaint has become, as literally as is possible, the foundation of France's continuing disciplinary apparatus, testimony to the state's desire to swallow up all that which resists its technologies of repression. In the United States, those ebon vines of Isabel's hair that arbor the dying figure of Pierre are a restaging of the black flowers of American civilization, and the speaking walls of the American prison confine another founding trope of bondage and revolt, another dispersed Saint Pierre.

Such foundational images of confinement are so pervasive within the Western text because bondage has been the condition of possibility for the American mythos of independence and freedom. Toussaint's revolution propels the (misdated) fury of Faulkner's Sutpen, just as Sutpen's dread that past transgressions of race and the history of slavery will one day echo in incest, the same fear that haunts Pierre Glendinning, brings down the walls of Sutpen's estate. The destruction of Sutpen's hundred is the logical outcome of its foundation in bondage, just as the self-imposed house arrest of Sutpen's heir figures the self-inflicted confinement within the prison house of race of American culture. In the end, Toussaint and Pierre are, as it were, confined together, each speaking the ambiguous message of their twinned imprisonments to the walls of history.

The figure of confinement is the yet to be fully acknowledged grounding trope of American letters, the figure that both enables and constrains the American narrative of free movement. As powerfully as the "madwoman in the attic" allegorizes the still inadequately read text of women in British culture, the confined African figures the as yet unspeakable possibilities of a future American text. Over and over our readings bring us to these narratives mingling memories of Middle Passage with bondage and revolution. We see it in the figure of Nat Turner, feared by so many American whites as an evangelizing replication of Toussaint L'Ouverture, as Turner sits confined in his cell speaking his history and his heresy to the blank walls and to the transmogrifying ears of Thomas Gray. We see that same figure more deeply imprisoned as William Styron renarrates Thomas Gray's reconfigurings of Nat Turner's unheard and still unread confessions. We find it again in the figure of Harriet Jacobs in her loophole of retreat, as Jacobs narrates her remarkable flight to a safe house deeper within the place of her enslavement. We see it again in Richard Wright's "The Man Who Lived Underground," and we see it reconstructed in the glare of the *Invisible Man's* subterranean loophole of retreat. Ellison redoubles the figure of black power within confinement with the trope of the ancient black man hidden away at the heart of Liberty Paints with his fingers on the controls of the enabling mechanisms of a whiter than white America. We view this figure repeatedly in works of John Edgar Wideman such as *Fever* and *Philadelphia Fire,* in the poetry of Edwin Arlington Robinson, in the surreal ancestral visions of O'Neill's *Emperor Jones,* and in the mirror image of Nat Turner's confessional scene that opens Sherley Anne Williams's novel, *Dessa Rose.*

The "madwoman in the attic" restores to view the prominence of the triangle trade in British literature as she fires the house of English culture, relinking African, Caribbean, and British histories even as the narrative in which she appears elides that linking. Just so the founding figure of Toussaint L'Ouverture's immurement, woven intertextually through the fabric of American writing, has kept Africa and the Caribbean in plain view, in evidence, even through those long periods of our literary history when criticism sought to confine black presence by refusing to read it. As *Absalom, Absalom!*, *The Confessions of Nat Turner,* and *Incidents in the Life of a Slave Girl* amply document, the Caribbean was truly the place of seasoning for the enslavement of the American consciousness and for American fears. Burying the body of Toussaint of Breda in a vault in the Jura Mountains could not prevent the appearance of a Nat Turner. In Edwin Arlington Robinson's poem, Toussaint makes a promise:

> There is an island
> Where men remember me; and from an island
> Surprising freight of dreams and deeds may come,
> To make men think. (230)

Robinson's allegory inscribes the logical inevitability of Nat Turner. James astutely recognizes, in *The Black Jacobins,* that the masses in motion, the thinking preponderance of people alive with dreams, form the conditions of possibility for the history that individuals such as Toussaint L'Ouverture and Nat Turner will make. The confinement and execution of Nat Turner—like the posting of an African's skull at Blackhead Corners in Southampton, Virginia, following Turner's rebellion, like the posting of Babo's mute skull high above the scene at the end of Melville's "Benito Cereno"—serve far less to chastise black aspirations for freedom than as testaments to both the savagery and the incomprehension of white power, and to the inevitability of revolution. C. L. R. James describes the repeated unwillingness of white power to recognize the realities of revolutionary African thought and action. "Feuillants and Jacobins, whites and Mulattoes in San Domingo," James records in words eerily relevant to the United States now, "were still looking upon the slave revolt as a huge riot which would be put down in time, once the division between the slave-owners was closed" (BJ 117).

In that same book, James observes that "one does not need education or encouragement to cherish a dream of freedom" (BJ 18), an observation James found to be continually borne out by his experiences and research. Still, as he was imprisoned on Ellis Island, it was a writer he remembered, as he had earlier remembered and studied the memoranda and letters dictated to his scribes by Toussaint L'Ouverture. James sees surrounding him on Ellis Island the society of meanest mariners, renegades, and castaways with their dreams and aspirations as narrated by Herman Melville, in James's estimation the author of the greatest English language text since Shakespeare. These castaways, a diaspora in the making, are federated along the single keel of a desire for freedom, and need no deeper education in their desire. Again this is an understanding that power refuses to take hold of. James remarks that "to the administration . . . these are just a body of isolated individuals who are in reality seeking charity, or a home in the United States which is a better place to live in than their backward or poverty-stricken countries. Of all the blunders I encountered on Ellis Island this is undoubtedly the most colossal" (MRC 159). But what particularly interests James as he writes the intertwined stories of Herman Melville, the world we live in, and James's own captivity narrative, is the revolutionary capacities of the written word. It is the possibility of the reiteration of the narratives of Toussaint L'Ouverture and Nat Turner that terrifies racist power, and it is the potential of the readable word to disrupt hegemonic ideology that most engages James. An understanding of this fact is fundamental to an understanding of this man who once said of himself that "Thackeray, not Marx, bears the heaviest responsibility for me" (BB 47). In his preface to *Beyond a Boundary* James makes clear the revolutionary role of a writerly rearticulation of colonial languages. "To establish his own identity," writes James, "Caliban, after three centuries, must himself pioneer into regions Caesar never knew" (BB xxi). It was as a writer and a speaker that C. L. R. James made his revolution, and it was as a black revolutionary writer and speaker that he was imprisoned.

C. L. R. James's literary judgments are sometimes difficult to accommodate to our contemporary modes of reading and critique. While we may appreciate the humor, few of us would now agree with him that "today Whitman's revolutionary attitude towards sex is a damp squib" (JR 205), nor would many of us agree with James that "no one except scholars and people specially interested in literature need read any of [Melville's] earlier books. They are not worth it" (MRC 77). It is often hard to remember that this same reader who felt that Muriel Rukeyser typified modern man's tendency to run away from the deeper emotions (JR 132), who could not "believe that the incessant soul-searching and wailing and misery that distinguishes so much of modern literature expresses any future" (JR 227), also pioneered the study of popular culture in film and soap operas, and was a fervent champion of such diverse writers as George Lamming, Wilson Harris, and Ntozake Shange. But James as a critic was an ever-evolving intellect who never lost his curiosity about the new. There was an obvious excitement in his voice as he and I discussed authors and exchanged books after school, James loaning me his heavily annotated personal copies of the then hard to acquire novels of Wilson Harris, and I bringing him a steady stream of the most avant-garde of contemporary American poetry. What remained consistent throughout James's work was his calling to read and repeat the revolutionary possibilities of languages.

It was purely by chance that James, at the age of fifteen, took as the subject of his English composition examination "The Novel as an

Instrument of Reform" (BB 19). (And when was the last time any American professor of freshman composition dared try that as an exam topic?) The essay so excited the schoolmasters that they reprinted it in the school magazine. This and another of James's first juvenile publications, an essay on an historic cricket match, set the pattern for his life's work. But while James was rewarded for this early effort he was always aware of the patterns of criminalization of writing that marked the progress of European power; he knew that the rewriting of radical inquiry leads to confrontation with the discursive powers that be. James learned in his studies that the French colonist Hilliard d'Auberteuil had written in 1784 of the minds of enslaved Africans that "no species of men has more intelligence," only to see his book banned by a hegemonic authority that reserved unto itself the power to set the disciplinary boundaries of the human intellect (BJ 18). It was as a writer, as a reiterator of discomfiting thoughts, that C. L. R. James came to be confined. It was his published books that the United States Department of Justice entered into evidence against him in the course of his deportation hearings. "This is my chief offense," James notes, "that I have written books of the kind I have written" (MRC 166). The Department of Justice brings all its power to bear upon this writer just as the outraged publishers of Pierre Glendinning's book descend upon him with all the weight of the law when they discover that he has composed a "blasphemous rhapsody" (*Pierre* 356). It is James's writing and reading, in the reading of the American judiciary, that mark him as profoundly un-American. James writes towards the end of *Mariners:* "It now appears that such work, serious work and some of it pioneer work, on some of the burning problems of the day, have [sic] unfitted me to become a citizen of the United States. This can mean only one thing: that the Department of Justice now assumes the right to say what a citizen or would-be citizen should study" (MRC 165). Similarly, it was because James published his disagreements with the political direction of the postindependence government of Trinidad that Dr. Eric Williams, whose own early writing owed so much to James, first confined James and then confined his books.

But James is equally insistent upon the ultimate futility of such attempts to surveil and discipline radical writings. As an epigraph to *Mariners, Renegades and Castaways* James reproduces Melville's aphorism from "The Encantadas": "Those whom books will hurt will not be proof against events. Events, not books, should be forbid" (qtd. in MRC 10). James learned, however, that the reiterative powers of the word may be proof against censure and derision. He knew Toussaint L'Ouverture collected a library and that among his books was a copy of the Abbé Raynal's *Philosophical and Political History of the Establishments and Commerce of the Europeans in the Two Indies*, a treatise that contemplates the inevitability of slave revolution. "It was a book famous in its time," James recalls, "and it came into the hands of the slave most fitted to make use of it, Toussaint L'Ouverture" (BJ 24–25). The circuit of this revolutionary intellectual correspondence was completed in later years when James learned that generations of South Africans with their minds set on freedom had read a library copy of the book in which he had recorded these facts. *The Black Jacobins*, published in 1938, before the accession to power of the Afrikaners' National Party, had somehow escaped the notice of the censorious Boers. James had also seen the circulation of his writings play a role during the freedom struggles in his own Trinidad. A colonial government commentator referred "to the writings of C. L. R. James as helping to stir up the people," and James was often told by West Indian students that "when the upheavals did take place these books were high on the list of those few that helped them to make the mental and moral transition which the new circumstances required" (BB 121). A yet more ironic completion of this circuit occurred during the years that C. L. R. James spent teaching at Federal City College. The college developed an innovative program providing inmates at Lorton Reformatory, the Washington, D.C., prison located in Virginia, with the opportunity to complete a degree program while completing their sentences. James was an important figure in this program and taught a number of inmate/students while he was at the school. There was even a tentative, but never funded, plan to endow a chair for C. L. R. James as part of the prison degree program; it might have been a fitting honor for the previously imprisoned scholar.

It is not enough today that we read more fully the yet to be explicated figures of confinement that articulate traditions of American literature. We must also, as James did in the last years of his life, return to our students and to our communities the sense of the powers of the word, the revolutionary capacities of reading and writing. We live in a time when books don't have to be impounded; they are either simply not published in the first place or they are rendered virtually unreadable by marginalizing literary-commercial modes and practices. As C. L. R. James came to the end of *Mariners, Renegades and Castaways* and prepared for his deportation from the United States as an undesirable, he wrote, "I have written all that I wanted to write" (MRC 7). He went on writing and speaking for another thirty-seven years. Even as the Department of Justice defined his writing as the very sign of difference, as the visible mark of his un-Americanness, James returned to the scene of his crimes, inscribing from his place of confinement a promise that is still to be kept and reiterated, calling upon our readiness to reread his texts beyond the boundaries of the defining and captivating law:

> I say here now that as soon as the opportunity presents itself, whether I am still on trial, in detention or out on bail, out of the United States, in the United States, with first papers, second papers or what not, I shall write my views of American civilization. I shall also give an accurate account of my political ideas, what they were, how and when they changed, and what they are today. I shall give you also an account of my political activities, in detail, what I see in the future, what if I can I shall do in the future. The Immigration Department and the FBI shall have their copies as soon as possible after publication. (MRC 172)

* * *

The critical reception of the works of C. L. R. James in the United States, and in other countries as well, has been hobbled by the fact that there has never been a time, at least since the publication of his third book, that all of his writings were in print in easily available editions simultaneously. Many of James's texts were fugitive publications or private printings, and others were internal documents circulated within small political organizations. While copies of such volumes as the mimeographed edition of *Notes on Dialectics* now command a substantial price among rare book dealers, too few students, critics, and working intellectuals have ever had the opportunity to read the book in any form. Still, with books such as *The Black Jacobins* remaining in print for long periods of time, each year new readers have discovered James's thought and begun the search for the rest of his works.

Though a significant number of James's texts have recently come back into print, and there have now been dissertations, two biographies, and several collections of critical essays devoted to different aspects of his life and works, readers often find themselves confronted with intriguing discussions of books they cannot find in print. *C. L. R. James: A Critical Introduction* is not meant as a summary of James's life and books, but it is intended to offer readers a critical study of his major writings illuminated by careful considerations of some of the more difficult to locate publications. James was an inveterate lover of the word, and this volume is intended as an extended investigation of the words he committed to print in the course of eight decades.

Some readers may be puzzled to discover that there is already a critical anthology titled *Rethinking C. L. R. James*. Coming just one year after the publication of Selwyn Cudjoe and William Cain's landmark anthology, *C. L. R. James: His Intellectual Legacies*, this new volume, edited by Grant Farred, suggests that it is already time for reappraisals of a writer and activist whom many are only now coming to know for the first time. It was ever so in James's life. The same intellectual and activist evolution that brought James into the international Trotskyite organization in the early part of his life brought him to a series of critical reappraisals in his later life that resulted in a sharp break with Trotsky's theories and the development of an independent revolutionary politics and cultural theory. By the sixth decade of his life, James, who came to the United States on a lecture tour sponsored by the Trotskyite Fourth International, was able to state his rejection of Marxist vanguardism with uncommon good humor. "Only two sets of people in the U.S. believe" in the conception of the vanguard party, James told his colleagues in 1963: "the first is the State Department. The second is the Trotskyists" (LO 44). The dialectical mode of critique to which James devoted himself called for a constant reappraisal of the ground he had covered, and so it should come as no surprise to us today that contemporary readers of James's writings are already engaged in a contentious process of rethinking the legacy of this phenomenal thinker.

Many of James's old friends have remarked the multiple Jameses that appear in critical essays that have been published in the past two decades. It is as if each intellectual discipline, having gotten hold of one portion of James's body of writing, constructs a James in their own image to fight off competing Jameses constructed in other areas of discourse. In this critical introduction I attempt to provide a coherent view of the trajectories James traced across several disciplinary boundaries. While my work is clearly undertaken from the point of view of a student of literature, and concerns itself primarily with what James has written, I have tried to work in such a way that the evolution of James's thought, rather than a particular contemporary critical technique, will guide the discussions. Kenneth Surin has argued that "there is a sense in which James is *sui generis*, and therefore not exclusively and exhaustively to be identified with a particular approach or method of cultural criticism" (203). Further, though James's Marxist historiography and philosophy is insistent upon the possibility of totalizing narratives, the Jamesian totality is not that against which so many poststructuralists have rightly railed. As Surin has pointed out in discussing James's *Notes on Dialectics*, "the totality invoked by [James], while remaining a whole, is one that is itself never totalizable because it is the 'whole' (i.e. not a 'unity' in the problematic 'Hegelian' sense) of an always displaced and decentered bundle of temporalities" (192). As James was able to theorize a universal that was subject to temporal change and was produced by the emergence of a determinate social class, so James's texts offer forms of "open" totality, and a critical introduction to James's works must in its turn offer an encounter with the totality of his thought without ever arresting that thought within an atemporal, confining, a priori mode of criticism.

But to say that there cannot be a totalizing poetics of James's texts is not to say that there are no describable features that form continuities across the breadth of his works. In his *Letters on Organization* James looked back to his entry into political activities some thirty years before. In 1962 he told his American comrades: "Up to that time I had been interested in literature, history, sports and general reading. I got interested in politics, local politics, suddenly, and my first decision was to write a biography of the local political leader, a biography, note it well, based on the history of the West Indies and of Trinidad, and including an analysis of different sections of the population, beginning with an analysis of the mass of the people. That was thirty one years ago. All that I have done since has been along those same lines" (12). James's work carried him into inquiries in the fields of literature, history, political philosophy, and studies of popular culture, but his trajectory was always along the lines here sketched out, as we have already seen in this introduction.

He began his publishing life as a literary man, but it is in the area of literary studies that his trajectory is least complete. James never worked out a final literary aesthetics, and to judge from his occasionally contradictory remarks about Melville, Whitman, Sartre, and others, he was till the end of his days very much still in motion from his starting point in literary realism toward an aesthetics that could encompass the formal revolutions of a Wilson Harris. What is clearest here is James's belief in the powers of the written word, and that is one of the threads that runs through all of his works. In his biography of James, Kent Worcester includes a description of the young James's home in Port of Spain, Trinidad. James's room was "'simply appointed: a table, a large orthophonic cabinet record player, and a bed placed diagonally across the room on which were always two opened books'" (18). When I first met James some four decades later his room (with the addition of a television set that never stopped playing) looked much the same. If it was not exactly a spartan existence, it was an existence built around sharing with others the revolutionary potential of the word. Worcester also describes "James's habit of purchasing multiple copies of books, magazines, and picture postcards to pass on to friends and acquaintances" (176), and anyone willing to read a book or look at a picture could be a friend of James. James's own life had been transformed by reading, and so had the life of Toussaint L'Ouverture, the subject of James's best-known book.

The other themes that pass through all of James's texts—not only the literary works, but also through his studies of history, his work in radical theory, and his examinations of popular culture—are the relationships between the one and the many. In the following chapters, no matter what the subject of James's investigations, we will see that he always has an eye on the question of how the intellectual relates to the masses of the people, how the individual in society is formed by a culture and in turn transforms the culture of which he or she is a part. James, whether looking at Melville's novels, Grace's cricket play, Griffith's movies, L'Ouverture's revolution, Hegel's philosophy, or at himself, always wants to know what are the conditions of possibility for the history that we make. The most important question in all of James's work, though, is how the masses of the people form the conditions of possibility for the future. In each of the fields of his writing that will form the subject of this critique, James is always attempting to locate those signs in the present shifting of social formations that show the way to the future that the people shall make for themselves, and this is the source of the spirit of optimism that marks James's writings from first to last.

Though James is known to the larger public primarily as a revolutionary historian and political activist, we can never underestimate the importance of recognizing that he accomplished all that he did through writing and speaking. While some readers may not consider literary analysis the best way to approach James's record of achievement (I would remind such readers that Consuelo Lopez's 1983 dissertation on James is a study of his rhetoric), in fact his own letters indicate just how important he thought writing and publishing were to his efforts as a revolutionary. In January 1963, as he reviewed the history of his political organization, his greatest sorrow was not that they failed to build a mass party but that they failed to complete their publication plans. "Whenever I think of what we were preparing to do on the Civil War," he writes, "I feel not bitterness, but the greatest regret for anything that was planned and didn't come off, more than I have ever felt about anything in political and mental life" (46).

James had long held that the Civil War occupied a position in American revolutionary history equal in importance to that of the French Revolution in Europe. What James had planned was not simply the writing of inspirational tracts or the offering of examples to contemporary revolutionaries. Rather, he believed that American revolutionaries could learn from study of the Civil War how to understand the relationships between independent black struggles and the revolutionary proletariat (NQ 142). As Marx had developed theory from his examinations of the French Revolution, James believed absolutely, American radicals would find that the Civil War, seen as an American bourgeois revolution, was "the theoretical basis for the coming social revolution" ("Education" 26). Publication of historical works on the Civil War by his group, he hoped, could provide the "theoretical axis of American analysis" (NQ 88). This revolutionary hope accounts for James's later expression of sadness at the failure of his organization to carry its program of writing and publication through to completion. Such is the efficacy even of James's informal writings that we can still feel today the pain of this regret. In the end, it may be that we simply can never understand the full complexity of James's political and philosophical theories until we have made a start out of close readings of the multiple openings of his texts.

In the following chapters, then, I offer preliminary critiques of James's written work in the fields of literary arts, historiography, political philosophy, and the theory of popular cultures. There is much more to do, but as an American poet, one of James's contemporaries, often said, one must make a start out of particulars.

C. L. R. JAMES

I

Spheres of Existence
What Maisie Knew

Read, read, read. Read till your eyes swim; get yourselves right.
C. L. R. James, *The C. L. R. James Reader*

I. DISCOVERING LITERATURE IN TRINIDAD

When C. L. R. James wrote a mock autobiography in 1944, parodically headed "Autobiography of a Man by Him," among the first memories he recorded, as he would again years later in the autobiographical opening pages of *Beyond a Boundary,* was the vision of his mother reading. His mother did have more material interests; James recalls that "she had a passion for dress," but it is the reading that seems truly to be a passion. In this early, humorous stab at a memoir, sent in a letter to Constance Webb, whom he was later to marry, James says of his mother, "She was a reader. She read everything that came her way. I can see her now, sitting very straight with the book held high, her pince-nez on her Caucasian nose, reading till long after midnight. If I got up there she was, reading, the book still held high. As she read a book and put it down I picked it up" (Buhle and Henry 19). James's first book, *The Life of Captain Cipriani,* was dedicated to the man most responsible for getting James to England and for getting his book into print, Learie Constantine, but James's first, and only, novel, *Minty Alley,* is dedicated to the same woman who had read and criticized his first childhood efforts at fiction, his mother. In an interview with Paul Buhle, James says that his mother was "the center" of his life, and that he "followed literature because of her" (Buhle and Henry 56). When James's mother read *Minty Alley,* her response was considerably more encouraging than when she read his earlier imitations of *The Last of the Mohicans:* "She thought it was fine. She read it and she was very pleased. To write for black people in the Caribbean was a distinction. And here I was writing well, and she was very pleased" (Buhle and Henry 57).

In retrospect, there is nothing more certain than the centrality to all of James's work of his two earliest passions, cricket and literature. *Beyond a Boundary*'s very first chapter, "The Window," places these passions in support of one another as James describes how, at age six, he would use the same chair to reach that titular window through which he could observe the action on the cricket ground directly opposite the house, and to reach the books his mother left stacked on her wardrobe. "Thus early," James notes, "the pattern of my life was set" (BB 3). Though the greater part of James's writings are nonfiction—works of history, political philosophy, and cultural criticism—James began and ended his career reading and writing about cricket and writing. Stanley Weir, in his essay "Revolutionary Artist," states what must be obvious to all who have read widely among James's texts: "it would be impossible to comprehend James without seeing him as an artist and literary critic first" (184). When Paul Buhle, curious about a noticeable gap in James's few autobiographical remarks, asked James what he had been doing between 1920 and 1930, the answer is as revealing as it is simple: "Reading books, that's what I was doing" (Buhle and Henry 58).

There were few models of the literary life for James to observe in his youth, fewer indications still that a life in letters was something to which a young black man in Trinidad might aspire. But there was his mother and her reading. When telling Constance Webb of his early attempts, at age seven, to compose poetry (the one genre in which he seems never to have excelled) he wonders: "Why I felt to write I do not know. No one wrote that I knew. No one had ever said that people wrote" (Buhle and Henry 19). As he grew older, James did encounter precedents for the career he was slowly moving toward in his voluminous and omnivorous readings. Among James's earliest publications is a 1931 article in the *Beacon* about the late Michel Maxwell Philip, a solicitor-general of Trinidad who was also among the first literary artists of African descent on the island. While in England studying for the bar, Philip wrote and published a book titled *Emmanuel Appadocca*. James promises in his essay that "on some future occasion" he will write about Philip's book, but the occasion never arrived. James declares Philip "the most brilliant native of his time and within memory." All James has to say of Philip's book here is "that all through it shows the powerful effect with which the misfortune of his birth weighed upon his mind" ("Philip" 17). There was also A. R. F. Webber, author of the novel *Those That Be in Bondage*. Though James may not have known Webber's volume, Selwyn Cudjoe has pointed out that James must have been aware of Webber himself, because

Webber "was an active colleague of Arthur Cipriani," the subject of James's first book ("Audacity" 49). And, of course, James knew well such nonfiction works as Jacob Thomas's *Froudacity: West Indian Fables Explained*. Thomas's book is not even now well known in North America. It is a beautifully accomplished refutation of James Anthony Froude's *The English in the West Indies: or, The Bow of Ulysses*. Froude was a friend of Thomas Carlyle and, as Thomas attests, "beyond any doubt whatever, a very considerable figure in modern English literature" (Thomas 63). Thomas, on the other hand, was, in James's description of him, a "Trinidad schoolmaster, without European or university education of any kind" ("Intellectual" 27), a schoolmaster who had already published *The Theory and Practice of Creole Grammar*. James's essay on "Discovering Literature in Trinidad: The 1930s" produces Thomas's book as an explanation of the audacity of Marcus Garvey, and of James himself. The attitudes Thomas so eloquently expresses in *Froudacity*, James posits as illustration of "the mentality in which I grew up, which was our inheritance of over a century" (SE 241). James's essay on "The West Indian Intellectual," which was published as an introduction to the 1969 reprint of Thomas's book, remarks that Thomas's success in refuting such a central figure in British letters as Froude "shows that the impact which the West Indian writers, our writers of fiction and the politicians and political writers of the day, have made upon the consciousness and the civilization of Western Europe and the United States, is the result not of the work of certain brilliant individual men, but is due in reality to our historical past, the situation in which our historical past has placed us" (27).

Not until later years was James to construct comprehensively this tradition of precursors to himself. While the article on Michel Maxwell Philip is among James's first publications, James recalls that the literary tradition inculcated in him through his reading and through his education was almost entirely a European legacy. Despite the fact of a Philip or a Thomas, there was little in the way of available literary institutions for James to build upon as he took his first steps toward the life of a writer. As is so often the case, James had to join together with other young literary talents in Trinidad to create institutions for advancing Trinidadian letters. With Alfred Mendes, James edited the journal *Trinidad* in 1929 and 1930, which, along with the *Quarterly Magazine*, stands as one of Trinidad's first modern literary journals. Mendes was at the center of an informal group of young writers that included James, Hugh Stollmeyer, and R. A. C. de Boissiere. When Albert Gomes, who had been studying in the United States, returned to

Trinidad, he used this group as an artistic core in founding his journal, the *Beacon*. Reading the issues of the *Beacon* now, it is difficult to see why the magazine should have aroused any animosity from the establishment, but it is important, if we are to understand James's development as a writer, to comprehend the extent to which colonial ideology exercised a powerfully hegemonic influence in all spheres of Trinidad's cultural existence. Brinsley Samaroo, in his introduction to the reprint of the *Beacon*, has described Gomes's publication as "an anti-Establishment paper, often boycotted by vested interests and under constant attack from the merchant and planter-controlled daily press" (i).

The *Beacon*, even though judged subversive by many in Trinidad's business community, and even though organized as a showplace for Trinidadian writing, was far from presenting a united front in cultural and political matters. Like the earlier *Trinidad*, it provided an outlet for James's writing, but the *Beacon* was not even of one mind about the writings of C. L. R. James. The journal published such important early essays as James's study of Arnold Bennett and his examination of Mahatma Ghandi's autobiography. When the *Royalian*, the magazine of Queen's Royal College in Port of Spain, which had published James's essay on "The Meaning of Philosophy" in 1920, attacked James's recently published short story "Triumph" in 1933, the *Beacon* came to his defense, sounding very much like James himself. The *Beacon*'s response declared their intention to "break as far as possible from the English tradition" and proceeded to make a particularly Jamesian prediction: "The day will come when we, like America, will produce our Walt Whitman; then and only then will the movement towards an art and language indigenous to our spirit and environment commence" (qtd. in Sander xxii). On more purely political issues, though, the *Beacon* published harsh criticisms of James with some frequency. Following the publication of James's first book, *The Life of Captain Cipriani*, the *Beacon* ran critical reviews in successive issues. The first, by Joshua E. Ward, titled "One Negro to Another," is one of the odder reviews ever printed in the magazine, with such tortured declarations as: "I am fed up with all this infuscated subreption" (18). Taking issue specifically with James's criticisms of the colonial English, Ward writes: "The negroes of this colony are in my opinion their own enemies: they oppress themselves when they are not oppressed by the white creole, by a selfish, relentless distrust and petty jealousy" (17). Ward characterizes James as being motivated by deep resentment, and closes his essay by likening James and the "varying coloured characters" to creatures in a barrel. "He is now," Ward finishes, "swelling for a charge at the throats of his comrades in the barrel" (18). Such subreptions, whether infuscated or not, seem to undercut somewhat Brinsley Samaroo's praise for the *Beacon*'s writers that they were able to debate race honestly, "but never descended to personality attacks" (v). The second *Beacon* review of James's book begins by welcoming James's biography at a time "when the people of the West Indies must develop a literature and philosophy of their own" (Mentor 15). On the other hand, the reviewer, Ralph Mentor, is displeased that James has not adopted the biographical methods of Boswell, and he is yet more displeased that "Mr. James has evinced such a rabidly anti-government mentality" (15). In Mentor's reading, James has been swayed by political bias and "has not attempted to give an impartial estimate of local politics." For that reason, Mentor cautions, the reader of this book "must peruse its pages with a discriminating mind" (17). Both reviewers of James's book present themselves as the objective, realistic observer offering correction to one who had allowed his politics to lead him into folly and error. Both reviewers, significantly, reveal a bias at the *Beacon* that they never acknowledge. Each makes a point of mentioning James's discussion of Cipriani's positions in the debate over divorce legislation, and each proffers this discussion as an instance of James's biased reporting. Neither mentions the fact that the *Beacon* group were, as Reinhard Sander puts it, "especially infuriated" by Cipriani's opposition to the divorce bill. The unsigned review of James's subsequent pamphlet, *The Case for West Indian Self-Government*, indicates that the *Beacon*'s editors themselves were not above "personality attacks" against a former collaborator. James's pamphlet, published by Leonard and Virginia Woolf, is described as "disgustingly one-sided and somewhat tiring," and the review proceeds to remark that "anyone who wishes to see how viciously prejudiced a man who sets out to rail against prejudice can be can turn with pleasure to this little pamphlet" ("Swan Song" 19). Strangely enough, given the nature of this attack, James is accused of being "far too personal" (19). One might have expected a work titled *The Case for West Indian Self-Government* to be one-sided, and one must wonder how James reacted to being condemned for not putting forward the other side. Stranger still is the fact that this review never quotes from James's text.

    Stranger yet by far is the exchange James enters into across several issues of the *Beacon* on the subject of Negro intelligence. Given the overheated nature of the *Beacon*'s reviews of James's work and the experience James had in the course of this episode, the real surprise is that so little sense of the negative side of James's relationships with Trinidad's early journals is given in his late essay "Discovering Literature in Trinidad: The 1930s." In that article, first published in 1969 in the *Journal of Commonwealth Literature*, James gives only a hint of the treatment he sometimes received from other writers he knew in his youth. Though James makes it clear that Alfred Mendes, for instance, could go to the United States to work "because he was white and had money" (SE 239), it will come as a shock to many readers to find that the last word from Mendes in response to James's defense of black intellect was a letter in which he wrote: "To tell me that the negro, as a race, has given to the fund of knowledge as much as any other race; that the raw material of his intelligence is as highly developed as the European's, is so manifestly absurd as not to warrant the slightest consideration" (27).

Knowledge of this early episode lends a certain poignancy to our reading of a passing note in James's *American Civilization*. In the portion of his prospectus dealing with "Negroes, Women and Intellectuals," James remarks that "it is instructive to read the old monographs, articles, volumes, disputes on Negro intelligence, tests, the shape of the head, the weight of the brain, etc. Today all that is dead" (AC 202). To read these lines again near the end of the twentieth century in the wake of such publications as Richard Herrnstein and Charles Murray's *The Bell Curve* or Dinesh D'Souza's *The End of Racism*, books that argue the genetic and cultural inferiority of black people, all the while disavowing racism, is to feel the most brutal tragedy. In consecutive issues of the *Beacon* in the summer of 1931 there appeared an essay titled "Race Admixture," by Sidney Harland, and a response piece by C. L. R. James under the title "The Intelligence of the Negro: A Few Words with Dr. Harland." The following autumn saw the *Beacon* publish an answer to James from Alfred Mendes and a lengthier rebuttal from Dr. Harland. Additional writers weighed in on aspects of the controversy, including Mentor and Gomes.

Harland was a British scientist who had come to Trinidad to teach at the Imperial College of Tropical Agriculture. In his initial offering, Harland begins by dispensing with general prejudices, which he describes as irrational, finding them unacceptable because they "have not been carefully scrutinized at the bar of reason" (26). In contrast to such prejudices he adduces what he takes to be fact, based upon his readings of the results of various intelligence tests: "that while it is not apparent to what extent the negro is inferior in intelligence to the white man, there is little doubt that on the average he is inferior" (26). Of course, Harland's own willingness to accept as fact that which has not been carefully scrutinized at the bar of reason leads him to report that "diabetes is said to be common among the Jews, but nearly unknown among negroes" (25). This pattern of prejudice disguised as reason also leads him to conclude his meditation upon miscegenation with a remarkable prediction: "It is possible that the distaste for marriage and parental responsibility which exists among many of the negroes will result in their virtual submergence in the other races, as it is clear that their rate of increase is very slow in comparison with that of the Eastern races" (29). In much the same way that Herrnstein and Murray decades later would point to the superior performance of "Asians" on intelligence tests in America without being at all clear about which Americans are gathered together in the name of "Asians," Harland reports another fact as cold comfort for readers of African descent: "There is little doubt . . . that the aborigines of Australia are innately inferior to the negro" (26).

C. L. R. James's "A Few Words with Dr. Harland" is immeasurably more measured in tone than the subsequent reviews of his own books in the *Beacon* might lead a reader to expect. Typical of James's humor is his comment near the end of the essay that he is "unlikely to see red on the race question, however much [he is] provoked to it by people who will not realize that the more they discriminate the less discriminating they show themselves" (10). The rhetorical strategy adopted by James is one that might be effective with an audience more interested in scrutinizing questions at the bar of reason than was Dr. Harland. James goes to his books to demonstrate that "in the short space of less than three-quarters of a century there has been a complete revolution in scientific and historical thought as to the relative quality of Eastern and Western minds" (6), a fact attested to by comparing the recent "facts" about Asian-American intelligence found in *The Bell Curve* to those proffered earlier in the history of racial debate. James suggests that this should be a humbling reminder. He proceeds to a careful debunking of Harland, using logic and counterevidence to make his case. James points to the undeniable existence of exceptionally talented men of African descent, men such as Toussaint L'Ouverture and James Weldon Johnson. More important, James points to the fact that Harland bases most of his argument on no evidence at all. Harland's comment about the inferiority of Aborigines, for example, is simply laid down as uncontestable common knowledge. Using Harland's own citation of the work of Francis Galton, *Hereditary Genius: An Inquiry into Its Laws and Consequences,* James established that by Harland's own warped statistical reasoning, since men of

L'Ouverture's level of genius constitute 1 out of every 4,300 of his population, Port of Spain alone should be expected to be home to no fewer than 15 such men; indeed, there must be at least 1 between Tunapuna and Tacarigua (9). James, it happens, was born near Tunapuna.

James states that he would have preferred simply to write about L'Ouverture but that he feels compelled to disprove Harland's arguments because "there may be negroes who might read his article and, misled by his reputation, feel some internal disquiet" (10). In the end, though, what James is really after is to expose the irrational and racist ideology that still grips those, like Harland, who present themselves as objective rationalists. Harland concludes his essay with a denunciation of prejudice that reerects racism as the social determinant: "The rise of racial hybrids to considerable economic power will be of increasing significance, and will further the rate of admixture. I close with the hopeful note that social distinctions, formerly based on family and now mostly on money, will have to give way to a set of new standards, and a scheme of social stratification based on biology" (29). Harland's vision of a heritable meritocracy precedes Herrnstein and Murray's similar vision by six decades. James's response to Harland is a good caution to bear in mind even now: "Where a man is so mixed as Dr. Harland is even before he mixes the races, we can guess at the nature of the racial admixture which he will wish to administer" (9). Before closing, James details a litany of errors in logic found in Harland's essay on the science of race. Conceding Harland's eminence in his own field, James catalogues the "vices of the unscientific" committed by this British scientist: "disregard of essential facts, large conclusions drawn from small premises, random statements of a patent absurdity; in fact . . . the very negation of the scientific temper, the very antithesis of the scientific attitude" (10).

The science that gets cited in Harland's answer to James's criticisms is telling. Since James had criticized his use of intelligence data constructed by Ferguson, Harland seeks to confirm Ferguson's conclusions by citing the United States Army's intelligence tests reported by Robert M. Yerkes. Harland does not report one fact that should pose an anomaly for his thesis. The results of the Army tests showed that northern black people on average scored higher than southern blacks, seemingly confounding an argument for nature over nurture. Further, some northern blacks performed better on the tests than did southern whites. These results certainly should trouble Harland's conclusions about the racial heritability of intellectual capacity, but he has in fact adopted a presupposition in common with

Yerkes to explain away such seemingly impossible persons as James Weldon Johnson. Harland, like Yerkes, attributes excellence and intellectual merit to white blood, even when it occurs in black people. Harland drapes this ludicrous proposition in thin, statistical veils. He calculates that "some 22,500,000 negroes have produced as a maximum 447 men of ability, while the 2,500,000 mulattoes have produced 4,267 persons of similar ability" ("Magma" 19). Not only does Harland's conclusion rest upon the most grossly subjective prejudgments, but it also requires a belief that the genetic material determinative of intelligence is somehow mystically and directly attached to the genes that determine melanin levels. Harland attempts no explanation of this strange mechanism of evolution, nor does he wonder why something like color should be correlated with intellect, but he does believe it. "I see no escape," he writes, as if he truly wished he could escape this painful realization, "from the conclusion that the germ plasm of the negro is not a valuable supplement to the germ plasm of the white" (19). Further, Harland belittles James's examples of Negro achievement: "A few eminent men have occurred in the negro group. No sane person would put them in the Newton, Kant, Shakespeare, Einstein class—that of genius, but they have done work good enough for sentimentalists like Mr. James to wax maudlin over their accomplishments. But—are these meritorious efforts due to the *negro* mendelian factors in their germ plasm?" (19). At least in Dr. Harland's view, Shakespeare *should* wince when W. E. B. Du Bois sits with him. The editors of the *Beacon* noted at the end of Harland's second essay that C. L. R. James would reply no further to these arguments. They indicated that the pressures of other business prevented his continuing in the debate, but it is easy to see that there was little to be gained from further reply. The more eloquent and brilliant James's performance, the more eminent the intellect he displayed, the more people like Dr. Harland adapted their racist theories to accommodate the phenomena rather than abandoning the racialist thesis. Harland has a ready explanation for James's own magnificent abilities: "through recombination of mendelian factors it was quite possible to have an association of negro physical characteristics combined with the mental faculties of the European" ("Magna" 19). Harland purports to have devoted himself to the fight "against untutored race prejudice" ("Magna" 20), but he is bent upon the propagation of tutored race prejudice. Alfred Mendes wrote in the September 1931 issue of the *Beacon* to protest Harland's biological explanation of natal incapacity, but like more recent writers such as Dinesh D'Souza, Mendes simply replaced the biological racialism with a cultural racialism. Though Mendes counters Harland's claims with reference to the "many intelligent negroes in Trinidad" he has known, he argues, unlike Pliny, that "out of Africa has come no literature, no painting, no music . . . In short, Africa has no indigenous culture to show the world" (27).

"But Prospero has not won," writes George Lamming. "For . . . this kind of victory would not be possible when the entire enterprise was founded on a Lie" (157). Lamming asks, "What is the real connection between James who knows Thackeray by heart and James who wrote the history of Caliban's resurrection from the natural prison of Prospero's regard?" (151). What Harland attributes to European germ plasm, James attributes to his black parents and their determination to provide him with an education, to the millions of other black people like them who had survived the Middle Passage to invent something new out of Africa and Europe, a New World culture. It is because of James's commitment to what he would in future years term the self-activity of the masses, and because of his ceaseless interest in the character of the individuals who comprise those masses, that, as Lamming puts it, "C. L. R. James shows us Caliban as Prospero had never known him" (119). Despite the internal dissension of the group of intellectuals with whom James associated in his early years, and despite the patent failure of some of his friends to understand the political dynamics of colonial culture as James understood them, what did unite James with Mendes, Gomes, Stollmeyer, de Boissiere, and the others was the desire to build an indigenous art and language.

The mode of this art was to be a literary realism directed toward narrating the lives of the laboring classes of the Caribbean. As was true of European and American realisms, this eventuated in an inherently ironic literary form, since few among the writers were themselves of the working classes. Still, the realism of the new writers of the West Indies in the first half of the century took on an explicitly anticolonial cast, because the shifting of class subjectivities in their art also signaled a shifting conception of national culture. Gillian Whitlock has said of Trinidad's *Beacon* group that their " 'realism' was interpreted as a focussing upon the life of the lower classes, which was seen to be more distinctively 'local' than the culture of the British-oriented middle and upper classes, and a means whereby a national literature could be nourished" (43). Though James has told interviewers that he was not fully aware of the political implications of his early fiction at the time he wrote it (*Kas* 33), this much he was quite assured of as he wrote, that the daily lives and thoughts of the masses of Trinidadians held an intellectual and aesthetic interest easily the equal of anything in Thackeray. It is James's belief from early on that West Indian peoples have something unique to bring to the literature of the English language both culturally and formally. In the beginning, James saw "that the African who made the Middle Passage and came to live in the West Indies was an entirely new historical and social category . . . there had never been people like that before and there haven't been any since" (SE 176). These remarkable people were joined together with Europeans, American Indians, East Indians, Chinese, and others to form not only an African diasporic culture but an international New World culture developing in the shadow of the setting sun of British imperial hegemony. This leads inevitably to that tremendously ironized sense of cultural doubling and redoubling, that position of being simultaneously insider and outsider, that James speaks of so frequently in his writings and interviews. James alludes to this quality, so much like the double-consciousness described by W. E. B. Du Bois, when he says to an interviewer for *Black Scholar* magazine in 1970, "I came from the Caribbean, and we there are a very peculiar people, you know" (36). James wants, in his fiction, to represent the unrepresented, to present lives and voices that are created within the communities previously sealed off from view by colonialist discourse. James Anthony Froude represented the West Indies to the English reading public in a mode that would silence the West Indies themselves. James, in his introduction to Thomas's *Froudacity*, writes: "Imperialism maintains a constant attack upon and a prevailing depreciation of the people it rules (or has ruled). The attack is not always malicious. Quite often it is worse, a genuine sense of outraged superiority stimulating political ignorance and myopia and not averse to plain lying" (23). For James, this discursive history of oppressive representations has become a part of the historical consciousness within the West Indies. When he states, in that same introduction, that the peoples of the Caribbean "are a people more than any other constructed by history" (46), he means not only that the populations of the West Indies have been specifically placed by describable historical forces, but that *as a subject* in history the Caribbean peoples are a contested construction. Lamming describes an "America that started as an alternative to the old and privileged Prospero, too old and too privileged to pay attention to the needs of his own native Calibans" (152), and describes James as a writer who "has always gone in search of those whose labor is a consistent rebuke to . . . monolithic authority" (153).

James also believes that a literature of realism attending to the lives and languages of the peoples of the West Indies may well instigate formal innovations within English writing. Frequently, as in "The Making of the Caribbean People," James pointed out to his audiences that writers from the Caribbean had played an important part in the creation of new aesthetic forms in European literary history, including names such as Alexander Dumas, Leconte DeLisle, Saint-John Perse, and Aimé Césaire. When, for a class James taught in the mid-1970s on South American intellectual history, I submitted a short, undergraduate paper on the subject of the rise of South American poetry in Spanish, I mentioned in passing a poet from the Caribbean named José Maria de Heredia. When James returned the paper to me I saw that he had marked a series of exclamatory lines in the margin next to that name. When I asked Professor James what it was about this poet that attracted his attention, he asked me (as if he thought I might really know), "Wasn't he one of the Parnassian poets of France?" I looked up the poet's biography in our small university library and, of course, James had remembered correctly.

There was nothing terribly mysterious about James's faith that West Indian writing would participate in the reformation of English letters. Long before reading Marx, James had recognized the importance of understanding literature as a social form, responsive to the transformations within the social world of which it is a part. In his later letters to Constance Webb he observes quite simply that "Shakespeare and the Elizabethans needed a new verse form to express a new world" (JR 138), something to which William Carlos Williams would agree enthusiastically, and one thing such a new verse form had to express was the metamorphosis in the English consciousness caused by the discovery and the possession of new territories of the New World. In his subsequent discussions of literature, James was often to remark the fact that many of the most important shifts in English writing had been instigated by writers from regions colonized by Britain, writing in forms of English that disrupted the metropolitan dominance of literary forms. In 1964 James was asked to deliver an address to the West Indian Students' Association in Edinburgh. As he addressed one group of colonial students on the ground of yet another once-colonized people, James spoke of "A National Purpose for Caribbean Peoples," and he built his discussion around the example of literary metamorphosis. "The criticism of literature, the break-up of the tradition of Wordsworth and Milton was done," James recalls for his audience, "by two Americans, T. S. Eliot and

Ezra Pound. They reorganized the poetic language of England" (RV 148). Similarly, James traces a history of innovations in English prose wrought by Irish authors from Swift to Joyce and Beckett. In his own lifetime, James not only contributed something of great originality to English prose, he lived to see novelists such as George Lamming and Wilson Harris build upon his foundation to bring into being new forms for the English novel. Of these two West Indian novelists, and others of their generation, James says: "There is nothing like them in English literature. Pull them out and English literature suffers tremendously" (RV 148).

Harris's own novels are easily as strange in comparison to most British novels at midcentury as Joyce's *Ulysses* was in comparison to the most popular British novels published during the modernist era. James describes Harris as the author of "the strangest books" he can think of (RV 148), and it is a justified appraisal. As it was true of Joycean English, Harris's language is a speaking back to the mother tongue by those to whom English was brought by the encroachments of empire. Even as James recounts an encounter with a reviewer for the *Times Literary Supplement*, we can see a small example of the West Indian reconstrual of English. When James wrote to the *TLS* editor, responding to a column that dealt with Caribbean literature, the editor told James that James held too high an opinion of the West Indian novelists, and he challenged James to produce in evidence a characterization in a Caribbean novel that could compare for understanding and artistry with Dostoyevsky's creation of Raskolnikov. Of course, James's original point had been that the same sort of national social transformations that had motivated the creation of a Raskolnikov were also inspiring the West Indian novelists. Almost in passing, though, James makes a linguistic point to his diasporic audience. Describing his final exchange with the *TLS* editor, James says that the man "took before, as we say in the West Indies, before before took him" (RV 149). It is a simple but profound point. Eliot, no matter how far he removed himself from his natal Missouri mud, had a history of hearing English differently, and that history of difference impresses itself upon what becomes the very model of a modern major poem, "The Waste Land." James's own fiction, which begins to appear in print only five years after "The Waste Land," does not signal so abrupt a change in surface style as Eliot's much redacted collage, but what James undertook within the existing framework of literary realism is the precursor to the far more unorthodox formal experiments of a Wilson Harris. James sets out in his twenties to change the subject of colonial realism, to change it by attending to the colonial subjects. Realism has a history of turning to the subject of the lower socioeconomic classes, of course, but James understood that for him to do so in his fiction was to add what Melvin B. Tolson terms the ethnic ambiguity to Empson's classic seven. Helen Pyne-Timothy has identified this as "James's major contribution to the literature of the Caribbean; the giving voice to the porters, prostitutes, carter-men, washer-women, and domestic servants of the city in their own language and surrounded by their African cultural values, belief systems, and cosmology" (56).

This, too, is what summoned the disapproval of the *Royalian,* where James's first writings had appeared. Not all of Trinidad was so interested in hearing Caliban's back talk, and not all who were interested shared James's delight in the phenomenon. D. Elliott Parris makes a telling opposition when he writes that "unlike Naipaul, James displays no hysterical embarrassment about Caribbean identity, but depicts it as it is with realistic candor and implied love" (200). It is not, though, the direct, unmediated voice of the masses that appears in James's pages. What we have instead is a writer who, somewhat like the protagonist of his novel, *Minty Alley,* attends to the lives of the masses with equal portions of curiosity, love, consternation, and confusion. This is crucial, because James believed, and he forms his novel in such a way as to dramatize his belief, that the middle and upper classes have much to learn from listening to the masses. But this is no *Sullivan's Travels;* James's middle-class protagonist is not simply enjoying an epiphany produced by his brief sojourn among the uncomplicated and lowly primitives. There is always more to be learned, as the masses themselves remain always in motion, always engaged in the struggle for happiness.

James, in Cynthia Hamilton's reading of his texts, presents culture as "a tool of preservation . . . In particular for those who survived the 'middle passage'" (438). This is a beginning point for James. Though Hegel had read Africa out of world history, and though the masters of slaves had taken great pains to separate Africans in the New World from their putatively nonexistent history, Africans had not been entirely dispossessed. Here, for James, is the degree zero of "The Making of the Caribbean People." As Africans arrived on the newly blanked slate of the Caribbean shore, they had in hand the cultural conditions of possibility for a future. James insists, "We had brought ourselves. We had not come with nothing" (SE 187). The something that they came with was manifested in the social practices that they created within their communities. In Hamilton's formulation, "Mass popular culture is that which existed 'before the word,' before it had been transformed into commodity" (439), or, as James might say, before before. What James wanted to write about was the popular culture of those whose labors and whose very bodies had been converted into commodities. If, as Cynthia Hamilton argues, "History was that which progressed from day to day within this cultural context of resistance," James wanted in his history and in his fiction to find forms within literary realism to represent that resistance.

II. MINTY ALLEY

He begins, as so many realists have, by turning to his own immediate experiences for materials. In his 1958 essay "On Federation," James remembers that when he was a small boy in Trinidad he used to hear news of the battles for control of nearby Venezuela between Castro and Gomez (RV 97). The narrator of "Revolution," first published in the *Beacon,* has the same memories. He tells a friend, "I had a vivid memory of ex-president Castro being pointed out to me in the street when, deposed and unable to land in Venezuela, he lived an exile in Trinidad" (RV 1). "Revolution" demonstrates how intimately the neighboring territories of the Caribbean and mainland South America were intertwined in their social lives. This had always been particularly true of Trinidad, with its successive waves of Spanish- and English-speaking colonists, its Africans, Indians, and Asians. More significantly still, the story is composed almost entirely of conversation, and its conversational mode comes to thematize its narrative. The Venezuelan exile to whom the narrator is introduced is marked in his very manner of speech by the exile's anxious attentiveness to possibility. "I noticed now," the narrator tells us, "that whenever he was not speaking there was an expectant air about him—the air of a man constantly on the look-out for news" (RV 6). The conversations that comprise the story become in their turn a sign of both freedom and dispossession. The characters, meeting in Trinidad, are free to speak, but that freedom underscores their exile's distance from freedom at home. In Venezuela, the exile explains to the narrator, "Nobody can say a word. As soon as you say anything, the irons on your feet" (RV 4). The exile is part of a furtive community of rumor, always speaking with an ear cocked for echoes from across the waters. The narrator, for his part, and this appears to be something that he has in common with his creator, craves more conversation, more narration. In the end, he appears more concerned with the experience of the exchange itself than with the actual disposition of affairs in Venezuela. It is the consciousness of his interlocutor that attracts his deepest interest. The narrator closes, leaving readers wanting more of the same thing he wants, with the remark, "I am not really concerned with Gomez and his rebels. What I want is to manage another interview with my Venezuelan friend" (RV 8).

James's first published short story, "La Divina Pastora," purports to be a nearly transparent report of oral tradition. The story was first printed in *Saturday Review* in 1927 and was selected by E. J. O'Brien for his *Best Short Stories* volume of 1928. It is easy to see how this very brief fiction, with its O. Henry style surprise ending, would exercise great appeal for a general audience. The story's opening, however, indicates that James had learned well from his reading. It is a most Melvillean opening, simultaneously teasing and revealing, like the opening of "Bartleby the Scrivener." Not only has James already become a master manipulator of point of view by the time of this earliest publication, but he has also constructed an ironic narrator whose positioning of himself as simple transmitter of the tale is not to be taken at face value. "Of my own belief in this story I shall say nothing" (JR 25), says the narrator, thus early suspending the willing suspension of disbelief. The narrator states that he has neither added to nor subtracted from "the essential facts," and yet his very profession of transparency is ironized. "What I have done," James writes, "is to put it down as far as possible as it was told to me, in my own style" (JR 25), and there is no subsequent untangling of this narrative knot. James at the same time promises readers that he is merely relaying a tale as it was told to him, lending it the authenticity of oral tradition, and that he will retell it in his own style. Thus, while it is no doubt to be believed, as he writes on the story's first page, that Anita Perez, his protagonist, "had no thought of woman's rights, nor any Ibsenic theories of morality" (JR 25), it must be assumed by readers that the people who first told the story to James told it without authorial intrusions alluding to woman's rights and Ibsen. This quick and seemingly innocuous aside is a sign of James's aesthetic modernity, and perhaps of his own political awakening. As the Venezuelan exile narrated his past to James, thus marking his and James's distance from events on the continent (even as the exile continues to influence those distant events), James's narrative self-presence in "La Divina Pastora" places both him and his readers in a self-conscious relationship to oral tradition, at once inside and outside the community of knowledge that encompasses Anita Perez.

That ironic opening of the story, by a narrator who, in effacing himself, only makes himself more conspicuous, is important too (or as James's characters so often say, "too besides") because it places us within the cultural context of pressures that are felt by the characters while also leaving an opening to the social outside from which the reader approaches the characters. Sylvia Winter, in "Beyond the Categories of the Master Conception," describes a Trinidad in which "the entire social structure is based on the acceptance and implementation of power-relations as the normative mode of relations" (77). One of those powers, for Anita, is the miraculous, and the possibility of the opening of the miraculous plays a role for her that the availability of the United States plays for James's much more audacious young woman character in *Minty Alley*, Maisie.

"La Divina Pastora" is built around a paradigmatically polysemous figure. In the town of Siparia, inside the Roman Catholic church, is a small, dark image that has religious significance to Christian, Hindu, *and* American Indian histories. In his story, James relates how this statue once figured at the center of an annual festival and describes its continued importance as the goal of pilgrims and supplicants. In a 1932 issue of the *Beacon,* Alfred Mendes published an essay in which he described the annual pilgrimage of East Indians to the Siparia shrine, detailing the syncretism practiced by diasporic Indians folding a Catholic image into their cultural practices. Mendes repeats reports of miraculous cures attributed to La Divina Pastora, but James is as ironic at the miraculous close of his story as he was at the beginning.

At its most basic level of signification, James's story illustrates the plain moral that one must be careful what one wishes for. However, the story also succeeds, with its deft characterization, in communicating the impossible tensions that cross the lives of people in Trinidad's colonial social structure. Helen Pyne-Timothy has argued that what James attempts in this story is "to capture the essence of the life of the descendants of members of the remnant Spanish community" (54) of Trinidad's past. Anita Perez and her mother are representatives of the laboring classes, working the local cocoa plantations six days a week. Sebastian Montagnio, Anita Perez's slow-to-speak suitor, is a step or two farther up the colonial hierarchy, the owner of "a few acres of cocoa and a large provision garden" (JR 25), a man whose four-room house seems a "mansion" to his neighbors. To Anita's mother, Sebastian seems an opportunity for escape from the fields. This is how he appears to Anita as well, but Anita also loves him and is tormented, as she ages, by her doubts of his love for her. It is at this point in the tale that the Perez family turns for aid to La Divina Pastora.

Anita's absence, while she is in Siparia seeking miraculous intervention, moves Sebastian at last to pronounce his love. Recognizing his need of her, he finally takes the step she is praying for in Siparia. The sudden nature of Sebastian's declaration shakes Anita's confidence. "Faith she had," James tells us, "but for this she was not prepared. It was too sudden, as if the saint had had nothing to do with it" (JR 27). This accession of doubt leads to Anita's casual and catastrophic second wish, which is granted as quickly as her first, bringing the story to its abrupt and mysterious end. Both the social order of the plantation economy and the universe of magic inhabited by the Perez family remain intact, perhaps even strengthened by the story's conclusion, but the ironized author's asides leave the story opening out at its end to a signifying as polysemous as the figure of La Divina Pastora herself. The authorial intrusions, like the presence of the reader, are in some ways as miraculous and as doubt-inducing as the seeming impossibility of the event that closes the story. The characters within the narrative live and die in a world suspended between the quotidian drudgery of the cocoa field and the sphere of the divine. The wearing world in which they seem fated to fade to their deaths gives onto another, equally dangerous world where wishes become material reality. This is a form of magic realism, though James had not yet read that term, and though more than a decade was still to pass before another Caribbean novelist, Cuba's Alejo Carpentier, was to give "magic realism" international currency with the publication of his introductory essay to his novel of Haiti (a subject of great interest to James), *El reino de ese mundo*. James does not suggest in this story that readers are to adopt the folk beliefs of the Perez women, nor does he indulge in the kind of nostalgic primitivism so evident in modernist depictions of the working class (and, it must be admitted, in some of the first world's reception of third world magic realism). But James writes with respect for the women's complexities, and he writes in such a way as to leave readers powerfully disturbed by a social order in which a woman's only mode of escape from virtual slave labor is either by marriage up the economic ladder or by miraculous means, both of which require that she become a commodity herself. That is not the thrust of the tale; it would be far less interesting to read if it were, but it is an ineluctable effect of the narration.

In each of his fictions James constructs similarly ironic narratives that, while presuming simply to report the local details of conversations and community tales, tend, almost without the reader's having noticed it, to restrict severely "the field of perception" (Murdoch 64), as H. Adlai Murdoch describes the technique in *Minty Alley*. In most instances readers receive information as it is unfolded to the narrator, and thus the relationships of knowledge and authority as they exist among James's characters are replicated in the relationships of reader to text. The same suspense that allows for the comedic effects of James's stories also places readers in a situation where the power of their social position, probably at a higher socioeconomic level than that of most of James's characters, is mitigated somewhat by their inability to know prior to information being related within the fictive community of the text.

This leads to a blueslike irony in stories such as "Turner's Prosperity" and "The Star That Would Not Shine." "Turner's Prosperity" appeared in the first issue of *Trinidad*, published at Christmastime in 1929. In this story, a working man and his wife, presented with an opportunity to consolidate their formidable accumulated debts, do what all practiced capitalists do; they begin plotting to transform their small debt into a larger one, to create capital from arrearage. Like the land-flipping savings and loan officers of America's Reagan-era boom, they even strike upon a fraudulent basis by which they might enter the entrepreneurial classes. The wife suggests that Turner and one of his creditors "make a false pro note and fix up things somehow. That will leave us with something substantial in hand. We could buy up a few necessaries with some and I could do some little business to bring in something to help. Send out an ice-cream cart perhaps. That is a paying thing—" (SE 13). In the end, though, a swift few paragraphs later, Turner's fantasized prosperity dissolves as he loses his job and his opportunity to stave off the creditors. The resolution of the story might seem to suggest simply that Turner's greed and lack of fiscal control have undone him, but his wife's dream of an ice-cream cart works against such a reductive reading. For just how does her dream of financing her family's entrance into business by means of debt, unrealistic as it may be under the circumstances, differ in nature from the business of Turner's employer, or from the leveraged propositions of venture capitalists? This is the sort of textual turn by which, according to H. Adlai Murdoch, "subjection to the discourse of colonialism has been inscribed in the text" (65). Turner and his wife, the chief subjects of James's story, are subjugated to a system of commerce and dominance that requires their continued positioning as subjects. Their debts may be moved about, increased, or diminished, but they, and thousands like them, are meant to remain in arrears.

James's 1931 story "The Star That Would Not Shine" is an amusing precursor to his later critical writing on cinema and mass culture. The story begins seemingly far from Trinidad, as the narrator describes an airplane landing that brings Douglass Fairbanks together with Mary Pickford and Maurice Chevalier. It turns out, however, that we are seated in a cinema in Trinidad. The narrative transition is yet another instance of Jamesian irony. As we leave Fairbanks and Pickford, the narrator tells us that "the scene shifted to another part of Hollywood" (RV 9), and while the remainder of the story is in the form of a conversation between two chance acquaintances in Trinidad, it becomes clear that the narrative space of the conversation is an ideological suburb of Hollywood, an extension of Hollywood's commercial apparatus. "The Star That Would Not Shine" is narrated by a man named James, who discovers that he has entirely "failed" to take the measure of the man sitting next to him in the cinema, Gonzales. At first James fears Gonzales will be one of those pests who insists upon revealing to his neighbors what is about to happen in the film. When that proves not to be the case, James supposes his neighbor to be a great admirer of Gloria Swanson, or perhaps he is just someone who is out to pass the hours. Learning that Gonzales prefers the great comics, Charlie Chaplin and Harold Lloyd, James decides that Gonzales looks "like a man who needed laughter in his life" (RV 9), a judgment that turns out to be true, though not for the reasons James has supposed. In fact, it is not the comedy of these greats that is their real interest for Gonzales.

As occurs so frequently in James's fictions, the character "James" has formed his judgments out of his presuppositions about familiar social types, and as a result he is wholly wrong about the thoughts and motivations of his fellow spectator. The neighbor, in his turn, suffers his own form of wrongness. Gonzales has been fully articulated with the Hollywood apparatus for the production of desire, but his response has narrowed to focus on the most abstract object of that desire. He knows, for example, just how much income tax was paid by Charlie Chaplin in the previous year, and this number has become a measure for him of his present distance from a missed opportunity. His son, Johnny, has also been swept up in cinematic discourse, but with a quite different result. Because other children have taunted him for his resemblance to Fatty Arbuckle, Johnny not only rejects the offered chance to become a child star, he refuses even to enter the movie theater.

As always, the humor of James's story points up a much larger issue. Decades later, writing in *American Civilization,* James remarked the emergent star-making machinery of Hollywood film. James describes the star system as "a complete denial of any serious creative effort on the part of the artist or audience" (AC 146). In "The Star That Would Not Shine," Hollywood has become a vehicle for miraculous economic salvation, as much as La Divina Pastora was for Anita Perez, rather than a vehicle for the expression of the deepest emotions and ambitions of the masses of the people. James's wistful interlocutor in "The Star That Would Not Shine," Gonzales, saw in the interest expressed by a film company in his corpulent child a momentary possibility of his wishes coming true, wishes created by his own measure of the social distance between his reality and that seen on the screen. His son, a star who refused to shine, has been the object of Hollywood's ability to create types and to fill the imaginations of millions with those types. Johnny's mother, though initially excited by the opportunities film offers her family, sees the Faustian nature of the proffered bargain: "Better I lose three hundred dollars a week than lose my child" (RV 12). She pronounces the end of negotiations and Gonzales repeats that ending to James, as if to end the tale: "It was the end, sir" (RV 12). But the story does not end there. We go on to learn of Johnny's successes in New York, and of his continued refusal to attend the movies. We see that Gonzales himself is happy with his son's course and that Gonzales continues his fascinated tracking of films and their stars' salaries. Most important, we see the story's sheer delight in conversation and in communal narrative; we see the cinema theater as a stage of interchange *among* the masses of the audience, a place where their own speech is as important (and in this case more compelling) as anything projected before them for their consumption. The story passed from Gonzales to James is far more entertaining than the distant doings of Fairbanks and Pickford.

As a literary artist, C. L. R. James has been best known, and most widely read, as one of the first authors to apply the aesthetic techniques of realism to the subject matter of life in Trinidad's barrack-yards. John Stewart has called James's work "a ground-breaking example of regional social realism" (104). D. Elliott Parris views James's early fiction as "a major forerunner of the Caribbean literary movements in English," with their marked "concern for class, color and race relations in the Caribbean that would be central to the works of writers who were to follow" (200). James notes, in an interview with Ian Munro and Reinhard Sander, that Alfred Mendes also published short fiction set in the barrack-yards, but those stories were published in the United States in the 1930s. James's story "Triumph," which he wrote in the late 1920s, is, then, among the very first narratives of what would soon become a recognizable genre, and while it was written around the same time as *Minty Alley,* James's novel was not to find a publisher till 1936. The effect of "Triumph" upon its first audience was swift and dramatic. As Kenneth Ramchand evaluates the responses, "episodes like this shocked the more respectable members of the Trinidad educated class, in much the same way that the Harlem writers of the late 1920's and early 1930's had shocked those Negro American conservatives anxious to be acceptable to White Americans" (9). Realism had begun by shocking its readers, in both Europe and the Americas, but the shock of James's fictions was redoubled by the political and social realities of race and colonialism. If one were to make a case for West Indian self-government, many felt at the time, one should not at the same time publish stories whose protagonists were poor people with active and unregulated sex lives. The editor of *Trinidad,* where "Triumph" first appeared, took note of the fact that many letters of protest had been directed to the *Trinidad Guardian* denouncing James and his "nasty" story (Ramchand 9).

The yards that are the subject of both "Triumph" and *Minty Alley* were common features of urban architecture in Port-of-Spain when James wrote. According to John Stewart, these barrack-yards evolved from the earlier estate model of the plantation era (104), and their North American counterparts might be the alleyway dwellings and courtyards that once were common in Washington, D.C., and New Orleans (living areas once reserved as quarters for the poor and the dark, now often transformed into comfortable condominiums for the newly capitalized). In the opening paragraphs of "Triumph" James describes the typical plan of these barrack-yards: "a narrow gateway leading into a fairly big yard, on either side of which run long, low buildings, consisting of anything from four to eighteen rooms, each about twelve feet square. In these lived the porters, the prostitutes, carter-men, washerwomen and domestic servants of the city" (JR 29).

This sort of sociological tourism marks the chief difference between "Triumph" and *Minty Alley.* More like "La Divina Pastora" than like "Revolution" or "The Star That Would Not Shine," the narration of "Triumph" enforces a certain social demarcation by means of its third-person omniscient narrative, a narrative that does not center in any individual character's point of view. This is not a matter of "epic tone," as Gillian Whitlock has described it (44), but James was conscious as he wrote of this distancing effect. "At that time," James subsequently recollected, "I somehow felt it necessary to introduce with a certain style, before I got down to it. But I got down to it, right down to it" (*Kas* 35). The opening of "Triumph" is in the familiar explanatory style of an early realism that undertakes to initiate a middle-class readership into the mysteries of life among the lowly, the same sort of impetus that caused so many novelists of the colonial era to attach glossaries to the ends of their works as a defining guide for the possibly perplexed reader, a guide that simultaneously underscored the linguistic difference of the characters while admitting readers to the characters' linguistic sphere. The descriptive opening of "Triumph" is the narrative equivalent of the narrow gateway leading into the big yard. It is in the form of a social travelogue. The rest of the story, though, works in a quite different direction. James's characters, as Sylvia Winter describes them, "refuse to accept their value of nothingness. Their lives are spent in constant combat to refuse this negation of their being, to affirm, by any means, fair or foul, usually the latter, that they have a life value and have powers that must be realized" (76). What James says of all the peoples of the Caribbean, that they didn't come with nothing, that they brought themselves, is at the root of his work of revaluation in these stories. As Winter has suggested, James does not contrive epiphanies for his downtrodden characters whereby they suddenly see where true value lies and join a political revolution, but his comic tales point to a desire for life values in the masses from which real revolutions do come. At the close of "Triumph," when Mamitz and Celestine produce a public display of paper money to confound Irene, their nemesis in the yard, some readers may be tempted to condemn these characters for their warped sense of value. But one cannot help, confronted with that florid display of currency, remembering that the ancestors of these characters came to the Caribbean as commodities, that commercial value had attached to them along with their chains, that they had been, in their persons, representations of exchange value. Within the comedic narrative of "Triumph," the characters' ingenuity and creativity are directed toward their own survival and prosperity, and thus their triumphs tend to be over one another rather than over the economic system that holds them in penury. As Sylvia Winter has shown, "The entire social structure is based on the acceptance and implementation of power-relations as the normative mode of relations" (77), and so, as in *Minty Alley*, most of the characters will secure their triumph at the expense of somebody else.

The short fiction of C. L. R. James has been reprinted in recent years in the various volumes of his selected writings, though it has yet to be gathered in one place. His novel, on the other hand, has never been printed in the United States, and while it has been maintained in print in Britain and the Caribbean by New Beacon Editions, its lack of widespread availability has meant that few literary scholars have written about the book. Among those who have there has been great divergence of opinion regarding the novel's merits, and considerable misunderstanding of its methods. When John Wickham reviewed New Beacon's republication of the novel in 1972, he adopted a condescending tone indicative of his inability to read the book as something more than thinly veiled sociology. Responding to Kenneth Ramchand's introduction to James's novel, Wickham complained that "an understandable nostalgia for that thirties period of the first 'Beacon' in Port of Spain of Gomes, Mendes, Frank Evans and their coterie need not lead us to claim either that C. L. R. James is a novelist or that MINTY ALLEY is a distinguished novel" (111). Wickham concedes a certain historical importance to *Minty Alley* as an event, "because C. L. R. James wrote it," and as a document, because it reveals "some of the social attitudes of the time" (112). Yet, Wickham seems alarmingly unprepared to read the novel as a novel, and hence seems to miss most of the book's ironies. In the end he can only see a form of homework in the book. "MINTY ALLEY is a valuable piece of social documentation," he concludes, "and certainly no student of West Indian literature can afford to miss reading it" (113), a misreading of a type common among those who have approached the novel primarily as historical documentary. Even in an essay on "The Literary Achievement of C. L. R. James," F. M. Birbalsingh demonstrates a remarkable disregard for the literary achievements of *Minty Alley*. "The characters of the novel are stereotypes," he believes; "the plot is a linear account of chronological events; and the dialogue is rather mechanical" (117).

Many of these negative evaluations of James's achievement in fiction are traceable to a lack of subtlety in apprehending the way that the novel positions its central character, Haynes. Haynes's name and social background are so similar to James's own that some critics have taken the social distance between Haynes and the other characters to replicate an unironic distance between the characters and their creator. It is true that James drew the materials for his fiction from the experiences of his own life. He had completed the manuscript of his novel before leaving Trinidad for England, though the book was not actually published till some years had passed, and the core events in the novel had been witnessed by James. As he told interviewers in 1972:

> I was about 27 or 28 at the time when I went to live in that household described in the novel. I was already engaged to be married; I went to live there, the people fascinated me, and I wrote about them from the point of view of an educated youthful member of the black middle class. The political implications I was not aware of. They seemed to be interesting people, and what was going on was very dramatic. So I wrote the story and brought it to a conclusion. Many of the things that took place in the story actually took place in life. The end—Maisie's going to New York and breaking with me—is fiction; furthermore, I never slept with Maisie. I didn't, but I imagine at 20 I would have found it very exciting to sleep with Maisie. I was about 27–28 when this was going on, but I made Haynes in the novel 20 years old. (*Kas* 33)

What these final remarks indicate in their amusing way is that we should read the same sort of ironized distance between James and Haynes that we can read between all the characters of his book. John Wickham reads and reifies that distance unironically, as a liability shared by James and Haynes. Reading the novel as a "social document," Wickham feels that "in spite of the accuracy one is reminded always of the distance between the author and his creatures—a social distance" (112). Yet, that very social distance is one of the novel's primary subjects, and James has thematized that distance by making it a structural property of his novel. Michael Gilkes has come to a partial recognition of this. Contrasting James's novel with De Lisser's *Jane's Career*, Gilkes describes James's narrative mode as one of "subjective involvement" (29). Still, Gilkes ends by viewing the character Haynes as "little more than a narrative device used by James to illustrate the essentially worthwhile and vibrant life of the slum community" (30–31). What Gilkes continues to overlook is the extent to which James's deployment of Haynes as a center of consciousness for this third-person narration stages James's lifelong examination of the relationships of individual to class, of the intellectual to the masses. This oversight leads Gilkes to declare Haynes "hardly credible" (32), because the critic takes Haynes as a failed attempt to present "a disinterested observer of the whole community" (32).

Other critics, however, have seen James's novel as one in which the narration renders problematic the interested voyeurism of the upper classes, in which the very desire of the better-off to project their desires onto the poor, to seek the simultaneous salving of their guilt and the titillation of their libido among the noble but primitive poor, is turned back upon itself. Gillian Whitlock views as the chief difference between "Triumph" and *Minty Alley* the fact that in his novel, James uses point of view to destabilize ideology.

"Here," Whitlock holds, "the narrator is self-consciously an outsider, the limited middle class perspective he offers is examined" (45). For H. Adlai Murdoch, this destabilizing begins with the social positioning of Haynes as center of consciousness, for "the character of Haynes . . . by virtue of his position as a member of both the ruling and the oppressed classes, may be said to mediate a simultaneous identification with the ideological position of the colonizer as well as participation in the fragmentation and dislocation of the colonized" (65). According to Sylvia Winter, what "the fictional system of *Minty Alley* reveals" is "the bourgeois telos of accumulation," and that revelation is borne home when Haynes "stumbles upon the realization of the social crime that makes his own standard of living possible" (79).

It is because he has lost the key support for his own standard of living that Haynes, who all his life has been dependent upon his mother and their servant, Ella, takes up residence within Number 2 Minty Alley himself, and even then he has relied upon Ella to locate these new, lesser quarters for him. Though the residents of Minty Alley all respect Haynes for his social standing in the community and for his education, though they turn to him for advice, he finds that he is poorly prepared to mediate their struggles. D. Elliott Parris concludes from this that "just as Mr. Haynes is depicted as lacking in confidence and as unprepared for emotional and physical involvement in life, the novel implies that the Caribbean petit-bourgeois class had been rendered relatively impotent by its education and stood to benefit from more exposure to the passions of the lower class" (202). If it were only the passions of the lower class that Haynes discovered this would be a more familiar study. But over and over again in this narrative, we see that Haynes has little knowledge of the facts of daily life in his own community, that he is reliant upon those who look to him for sagacity for the most basic knowledge of day-to-day human interactions.

Haynes's mother had sought to prepare her son for an independent existence in his colonial society, and so she had prepared him for professional training in England. "You are black, my boy," she tells him, " . . . and in these islands for a black man to be independent means that he must have money or a profession" (MA 22). His mother's death occurs before either enough money or sufficient training has been accumulated to make Haynes independent, and we read, as Haynes completes the calculations that determine his economic future, that even these initial steps toward independence have been secured upon the lack of independence of other people. When Haynes totes up his fiscal prospects, we learn that he receives some of his income in the form of "rent from two or three rooms in the slum quarter" (MA 23). Even the insignificant job Haynes holds at a local bookstore was arranged for him by his mother. The accident that leaves Haynes with idle hours to devote to watching the comings and goings at Minty Alley underscores the extent to which his bookish life has incapacitated him for life's daily struggles. He is bruised severely when a case of books fall on him (MA 41). Haynes's social distance from the other residents of Number 2 Minty Alley is further signaled by his voyeurism. He has gone to some lengths both to enlarge and to camouflage a peephole that allows him to spy out onto the barrack-yard from within the privacy of his room. Mrs. Rouse, his new landlady, has promised Haynes privacy in his room, hinting that nobody would disturb him if he chose to bring a female guest into his quarters. Haynes in fact uses his privacy to invade the privacy of his neighbors, to spy upon their romantic interludes and arguments when they think nobody is watching. In effect, Haynes literalizes the panopticon effect of social hierarchy in the colony. His is the surveying eye of middle-class morality enviously scanning the daily lives of the lowly.

In other ways, too, the architecture of Haynes's living area, like the architecture of James's novel, reproduces the social structures of Trinidad's colonial society. We learn early on that Minty Alley, that yard enfolding the lives of so many people who might appear inconsequential to the governing eye, gives onto a major thoroughfare, Victoria Street. As Trinidad is to England, then, a marginalized outpost of the empire that in fact makes possible the empire of Queen Victoria, so Minty Alley appears an offshoot, and an eccentric one at that, of the colony's main business, but proves in the end to be its heart and soul. For the rest of the residents of Minty Alley there is little real distinction between inside and outside. In the same way that their movements carry them rapidly back and forth within the yard, and from room to room of its perimeter, their daily lives carry them in and out of the yard itself and throughout the surrounding environs. It is Haynes, the educated man preparing to administer the lives of others, for whom the yard truly is an enabling structure. Haynes turns off Victoria Street only when driven by necessity, and as he enters Minty Alley he comes for the first time into full contact with the life of his island. For the first time he is in the thick of it. "He was uncomfortable, and wished he was elsewhere. But it was life, he thought" (MA 73).

Near the end of the book he despairs of ever leaving. "I am going to die in this damned house" (MA 241), he tells himself, and yet he also sees that it is Minty Alley, and his relationship with Maisie, that has made him more "human" (MA 202). There is a sexual element in this as well. Haynes has lived an isolated life and has never kissed a woman who was not related to him. Obviously, part of his excitement about living at Number 2 Minty Alley is his illicit pleasure in the illicit pleasures of its residents, and his fervent hope that he might himself have an affair. At the close of chapter 10, as Haynes announces to Maisie his intention to remain at Number 2, he begins to view the seventeen-year-old niece of his landlady, Mrs. Rouse, in a new light: "a new aspect of Maisie, vaguely present for some time in the background of his mind, suddenly emerged clearly. She was a damned, pretty girl, and would be very nice to sleep with" (MA 78).

This much seems typical of much literature of the period throughout the English-speaking world, the symbolic linking of carnal knowledge to social knowledge and the desire of the middle-class intellectual to "find himself" among the lower classes. What James makes of this, though, is considerably more complicated. In Cynthia Hamilton's estimation, James is one of those novelists who worked out in his fiction "the conditions of consciousness of the colonized" (438), and he accomplishes this with a sustained bit of comic epistemology. Haynes is a colonized subject who views himself as existing apart from the masses of colonized subjects. His destiny is to occupy that middling administrative ground allotted to a tiny middle class of black people under British rule. Still, as was true of the governors of Trinidad themselves, he is utterly reliant upon the lower classes for the most basic intelligence of colonial society. In James's construction, Haynes is seen to reproduce at another level the most petty jealousies and aspirations of the masses. While Haynes never quite fully recognizes that fact, he does come to recognize the ways in which colonial class structures come to divide him from himself.

Haynes is, of course, known and respected in his city as a man of learning. Ella, though she has been a second mother to him, is too self-conscious in the presence of his erudition to permit him to see her attempts at handwriting. One of Haynes's fellow tenants at Number 2, Mrs. Atwell, takes pains to let him know that, while she has little formal education, she was a great reader of novels in her day (a day that seems to be long past). After returning a book Haynes has loaned her, Mrs. Atwell, who appears really to have knocked at Haynes's door to see what he is up to with Maisie, effuses: "I pass through the Universal Spelling Book at school, Mr. Haynes, and when you pass through that you know something, you can take it from me. And I can tell you, Mr. Haynes, it was a real good book. A1 and no mistake. High, high class. But how do men think of such things, Mr. Haynes? Education. That's what it is. Education. If I had a child I would sacrifice anything to give him education" (MA 152). Haynes's mother has sacrificed, as have the renters of certain rooms in the slum quarters, so that Haynes might have an education. Still, he frequently appears to know much less than those around him.

An early indication of Haynes's lack of social knowledge comes when he is first introduced to Mrs. Rouse. Though he has never previously spoken with any of the people living in Minty Alley, they know him. "We know you" (MA 25), announces Mrs. Rouse. "We see you passing up and down." Despite Haynes's extensive learning, though, his new neighbors often are caught off guard by his failure to comprehend his immediate surroundings and culture. It is much as though he had passed up and down Victoria Street without ever having looked into the yards he was passing, without taking in what was all about him. One day, as Miss Atwell narrates the wedding of Mrs. Rouse's former lover, Benoit, to the light-skinned nurse who had earlier lived at Number 2 with the rest of them, Haynes interrupts to ask what Miss Atwell means when she declares that the nurse has "fixed" Benoit. "What?" Miss Atwell responds incredulously. "You a Creole and don't know these things? Mr. Haynes, you are a young man and should take my words to heart" (MA 108). This is the sort of knowledge Maisie brings to Haynes as accompaniment to his sexual initiation, and in many ways it seems this accession to social comprehension makes a more lasting impression upon Haynes than the delayed advent of his sexual life. From the very beginning of his stay in Minty Alley, it is Maisie who bears knowledge to Haynes and offers interpretation. It was invariably Maisie who "came up to him and told him what happened" (MA 74). In the end, what Maisie knew is far more important to Haynes than what she offers him sexually, though that is certainly impressive as well. In those intimate conversations that follow their lovemaking in Haynes's room, "they scarcely talked about their relationship, but about No. 2 and the people who lived in it" (MA 169). What Maisie knew was what made her Haynes's first new friend.

The actual mechanisms of Maisie's knowledge are not in the least mysterious, as Haynes finally learns when he inquires directly about her sources. As Maisie narrates the wedding of Benoit and the nurse in elaborate detail, Haynes interrupts and asks, "But how do you know all this, Maisie?" Maisie patiently explains, "The girl she buy the dress from in the store tell people. And we know plenty who Mrs. Robinson does sew for. And when they go there she tell them about it" (MA 100). Maisie's use of the first-person plural in this account is revealing, for while Haynes has as much opportunity to know these people as do the others in the house, this is all news to him. It is news to the novel's readers as well. James's tightly controlled flow of narrative information is directed almost exclusively through the person of Haynes, so readers only learn of what is already common knowledge to all the others as Haynes learns of it. Maisie's "we" does not include us, though the implication of the narrative is that it could. One of the reasons that Haynes identifies both the household at Number 2 and the barrack-yard itself so intimately with Maisie, to the point that he comes to feel that "No. 2 without Maisie would now be unbearable" (MA 194), is that Maisie has become the personification of all that Haynes finds disturbing, titillating, tragic, and inspiring at Number 2. "Through her," we learn, "Haynes knew immediately every single thing that was going on in the house" (MA 209). We see just how sad and telling this fact is when we remind ourselves that this is said of the house in the yard where Haynes lives, a house to which he has ready access. In a way, Maisie has become an extension of his peephole, both bringing him closer to understanding of his neighbors and further distancing him from them. The fact that Maisie is the bearer of all household knowledge to Haynes marks the extent to which Haynes remains apart from his neighbors, and even from his lover. It is Haynes, not Haynes's creator, who is always so distanced from those with whom he lives, and that distance is tragically measured at the novel's conclusion.

One additional thing that Maisie knows from the outset is that Haynes is not the type to rebel wholly against his deceased mother's expectations and marry a woman of Maisie's class. When Haynes rashly promises that he will never forget her, Maisie promptly places things on a more realistic plane:

> "Me, Mr. Haynes. You'll never forget me? You, mustn't say such things." She was smiling, but she was serious. "Why mustn't I say such things?" said Haynes, but he spoke mechanically.
> "Because they aren't true." (MA 172)

It proves finally to be true after all that Haynes will never forget her, but he intends no more than a temporary liaison while at Number 2, and Maisie knows this. She is to be his initiator, his youthful fling before the serious business of adult marriage. Maisie knows that Haynes has hoped to learn something of life from his sojourn in Minty Alley, but Maisie knows that he will not learn the one thing that might make a life together for them possible. In the end, Maisie has far greater faith in her prospects for making her own way in the United States than for anything that might advance her materially to come from the likes of Haynes.

And she has him pegged precisely. Haynes, who has filled himself as full of romantic ideals as ever did Emma Bovary, dreams of a perfect mate, one of his own social order. Even when he comes to understand what Maisie means to him, he cannot abandon his class-conscious idiocy: "He wondered if the girl of his dreams, the divine, the inexpressible she whom he was going to marry one day, he wondered if in some things she would be to him what Maisie was in all" (MA 212). Haynes, having passed his early years in the cloistered order of his mother's house, with Ella and his books for company, has at last found someone with whom he can truly live, yet he cannot live with her: "It wasn't only the sleeping with her. They met elsewhere for this purpose and that could continue. But for the first time in his life he had a friend. If she left this life was over" (MA 194). For the first time in his life Haynes has had the temerity to become a part of the lives of others (though he hasn't become much of a part), and he yearns after the kind of friendship that could be his could he but allow those others fully to join him in his life as equals, but he fails to formulate even the first opening in that direction; he only opens peepholes.

At the novel's end Haynes is again left bereft as he was at the beginning, but this time his loss is of his own devising. Benoit has died and Mrs. Rouse has sold Number 2 Minty Alley. The nurse has gone with her son to live in North America. Maisie has, by her usual mischievous means, managed to translate herself to the United States. We learn by a last letter from her that she has jumped ship and has landed among friends, and who would doubt that she would know what next to do? Haynes misses her most as the tangled lives of Minty Alley reach their communal denouement, as he wonders what Maisie might have made of all this. In John Stewart's reading of James's novel, Haynes has learned at last that there is another world adjacent to his own realm of comfort and abstraction. That, though, is the conclusion to all too many tales of middle-class slumming. Stewart also believes that life in the barrack-yard teaches Haynes "his own capacities for honesty and integrity, and he acquires a lasting appreciation of the palpitant tragicomedy which underlies upper-class posturing" (106). Here it would seem that the critic has conflated the understandings reached by Haynes with those reached by the readers of Haynes's tragicomic trajectory. Maisie knows the limits of Haynes's honesty and integrity, though she is herself a practiced liar. To the very last, Haynes is not wholly honest with himself as he thinks about Maisie: "He would sometime or other find another girlfriend. But another Maisie, never. Why had he let her go? But how could he have kept her?" (MA 228). Just how rhetorical that final question remains is something Haynes cannot allow himself to contemplate. Its answer is the ground against which the novel's last scene assumes its tragic proportions.

In the last paragraph of his novel, James returns his protagonist to the ominously named Victoria Street. Though young Haynes has been transfigured by his experiences, he has not truly grown into his own capacities. So concerned is he still with keeping the pathway to his independence cleared of impediment that he does indeed stand alone. Again he is seen looking into Minty Alley from the outside. Standing in Victoria Street he once more gazes unseen at the life within. The new residents of Minty Alley, like the old, live with their windows and doors open to the world. This time there is no Maisie to bring Haynes news of the intimacies lived out all around him. What Maisie knows, he will not know again. Haynes is left in solipsistic whimsy as the last sentence of *Minty Alley* leaves him "looking in at the window and thinking of old times" (MA 244).

In his critical writings, James said again and again that the truly great novelist is the author who sees that one great age is passing and that the next is visible within the lineaments of the present. For James, such novelists present their vision "primarily in terms of new types of human character with new desires, new needs, new passions" (MRC 124). In creating Maisie, James was delineating evolving types of human characters, individuals who were not content to live out the lives plotted for them by the circumstances of their birth and the oppressive weight of colonial history. She is not a revolutionary, but out of her desire for a better life comes the force that leads to revolution, and that has already set millions of people in motion across the breadth of the globe. Haynes is not a revolutionary either. What James once wrote of Herman Melville's character Pierre could be true of Haynes as well: "Violently alienated from the old world by its corruption and its selfishness, he would turn to the poor and the humble, seeking to regenerate the world by new discoveries in Truth and Wisdom and ethical principles. There are none such to be found anywhere. Hence Pierre clung to the old conceptions, could not break once and for all with his father's world" (MRC 111). Haynes is unable to break from his mother's world, which really died with her, and so he ends friendless in the middle of a crumbling imperial road, looking on wistfully as others make a life for themselves out of the materials at hand. C. L. R. James never published another novel, not, as John Wickham would have us believe, because James was not truly a novelist, but because he sought to regenerate the world by new discoveries, and he devoted himself to the prosaic tasks of building among the people towards that regeneration. Literature remained for him a source for discovery, though, and four decades later he was still reading and arguing about the newest literature of his day.

III. PREFACE TO CRITICISM

An artistic, a social event does not reflect the age. It is the age.
C. L. R. James, *Cricket*

Few critics in America were as well situated as C. L. R. James to recognize the social and historical significance of the publication and reception of Richard Wright's *Native Son* when the book first appeared. James had known Wright from the early years following his arrival in the United States and his friendship with the North American novelist was to continue for more than two decades. Margaret Walker, in her biography of Wright, suggests that "perhaps the most significant friendship that Wright began in 1938 was with the West Indian writer and advanced Trotskyite C. L. R. James, author of *The Black Jacobins*" (120). The subsequent appearance of *Native Son* was greeted by James not only as a major literary achievement by a close friend, but as an event that marked an epochal moment in American cultural history. Writing in his regular column for the *Labor Action* newspaper, under the title "The Negro's Fight," James remarks on May 27, 1940, that "six weeks after publication, *Native Son*, a novel about a Negro by a Negro, Richard Wright, had sold a quarter of a million copies. This is not only a question of literature. Whatever brings a nationally oppressed minority to the notice of the oppressing majority is of political significance" (NQ 55). James, of course, appreciated *Native Son* as a powerful accomplishment of narrative art; indeed he regards Wright's book as "one of the most powerful novels of the last twenty-five years" (NQ 56). Still, James had never adhered to a simple reflection model of base and superstructure. He believed that the novel was a mode of social and political action, one with far-reaching cultural consequences. In James's reading, at the end of Bigger Thomas's story "Bigger stands in the dock and is sentenced but it is the American social order which is on trial" (NQ 56). The fact that millions of white Americans would read Bigger's sentence and contemplate uncomfortably the questions it raised about their society was, for James, equal in importance to the novel's aesthetic triumphs. Decades later he was to have a similar response to the nationwide television broadcast of the miniseries *Roots*. As a professional historian and novelist himself, James had certain qualms about Alex Haley's work, but, as he told his students at Federal City College, nobody should underestimate the historical importance of the fact that millions of white Americans were attending, however shallow that attention, to an epic narrative of the lives of black Americans.

In the years intervening, few scholars knew of James's importance to the career of Richard Wright or of his continued critical engagement with literature, largely because of the fugitive nature of James's publications and of his life. Thousands of people read James's remarks on *Native Son* in 1940, but they were published under his pseudonym J. R. Johnson, a thin veil drawn over James's illegal continued presence in the United States. Thousands, too, at one time or another heard James speak in public of his critical readings, but his writings on literature were scattered and remained out of print for years at a stretch.

Typically, one of the great near-events in American cultural life was a magazine that was never published. Following the release of Rayford Logan's anthology *What the Negro Wants* and the controversy spurred by that book, Richard Wright began making plans to edit a volume of essays by African-American scholars, including Saunders Redding, St. Clair Drake, E. Franklin Frazier, and C. L. R. James. When that plan didn't work out, Wright began meeting with James to outline a proposal for a magazine, to be titled *American Pages*. Other writers, including Ralph Ellison, Melvin B. Tolson, Horace Cayton, and James T. Farrell, were involved in the planning stages, and soon a prospectus for the project and a few initial commitments of funding were in place. Wright and James had agreed that *American Pages* was to be a popular magazine, with features on entertainers of the day, fiction, and poetry. In the words of James's second wife, Constance Webb, the magazine would bring the middle-class reader "face to face with the simple outlines of his culture as it really was, with the attempt to forge a knowledge of the emotional cost among majorities and minorities alike of what it was like to live in America" (219). Despite early enthusiasm and the pledged financial support of such well-to-do liberals as Mrs. Clara Florsheim, the magazine project eventually withered on the vine as Wright found himself stalled by other potential supporters, Marshall Field among them.

Because the literary criticism of C. L. R. James remained largely out of print till the last decades of his life, there is considerably more confusion about this aspect of his career than there is about his work as an historian. James's one separately published critical book, *Mariners, Renegades, and Castaways: The Story of Herman Melville and the World We Live In,* is a case in point. In a report delivered to a conference on West Indian affairs meeting at the University of Montreal in 1965, Martin Glaberman, a longtime colleague of James's in political activities, wrote that "MARINERS, RENEGADES AND CASTAWAYS . . . is now one of the standard texts of Melville's criticism" ("Man" 22). A quarter of a century later, however, this wishful thinking was still a good distance from the bibliographies of most Melville studies, and Darrell E. Levi observed that "*Mariners* seems to have had little, if any, impact on subsequent Melville scholarship" (495). Levi sees James's study of Melville as being, like Charles Olson's *Call Me Ishmael,* a valuable text that occurred at an eccentric angle to traditional Melville criticism. For Levi, "*Mariners* can be seen as a preface to the extensive, provocative, political Melville scholarship of recent years" (496), even if that preface has gone largely unread.

Mariners, though available in many American university libraries, was not available in a well-distributed edition for two decades following its first publication by James and his political group in the early 1950s. Even now, when versions of the book have been republished in two subsequent editions, it has never reappeared in its entirety. With the book's republication, more readers of Melville have come to know of it and to regret that it has not been better known. William Spanos, in his recent study, *The Errant Art of Moby-Dick,* cites James's midcentury Melville work and terms it an "unconscionably neglected book" (100). All the same, the dropping of segments from the end of *Mariners* in its republished form causes critics to miss much of what James is up to in his hybrid volume of literary criticism, cultural studies, political polemic, and plea against deportation. The version read by Spanos is the 1978 text, and this is why he is able to cast the book as one that looks at *Moby-Dick* "from a non-American perspective" (350n). It is true that James was legally an alien, and he notes, near the end of his study, that even though he is a foreigner, it was from him that many

Americans "gained their first enthusiasm and interest in Melville" (168). What Spanos does not know, though, because this last chapter was not reprinted in the 1978 edition, is that James presents his reading of Melville as a transformative, perhaps even Americanizing experience. He says of his life in America that "from that beginning, stage by stage I have spared no pains to understand the United States and become a part of the American people" (167). The end of James's book on Melville, in other words, argues that the Melvillean text has made of James an insider, so much so that he produces his readings as evidence of his Americanness, and he believes Melville can serve this function for others as well.

Not only had significant numbers of Americans, particularly radical, working-class Americans, come to Melville through James, but many others throughout the world have been influenced by James's work as a literary critic, even when that work was not readily at hand in a printed form. He began his work as a publishing critic writing book review columns in the *Beacon* as early as 1931, and nearly a half-century later he was still contributing book review columns to *New Society* and other magazines, turning his attention to recent works of history and politics and to such novels as Michael Thelwell's *The Harder They Come*. Much of that work remains uncollected to this day, but scattered through the volumes of James's selected writings one finds commentary on canonical authors such as Shakespeare, Thackeray, Melville, and Whitman, as well as occasional commentary on newer writers, including Derek Walcott, Wilson Harris, Aimé Césaire, Alice Walker, Ntozake Shange, Toni Morrison, and others. Often James's literary commentaries are delivered informally, as in his report of an encounter with Edith Sitwell that he published as part of a series of articles for the *Port of Spain Gazette*. The early James, while his characteristic tone is much in evidence, shows himself as one who is resistant to novel formal experiment, though he will later speak favorably of such powerfully innovative artists as Beckett, Césaire, and Harris. Recounting his conversation with Sitwell in 1932 to his Trinidad audience, James makes clear his early commitment to a thematic study of literature and his preference for traditional modes and realism. That James chose Edith Sitwell as his foil for a debate on form (they conclude, in James's account, agreeing on more points than one might expect) is again characteristic. James nearly always produces transformative readings, as William Cain argues, making authors and texts "serve his own social, political, and historical purposes" (270). James's approach to Sitwell is, as Cain describes James's readings of Shakespeare, a "subversion of the natural, the obvious, the taken for granted" (270).

Though James continued his thematic emphasis in literary criticism, he cared little for reductive readings that attempted to glean great ideas from books while leaving the art behind. For James, such utilitarian readings were fatal because, as he writes in *Mariners, Renegades and Castaways,* "the social and political ideas in a great work of imagination are embodied in human personalities, in the way they are presented, in the clash of passions, the struggle for happiness, the avoidance of misery" (MRC 122). This accounts for James's emphasis upon character and context. In his view, great authors presaged the coming social changes in their dramatization of new forms of human organization and character within the struggle of daily life. In his essay "The Artist in the Caribbean" he remarks that "an artistic medium is a thoroughly artificial construction, through which an individual is able to see and to express the world around him" (FP 183). His underscoring of the artifice of art is crucial here. James did not read literature as a mirror held up to society but as a metamorphosing lens revealing that which is invisible to the naked eye, and that which is yet to come. Despite his occasional resistance to formal experimentation in modernist literature, he always contended that the artist's ever-shifting cultural context required the creation of new forms. Just as Shakespeare had required a new form to "express a new world," he wrote to Constance Webb in 1944, the American circumstance called upon artists to create new measures. For James, the importance of Whitman was that "he consciously saw that the society of America, *without the European roots* and more democratic in its social life than any European society, needed a new verse form" (JR 138). As a dialectician of history, James naturally tended to view the formal evolution of poetry as responsive to the same cultural forces that drove other ruptures and syntheses. In another letter to Constance Webb in that same year James sketches parallel lines of intellectual history: "What is most exciting is that the sequence from Hume to Marx which I have been studying for the last three years and which now has had an effect on my thinking and on my personal life beyond all explanation, this I find repeated with an almost photographic exactitude in modern poetry. Yes, modern poetry!" (JR 140). This reading of literature as a dialectical progression of contending social forces finding their forms in great art is a constant theme in James's commentaries. It was never, however, merely a belief that the economic structures of a society inevitably produced a particular culturally dominant literary form. James knew that Marx was an inveterate reader who learned from literature, and as James himself learned from Marx, so did other writers. Literary works were not just answers to what the age demanded, they helped to shape the age and its demands. They were events in history, not simply writing formed by history.

This mode of conceiving of literature as socially transformative, and James's characteristic act of transforming the accepted conceptions of literary works in his reading of them, were both rooted in his own early experiences of returning with his readings to the colonial center. That trajectory can be readily traced in two talks given under the same title, "The Old World and the New," one of which has been published among James's volumes of selected writings, the other having been circulated by his political associates in the United States in the form of a long-playing record. (This recording may be distinguished from the printed speech by its subtitle, "Shakespeare, Melville and Others.") In the published speech, which is largely autobiographical, James recalls the double reading of canonical English texts that confirmed his revolutionary politics: "Those few of us who got an education were able to read Thackeray, Dickens, Shakespeare, Hazlitt, a whole lot of people who had liberal ideas and put forward conceptions which were absolutely opposed to the kind of society in which we lived and the subjugations which were imposed upon us. Therefore we had a conception from the books that we read. The result was that when we came to Europe and saw that society did not correspond to what we had read, without exception we revolted against it" (RV 205). It would be difficult to overstate the importance of this statement, made late in James's life, to our understanding of postcolonial literatures and cultural theory. It was through a thorough reading of the canonical texts of the colonial language that James's thoughts moved toward a radical conception of what a truly democratic society might be; which is not, James would insist, to say that the ideal could not have been located elsewhere. It was because of the contingent circumstance of James's birth in a British colony that he was given to reading these particular texts and this particular tradition. He comments in passing in this same speech, "I have sometimes wished that I had a native language but I find English good enough to go on with for the time being" (RV 202). It was James's reading of the distance between that democratic ideal and the social realities of the culture that claimed to have birthed it that confirmed James in his determination to revolt against the colonial powers of the capitalist West. Many might insist to James that he had misread

Shakespeare and Thackeray if he claimed to have found an anticolonial text in his study of those authors; James would claim in response that it was British society's misreading of its own greatest art that caused it to cling so tenaciously to imperial privilege, and that caused its literary arts to enter a period of decline.

In the recorded speech "The Old World and the New," James offers Shakespeare and Melville as representative figures of what had once been a great European culture and what was now great in New World writing. Reading through Shakespeare, Defoe, and Blake, James posits an evolving empiricist foundation to later British literary arts. Though English writers might soar to Romanticist heights of mysticism, James believes, they invariably return to the reality of their social placement. English writers, James argues, are always aware of the social system they are a part of, and of their place in it. James turns at this point in his lecture to Marx's first volume of *Capital* with its bemused critique of the political economy of *Robinson Crusoe*. Visiting Crusoe on his island, Marx finds a textbook example of the essential empiricist, and of the division of labor. According to Marx: "Necessity itself compels [Crusoe] to apportion his time accurately between his different kinds of work. . . . This our friend Robinson soon learns by experience, and having rescued a watch, ledger, and pen and ink from the wreck, commences, like a true-born Briton, to keep a set of books" (*Capital* 1: 88). Crusoe is the kind of character so often seized upon by James in his readings, a character, like Melville's Ishmael and Ahab, in whose confrontation with his environment we can perceive the emergent reconfigurations of future society. Marx finds Crusoe, alone on his island, reproducing in his own person an entire social order, a structure that leads almost inexorably to the enslavement of Friday.

James conducts a similar reading in the plays of Shakespeare, finding, to the surprise of some other readers, that "from the beginning of his writing to the end Shakespeare was dominated by one subject, to attack the conception of monarchy" (n.pag.). This is the sort of criticism that leads William Cain to say of James that "it is less that he *fails* to read Shakespeare rightly than that he *refuses* to abide by the words of the text alone" (269–70). James must have frequently encountered such objections, for in his speech he takes a certain delight in detailing for his audience how he has parried similar criticisms precisely by citing the words of the text alone. With a series of beautifully recited extracts from the major plays, James makes the case that again and again Shakespeare places speeches about the unsatisfactory nature of monarchy into the mouths of royalty themselves. (Though James could not have known of it at the time, the American poet William Carlos Williams had reached similar conclusions. In his posthumously published manuscript titled *The Embodiment of Knowledge,* Williams had written in the decade preceding James's arrival in the United States of his exasperation at the dominant critical view of Shakespeare's texts. "Can't they see," Williams asks, "that the decay of the monarch all through his work is one of the most important documents in existence" [28].) While his reading may be far from proving that this formed the one subject dominating Shakespeare, it is rhetorically forceful and leads to James's larger point in distinguishing the great writing of the Old World from that of the New. James reads those authors he considers at the forefront of English letters also to have been at the forefront of significant social transformations, and he feels that contemporary British authors are no longer able to place themselves in that position. "They had the tradition since Chaucer," he argues, "of writing in relation to a social structure. By the end of the nineteenth century they couldn't do that. And this tradition which they had for many centuries, one of the greatest literary traditions in the world, had gone to pieces" (n.pag.).

With the colonization of the New World, James holds, Western culture opened upon an uncertain future, one that European artists found increasingly difficult to address in their work. In his lectures on the Guyanese novelist Wilson Harris, James says that "European civilization for many centuries had a fixed assumption and classification of material achievement and corresponding philosophical assumptions. Harris says that America is not like that" (SE 168). The difference, as James delineates it in "The Old World and the New," is that "the American writers are very much aware of the instability of the society where they are, and of the fundamental unsoundness of the whole structure of human existence" (n.pag.). Where the literature of the Old World took the structures of human existence as a given, American writing takes the fundamental unsoundness of human existence as its structuring principle. James is acutely aware of the dangers of essentialism in such remarks. He tells his audience that he wants them to understand that he is only describing trends, intellectual currents, that allow him to steer a course for the future.

This New World structuring that James describes is most evident in the intellectual and aesthetic tension between the individual and the mass. Sounding much like Antonio Gramsci, James writes that "the intellectual was an organic part of rationalist society and Hamlet is the organic intellectual" (JR 245). James sees Shakespeare as having lived at a transitional time when it was possible for him to exist, through aristocratic patronage, as an intellectual of the medieval type, while at the same time working in a commercial milieu as one of the first intellectuals "whose life has been shaped by the communication of ideas to the general public" (JR 245). Hamlet is not simply a character with an Aristotelian flaw in his personality; his personality exhibits "a flaw in the whole construction of civilization" (JR 245). American literary artists work at a geographical and social point of still greater transformation. They are "the first to face as a practical question the beginnings of a problem which has been fully recognized during the last twenty years," James writes in 1950. That problem is "the relation of individualism to democracy as a whole" (JR 202). James here strikes the theme that was to be followed through by Ralph Ellison in his later collections of essays, *Shadow and Act* and *Going to the Territory*. Both writers read an American body of texts whose structuring tensions were built from the very beginning around the difficulties of reconciling a commitment to the freedom of the individual with the democratic ideal of majoritarian governance, around the dramatic conflicts of individual conscience and the political expressions of the masses, around the tasks of rescuing a possible democracy from the legacy of a governing apparatus that oppresses minorities.

Though James views Whitman as a great lyric poet, one whose finest work had not yet been surpassed by any European poet (JR 203), he feels that Whitman ultimately fails to comprehend fully those contradictory commitments. Whitman, according to James, remains an isolated individual, but one "who craves free association with his fellows" (JR 203). In this, Whitman is a representative American, and America is, again, one of those first sites for the emergence of this problem as the problem of modern peoples and the problem of modernist arts. Despite Whitman's epic lists, despite his monumental cataloguing of his fellows and his assertions of identity with them, James believes that Whitman, "the greatest of American poets, . . . wrecked himself trying to achieve the impossible" (JR 204). The very thinness of Whitman's great lists, though they teem with closely marked detail, becomes for James a sign of shallowness in Whitman's Romanticism. The constant identification with everyone and everything he meets becomes an emblem of the isolation of Whitman, of his apartness. Whitman remains, at the last, himself an isolato.

James contrasts Melville to Whitman on exactly these grounds: "He sought not the violent self-expression of individuality which is so peculiarly American, but that conviction of the need for communication with all types of men which is also so peculiarly American. Many European intellectuals write for common men, organize for them, will readily die for them—do everything for them, except meet them as men. Melville described common people as they have been described in no modern literature; but he saw no way for them to form a harmonious society and drew a society which would crash to its doom by individuals" (JR 210). While Whitman catalogued the charged details of trippers and askers, and while he sang of occupations as no poet had before, Melville showed men occupied, and dramatized their occupations with one another. Rather than indite a tempting vision of the American dream hovering above the horizon, Melville found, in the concrete proceedings of daily life, the future in the present, and so was able, as Whitman was not, to demonstrate in the engagements of his characters with one another those difficulties that would come to typify the succeeding age.

Melville was also able to see the extent to which the narrative of the American dream held even so great a visionary poet as Whitman from finding his way to practical resolutions of his democratic ideals. The fact that the same poet who writes so movingly of the escaped slave could also at times exhibit "copperhead" sympathies would not have surprised Melville, for Melville also had seen clearly a characteristically modern plight of the intellectual. Reading Melville's *Pierre,* James finds that "what Melville saw was the way in which the traditional, the accepted, the established, however admittedly corrupt, retains its grip on those who want to break with it, or seem to have broken with it—and the consequences to personality" (MRC 110). This may be a distinguishing trait between James and the earlier scholars of the Melville revival, or between James and his contemporaries among cold war liberals who reproduced *Moby-Dick* as an allegory of the contest between freedom and totalitarianism. Like the revivalists, James saw the *Pequod* as the ship of state making a revolutionary voyage into the frontier of human possibilities. Like many cold war liberals, James tended to read Ahab as a premonition of the totalitarian psychology that has terrorized the twentieth century. But in reading Melville's texts as also staging the complicity of the individual intellectual, James was reading what William Spanos has termed *Moby-Dick*'s "errant art." James reads *Moby-Dick* as a novel that resists domesticating political allegories, even his own.

As William Cain has pointed out, James is not entirely comforted by Melville's errant art, for not only does Melville never overtly propose a mode of reconciling these powerful conflicts, he seems to suggest that they may not be reconciled. James writes that "Melville saw, and indeed on the basis of his experiences, could see no solution whatever" (JR 218). For Cain, this signals a "deep conservatism in Melville that runs contrary to James's own trust in the innate decency and inventive power of working people. Melville is less James's ally than his opposite, the Other whose pessimism about human nature James must override" (267). There is a great deal of truth to Cain's observation, but there is another and simpler distinction which is drawn by James himself. "Melville did not write political treatises" (JR 214), James reminds his readers so as to keep clear the differences between what Melville has done as a novelist and what James may choose to do with his study of Melville's text. In fact, James believes that among the most remarkable aspects of Melville's writing is his willingness to pose unanswered questions about his historic moment.

James's chief example of this, in his discussions of *Moby-Dick*, is Melville's exploration of the relationships between the *Pequod*'s crew and their captain. The fact that Ahab's crew do not revolt against him is not fully explained by their spiritual investment in Ahab's search for the great white whale. But neither are things quite as straightforward as William Cain reads them. Cain believes that "*Moby-Dick* is, or should be deeply disturbing for James and for those who share his faith in common people and their capacity for political resistance" (265). Cain's reading of James's critique, though, misses just how disturbing James does find the novel. In Cain's reading of *Mariners, Renegades and Castaways,* "The workers of the 'Pequod' do not revolt, James contends, because they *cannot:* Ahab's totalitarian power and Fedallah's terrorism are too extreme, too absolute, for the men to break free" (265). Cain feels that "this is not quite satisfactory," but it isn't satisfactory for James either. In the notes on *American Civilization* that James wrote prior to *Mariners,* he describes this most confounding passage of Melville's narrative. According to James, Melville was "deeply concerned with the inability of the crew to put an end to the mad captain by revolt" (JR 214), but in a passage of *Mariners* not cited by Cain, James goes on to argue that "Melville took great pains to show that revolt was no answer to the question he asked" (MRC 60), and it is important that we register those last four words. It is not that Melville thought revolt impossible, nor did he think revolution could answer nothing. Rather it "was no answer to the question he asked."

James poses this part of the plot as an open question when he discusses Melville's role in nineteenth-century American intellectual life: "Why didn't they do it? Here Melville does a most extraordinary thing. He says frankly that he doesn't know. . . . Melville cannot understand why. It should be obvious by now that behind this marvelous sea story, this writer was digging into problems of far greater social significance for us today than were Flaubert, Dostoyevsky and Rimbaud" (JR 214). In *Mariners* itself, James points to a subnarrative in *Moby-Dick* that demonstrates why this text is so profoundly disturbing. When Melville introduces into his narrative the story of a revolt on another ship, a successful revolt instigated by one Steelkilt, the sub-sub-librarian's subnarrative shows why Melville felt a revolt would not answer his deeper questions. As James describes this passage: "Steelkilt and some of his fellow-mutineers escape and get back home again. That's all. Everything goes back to just where it was before. That is exactly what would have happened in 1851 if there had been a revolt on the *Pequod*. We would have been left in the end exactly where we had been at the beginning" (MRC 60). James suggests that Melville believes such a revolt, a revolt directed solely against the particular monomaniac at hand, would leave the social and political structures within which Ahab seizes power intact, that the crew would return to inhabit (and be judged by) the very orders that had constituted Ahab as the captain of their fate. And yet, Melville has not created a crew who believe this themselves, and so the mystery lingers, and both Melville and James make room for its disturbing, even errant mystery.

There is much that James admires in Melville, but this above all: that "with an almost mathematical logic, Melville took individualism to the extreme limit of what it could accomplish and then faced it with the crisis which he inevitably foresaw would result" (JR 217). James had already composed his prospectus for *American Civilization* before he wrote *Mariners, Renegades and Castaways*. The promise he makes to his readers at the conclusion of *Mariners*—to publish his views on American Civilization (MRC 172)—is an unfulfilled promise to complete the work of that prospectus. Though hints are given elsewhere in his speeches and writings, and short excerpts appeared in radical newspapers here and abroad, it was not until *American Civilization* was published posthumously in 1993 that many readers found James's outline for a discussion of a group of American intellectuals who "had found what both Whitman and Melville had failed to find" (AC 87). James made this discovery in a body of texts that few literary scholars at the time had paid much attention, the literature of the American

Abolitionist movement, and here we can see more readily and more fully the postcolonial context of James's later writings on Wilson Harris, George Lamming, and Toni Morrison.

In an era when the very few literary scholars who studied the slave narratives faced great difficulty in finding publishers for their work, and when the writings of most nineteenth-century abolitionists, black and white, were routinely ignored in literature and American studies programs alike, James proposed a thorough study of the Abolitionists as "intellectuals whose whole intellectual, social and political creativity was the expression of precise social forces" (AC 85). While James acknowledges the multiplying doctrinal disputes within the Abolitionist movement (and in his 1949 essay on "Stalinism and Negro History" he attacks Herbert Aptheker for neglecting to historicize adequately the oppositions between white and black Abolitionists [RM 198–99]), he tends to smooth over the racialized particulars of these sectarian debates in order to focus his discussion more closely upon the Abolitionists as intellectual expositors of revolutionary aspirations emanating from the masses of the slaves themselves. Thus, for example, James mentions William Lloyd Garrison's rejection of the authority of the United States Constitution without mentioning, at least in this preliminary sketch, that this was one of the points of contention upon which the working relationship of Garrison and Frederick Douglass foundered. Like W. E. B. Du Bois in his book *Black Reconstruction,* James described the social movements leading up to the Civil War and the end of legal slavery as a political revolution of the modern type. As in his history of the slave revolt in San Domingo, James wrote the history of Abolitionism as a narrative in which the intellectual leadership of the political movement were constantly prodded to ever more radical actions as the result of their working contact with the masses of African Americans. Because James perceives the political leadership as the mode of expression of the liberatory thought of the free blacks and slaves, he argues that "any kind of analysis of the Abolitionist intellectuals must . . . begin with the slaves" (AC 85), and he is right even if he does elide the substantial levels of racism among many white Abolitionists. James draws a parallel between the social upheavals of Jacksonian democracy and Denmark Vesey's uprising. Looking at such phenomena as David Walker's "Appeal," Nat Turner's rebellion, the evolution of the Underground Railroad, exactly the sort of revolutionary "self activity" he had earlier outlined in his *History of Negro Revolt,* James finds a gathering coalition of intellectuals and revolutionary masses, and he describes how this coalition began to express itself as a mass movement in such media as the Abolitionist press and in such innovative publications as *Freedom's Journal*, which James identifies as "the first Negro newspaper in the United States" (AC 86).

Working, usually for the first time in their lives, with black intellectuals, responding to reactionary attacks upon even their most moderate proposals, white Abolitionists moved toward increasingly disruptive positions. Their proposals for immediate and unconditional abolition of slavery were expressed in progressively more violent language as they attempted to "startle the South to madness" (qtd. in AC 89), and eventually, in response to such outrages as the Fugitive Slave Act, they were to deny the legitimacy of their own national government. They sought to lead a mass party and they intended theirs to be an international movement. James plans, in the book that was never finished, to relate Emerson, Thoreau and the Transcendentalists to Whitman, Melville and the Abolitionists, for he sees the literary arts produced during this period as being "complementary parts of the same movement" (AC 87). For decades after James proposed these analyses, graduate students in American literature continued to read Emerson without reading William Wells Brown, to study Henry David Thoreau's essay on John Brown without examining the writings of William Lloyd Garrison, and to read Walt Whitman without reading the remarkable prose works of that great Abolitionist and inept reader of verse Thomas Wentworth Higginson. Though students of literature would read such nonfiction political prose as Thoreau's "Civil Disobedience," few could be found in that day who also read the works of Wendell Phillips, whose texts were to prove so important to such later writers as James Weldon Johnson. What James proposes, then, is a much-needed revisionary view of the American Renaissance, one that would demonstrate the integral importance of African-American thought and expression to the canonical texts of what has too often been produced as a white Renaissance. As he proposes in *American Civilization:*

> What we have to show is that if Whitman anticipated the new loneliness of the American character, its passion for the old free association which it was losing, the powerful but false ideals which it tried to substitute for many years; if Melville brushed aside the slaves and painted a picture of impending catastrophe for America and the whole world, whose significance we are only today able to see; then the Abolitionist intellectuals in their political action showed a solution that corresponded in range and intensity to the inspired vision of Melville. (AC 87)

It is not that James would substitute the reading of political treatises for the reading of *Moby-Dick* but that he believed the writings of the Abolitionists were in correspondence with the vision of Melville, that our readings of one would inform and transform our readings of the other, and that we could not fully comprehend America's cultural history without a fuller reading of both. In his commentaries on the experimental novels of Wilson Harris, James singles out for praise "Harris's clear recognition that we are the product of a very complicated historical past and all of it is in us *stirring or at any rate ready for expression*" (SE 170). In proposing that we reread the correspondence between the writings of the Abolitionists—in which James thought to read a joining together of America's zeal for individual freedom and its yet to be honored promise to its own masses of radical democracy—and the texts of America's continually revised canon of Renaissance and Jeremiad, C. L. R. James was proposing that we undertake a more comprehensive reading of the history of our own self-expression.

This was neither the New Historicism nor the old Marxism. James outlines, but never completes, an aesthetic that views literature as history, as event, as the text in which we read our own future in the present. This is why, when he reviewed the first volume of James's three-volume selected writings, Farrukh Dhondy declared, "James has built a stairway in the house of marxist aesthetics" (116). Dhondy's imagery is uncannily apt, for in his own political writings James had spoken movingly of the need to throw open to public view the unexplored foundations of Marxism itself. In calling for a renewed reading of the American past, James proposed an exploration of long-neglected passageways in the superstructures of American literature. In his explorative, audacious correspondence with the American text he continually turned up useful treasures. As he read in the collected writings of Wendell Phillips, for one, he came across a passage that must have seemed particularly propitious to a political writer such as James, who was even then in correspondence internationally with a group of radical theorists who published their works under the slogan of "Socialism or Barbarism." Predicting that the struggle against slavery in the New World would only be settled by force of arms, Wendell Phillips, that great nineteenth-century orator whose address on the life of Toussaint L'Ouverture was to be invoked in so many African-American texts across the generations, concluded that "Our struggle . . . is between barbarism and civilization" (qtd. in AC 94). C. L. R. James, that inveterate reader of American letters, who had begun his childhood practice of writing by imitating the tales of James Fenimore

Cooper, and who devoted himself to a critique of the greatest novel of Herman Melville while awaiting trial and deportation, when he had finished his reading of Wendell Phillips, wrote this about Phillips's text: "seen in its context, it is perhaps the highest peak reached by the United States intellectuals in the foreshadowing of the future of the world of today and in indicating how deeply all great world currents are integral to the United States as a nation" (AC 92). In this judgement, it would seem, C. L. R. James is still ahead of his time.

At the Rendezvous of Victory

> *The masses do not learn history, they make it. More accurately, they learn it only when they make it.*
>
> C. L. R. James, *C. L. R. James and Revolutionary Marxism*

> *Black Studies means the intervention of a neglected area of studies that are essential to the understanding of ancient and modern society.*
>
> C. L. R. James, "The *Black Scholar* Interviews"

> *Some of you may believe that you have read [*The Black Jacobins*]. I did more than that, I wrote it. But it is only in late years that I am able to understand and to appreciate the full significance of what I wrote in that book.*
>
> C. L. R. James, *Spheres of Existence*

I. THE PHILOSOPHY OF HISTORY AND NECESSITY

Writing in 1975, in a review essay for the magazine *Black World*, C. L. R. James noted with some satisfaction that "for some years now, a few historians have recognized that one only begins to write genuine history when one writes about the great untutored mass of the population" ("Maroons" 67). Though he does not here mention the fact, James himself could claim a considerable portion of the responsibility for this transformation in the practice of writing history, and it is important for us to note also in this passage James's emphasis upon the nature of history *as* writing. James was not all that bashful about remarking his own accomplishments, but most moments of self-credit in James's essays are playful. In a 1943 article published in the *New International,* James refers readers to an essay written by J. R.

Johnson on the subject of Trotsky's place in history (SE 53). "J. R. Johnson" was, of course, James writing under a pseudonym, and his *New International* article on "The Philosophy of History and Necessity" was itself signed with the pseudonymous initials "A. A. B." Readers who took the advice of the mysterious but well-read A. A. B. and secured a copy of "Trotsky's Place in History" would have found J. R. Johnson, in a footnote, recommending to their attention the introduction to *The Black Jacobins*, by one C. L. R. James (RM 120). Likewise, in an essay on "Capitalist Society and the War" that appeared in the July 1940 issue of the *New International*, J. R. Johnson quotes approvingly from the first page of *World Revolution*, by C. L. R. James (121).

There is no shortage of testimony from hands other than his own to the importance of James's contributions to historiography. Anna Grimshaw argues that *The Black Jacobins* "raised, implicitly, a challenge to certain assumptions which were commonplace on the revolutionary Left. First of all, he cast doubt on the assumption that the revolution would take place first in Europe, and in the advanced capitalist countries, and that this would act as a model and a catalyst for the later upheavals in the underdeveloped world. Secondly, there were clear indications that the lack of specially-trained leaders, a vanguard, did not hold back the movement of the San Domingo revolution" (JR 7). In Robert Hill's estimation, *The Black Jacobins* can be said "to have revolutionized historical writing in ways dealing both with conception and method" ("In England" 79). Hill notes that James effectively dispensed with the prevailing scholarship on the Abolition movement in England and the end of slavery in the colonies, in the process laying the foundations for such important later histories as Eric Williams's *Capitalism and Slavery*. Further, "James's work laid the foundation for the later systematic analyses of slave and colonial resistances, as well as the factor of the radical consciousness realized as self-activity" (80). Finally, Hill sees James's work in history as complementing a book James was often to speak of in his later years, W. E. B. Du Bois's *Black Reconstruction*. Both Du Bois and James, at nearly the same time, advanced the thesis that black emancipation played an essential role "in effecting the course of . . . wider historical changes in which it was enmeshed" (80). In this judgment Hazel V. Carby concurs, finding in James's histories the argument that "the political, social and cultural issues of the West Indies, of African exploitation, of underdevelopment, and of colonialism in general were not marginal but central to the formation of Western civilization" (45).

When James left Trinidad for England, he took with him the completed manuscript of his novel, which was to become one of the first of the new West Indian novels to be published in England. It was also the only novel he ever published, as his work was directed increasingly to writings in politics and history. Almost immediately upon his arrival James published his first widely disseminated anticolonial texts, *The Life of Captain Cipriani* and *The Case for West Indian Self-Government*. He had come to England under the sponsorship of Learie Constantine, in part to assist Constantine in producing an autobiography, and in 1932 that text was published under the title *Cricket and I*. In 1936, *Minty Alley* was printed, and then, in the space of just three years, James published *World Revolution*, *The Black Jacobins*, his English translation of Boris Souvarine's biography of *Stalin*, and *A History of Negro Revolt*, which first appeared as a special issue of *Fact* magazine ("a monograph a month" was *Fact*'s slogan) in September of 1938. This level of production is all the more impressive when we remember that during this same period James was writing regular cricket columns for the *Manchester Guardian*, helping to organize the International Friends of Abyssinia and the International African Service Bureau, and carrying out a dizzying agenda of speaking and organizing activities for anticolonial and leftist organizations. This span of years marks both the movement into Marxist politics and philosophy that set James's course for the rest of his career and the beginnings of his career as a writer of history.

C. L. R. James has described himself as one who arrived in England with a set of abstract Labour and Socialist ideals clustered around a firm commitment to the goal of self-government for the peoples of Trinidad. In the company of Learie Constantine in Nelson, Lancashire, James met frequently with working-class radicals and leftist intellectuals who challenged his still somewhat vague politics. James, always intellectually curious and an omnivorous reader, set himself a rigorous program of study in political philosophy and in history, and soon joined the international Trotskyite movement. While he has spoken variously of the events leading to his commitment to Marxism, the events of his reading and thinking were as important in this political evolution as were his own experiences as a colonial subject and a member of an oppressed racial group. He told one interviewer: "I became a Marxist through the influence of two books I read. One was Trotsky's *History of the Russian Revolution* and the other was *The Decline of the West* by Oswald Spengler" (qtd. in Le Blanc, RM 3). James's readings of history are, then, intimately tied to the maturation of his political thought. As James read the radical historiography of French writers such as Michelet, Aulard, Mathiez, and Lefebvre, Robert Hill argues, "it was instrumental in helping him to make the transition from literature to a political consciousness, and from a West Indian to a world consciousness" ("In England" 68). However, the increasing emphasis upon historiography in James's career was not so much a transition from literature to political consciousness as it was a transition to the literature of political consciousness, from a potential career as a novelist to a vocation in an equally demanding form of writing. James continued his avid interest in literature, as we have seen, and as an historian he was always vitally concerned with the uses of the literature of history.

As a Marxist historian, James believed in the usefulness of historical writings to revolutionary activity, and he believed in a dialectical movement of human progress toward an inevitable telos. He based his philosophy upon "the destruction of barbarism by the inevitable triumph of the socialist revolution" (JR 159). James insisted that his materialist teleology was, in fact, more objective than the views held of history by those among his contemporaries who rejected historical determinism as idealism and theology. If one recognizes the "bankruptcy of bourgeois democracy," so goes James's argument, but rejects the inevitability of socialist triumph, then one truly does indulge in a defeatist mysticism and quietism, for then one is left with only two choices: "Either the inevitability of barbarism, that is to say the acceptance of the principle of inevitability which they have just rejected or the hope, the faith, the belief that history will offer some way out of the impasse" (JR 159). This is a characteristic Jamesian turning of the tables, and while it may not hold up to the close scrutiny of logicians, its rhetorical power is manifest. What James insists upon here is that to accept the inevitability of the present barbaric modes of social organization is far more of a mystification than a belief that the historical forces of class conflict will ineluctably bring us to socialist revolution.

James's Marxist historiography was, still, never the dogmatic determinism so often found in Communist Party documents. "Like Lenin," A. W. Singham has noted, "but with more concrete evidence, James stressed the flexibility in the stages of history of different societies, as opposed to Stalin's rigid formulations" (85). According to Singham, James's studies of West Indian history had brought him to a significant revision of Marxist economic history. Marx's "Asiatic" mode of production was clearly not an adequate explanatory model for what had developed through the colonial era in the

Caribbean. There, Singham suggests, a capitalist mode of production, the plantation, had been superimposed upon a "pre-feudal structure of slavery" (85). "While Marx, Lenin, and even Trotsky and Luxemburg saw traditional states of Africa and Asia as reflecting the 'Oriental' peculiarity, James showed how the Caribbean was the first modern society to arise outside Western Europe, where both institutions and populations had been transplanted" (86). James's recognition that the hybrid economic modes of West Indian colonialism signaled new contradictions that opened up new revolutionary possibilities is seen by Singham as marking "the beginning of Caribbean social theory" (86).

It is true that Marx had not completely understood the radical potential represented by West Indian modes of economic organization, but he had kept an interested eye on developments in the New World. In an exchange of letters among James's political allies in the United States in the late 1940s and early 1950s, James's correspondents evinced great interest in tracking Marx's study of events in the Caribbean. Raya Dunayevskaya wrote a letter to James on June 7, 1950, in which she reports on her studies of the Marx-Engels correspondence. She tells James of a significant letter, dated November 20, 1865, in which Marx addresses colonial outrages in Jamaica. "The revolts of the West Indies Negroes," Dunayevskaya writes to James, become "part of the history surrounding and sending out 'impulses' to Marx rewriting Capital along the lines of his new thesis" (*Dunayevskaya Collection* 1720).

James recognized the importance of New World African slavery to the rise of international capital, and following Marx's own interest in workers' struggles in the Western hemisphere, James set about researching and narrating the importance of black revolt to the history of world revolution. Patricia J. Williams has recently remarked that "the transformation of slavery's rationales from one discourse to another has been . . . an extraordinary force in the shaping of the modern world. While the master-slave dialectic about which Hegel wrote so evocatively is an ancient philosophical paradox, the life-and-death struggle with which the legacy of the actual slave trade marked contemporary political life is resoundingly modern" (230). Among the sharpest resonances of this passage is its response to the call of C. L. R. James's *The Black Jacobins* and W. E. B. Du Bois's *Black Reconstruction*, among the first books by black writers in the Americas to contest effectively the hegemonic discourse of white dominance put forward by earlier historians. James argued, as did Du Bois, that "any history of the Civil War which does not base itself upon the Negroes, slave and free, as *subject* and *not the object* of politics, is ipso facto a Jim Crow history" (RM 202). In this observation James counters not only the histories authored by the Stalinist party scholars who were his immediate targets but also the dominant American school of thought on the Civil War and Reconstruction, the so-called Dunning school of historians, centered around Columbia and Johns Hopkins Universities in the early decades of this century, as well as the dominant view of white, antebellum abolitionist writers, who so often appeared more concerned with what had been done *to* black people than with what slaves and free black people had accomplished and might still accomplish in the future. James went further still and argued for the centrality of New World Africans and their struggles to the course of development of the modern West. James holds that:

> The wealth which enabled the bourgeoisie to challenge those who were in charge of society and institute the power-building industrial regime came from slavery, the slave trade, and the industries which were based upon that.... The vast change in human society came from the slave trade and slavery. All the historians tell you that. Marx also. His *Poverty of Philosophy* has the section on slavery. It was slavery that built up the bourgeois society and enabled it to make what Lévi Strauss thinks is the only fundamental change in ten thousand years of human history. The blacks not only provided the wealth in the struggle which began between the old society and the new bourgeois society: the black people were foremost in the struggle itself. (JR 396)

James made these observations in 1969. At the time years earlier when he wrote *The Black Jacobins* this was not what all historians told one, and James's theses were hotly debated. Subsequent historians have differed with James and Williams on questions of the exact amounts of capital generated by slavery and made available for industrialization, but there is little question that slavery was central to the evolution of modern capitalism and industry, just as there is no doubting the revolution in historiography represented by James's analyses of the role of black people in the rise of modern Western culture and the importance of Pan-African revolt to our future understanding of revolutionary possibilities.

In a 1949 column in the *Militant* titled "Negro History Week and the Workers" and contributed under the name "J. Meyer," James addressed the fundamental changes in historiography wrought by black scholars: "They began solely with the need to right their own historical wrongs. But now after some thirty years they have not only undermined the vast structure of bourgeois lies about Negroes. They have done more. They have undermined the foundations of American historical writing, not only about Negroes but about crucial aspects of American history" (3). During his years in the United States, James developed a number of critical positions on the writing of American history and on the political significance of that work of research and writing. Many of those publications remain uncollected, but they are integral to our comprehension of James's view of the relationships between his work as an historian and his work as a revolutionary activist. As he neared the conclusion of a speech to the Socialist Workers Party in June of 1949, James spoke of the direct use of historical analyses in the effort to affect the thinking of black Americans. While the descendants of the Dunning school still held great influence among educators in the field of history, many younger historians were reexamining the Civil War and the history of racial politics in response to new works by Gunnar Myrdal and Herbert Aptheker. James tells his colleagues that, as the Communist Party intellectuals had shifted their official positions on "The Negro Question," they had also increasingly taken positions of leadership in the rewriting of American history. James argues that if his group is to "win over Negroes, both intellectuals and advanced workers" ("Speech" 15), they must make plain the differences between themselves and the Stalinist intellectuals.

With midcentury approaching, James saw African-American intellectuals who searched for histories with greater explanatory power in analyzing America's racial present as caught between two alternatives: the Communist approach, practiced most effectively by Herbert Aptheker, and the liberal idealism represented by the work Gunnar Myrdal and his associates accomplished in producing their book, *An American Dilemma*. In "The Revolutionary Answer to the Negro Problem in the United States," issued the year before his speech on the Negro Resolution, James had summarized this situation: "During the last few years certain sections of the bourgeoisie, recognizing the importance of this question, have made a powerful theoretical demonstration of their position, which has appeared in *An American Dilemma* by Gunnar Myrdal, a publication that took a quarter of a million dollars to produce" (RM 179). At the same time, as James outlines for his colleagues in 1949, intellectuals aligned with the Stalinist party organizations in America were beginning to dominate "the field of the Civil War with special reference to Negro history" (15). Ticking off recent publications in the field, many by Aptheker, James itemizes pamphlets on Wendell Phillips, Harriet Tubman, Thaddeus Stevens, Frederick Douglass, Abraham Lincoln, pamphlets on *Lincoln's Third Party* and the *War Elections, 1862–1864* in connection with Henry Wallace's election campaign, and a special pamphlet attacking *An American Dilemma*. James warns his audience: "You can see the immense advantage the Stalinists hold. Along with their maneuvers on policy they have this solid basis of constantly growing material. . . . It is widely spread among the Negro intellectuals" (15).

Pointing to scattered signs of dissatisfaction among black intellectuals with Aptheker's work, James begins a critique that is continued just months later in "Stalinism and Negro History." He quotes at length from a 1948 *Phylon* article contributed by E. Kaiser, of the Schomburg collection, in which Kaiser had attacked Aptheker's historiography as representative of Stalinist approaches. Condensing Kaiser's objections and adding a few of his own, James builds to the conclusion that the errors of Communist Party history are the same errors that lead to the Party's propaganda slogan of self-determination for a black belt region of North America: "Aptheker consistently refers to the heroic qualities of the Negroes, their struggles for freedom, their great deeds, but all of it is general. Despite reservations here and there, his attitude is that of showing that the Negroes *were* human because, look, they fought heroically for freedom. But that the Negroes were a class, in production, at a certain stage; that they made special contributions to the struggle, conditioned by their social role—these things are absent from Aptheker's work" ("Speech" 17). Though some of this is no doubt unfair to the facts of Aptheker's texts, it does render in sharp contrast the difference James perceives between Stalinist historians and the Marxist mode of historiography. The Stalinist view of "the Negro problem" lays its emphasis upon the status of black Americans as an oppressed national minority, without sufficiently examining the history of black actions in class struggle. This eventually has the odd effect of enabling the Communist Party to subsume the Negro question beneath the class question. Though he does not venture an answer in his outline in *American Civilization,* James also underscores for his audience at the Socialist Workers Party meeting the importance of analyzing the causes of "the historic quarrels between Negro Abolitionist and white" (17). It appears from the context in which James raises the issue that he believes the answer to that question will have much to tell black intellectuals about the inadequacies of the Popular Front advocated by the Communist Party in his own time. James proposes to his party colleagues that they enter into the disputes about history in an organized manner, not only with articles in their own magazines and newspapers, but through contributions to the black press as well. James predicts "we shall be able to show that if you do not adopt a strictly Marxist position on the Negroes in the Civil War, you fall not only into idealism, but into white chauvinism" (17).

In his article on "Stalinism and Negro History," first published over the signature "J. Meyer" in *Fourth International* and now reprinted in *C. L. R. James and Revolutionary Marxism,* James claims that Aptheker and other Communist historians fell into both errors. Citing the work of Richard Enmale, James shows that this historian's tendency to ignore the breadth of contributions to the Civil War effort made by black Americans is parallel to his chauvinism with regard to contemporary black intellectuals. Enmale, James charges, leaves out of account the works of African-American historians, and thus "the contemporary Negroes were kept in the background, theoretically and politically, in the role reserved for their ancestors in the actual conflicts of the Civil War" (RM 189). In the same way that the white Abolitionists of the nineteenth century sometimes told former slaves appearing on the speaking circuit that they should stick to the facts of their experiential narratives and leave the theory to the whites, historians such as Enmale were only interested in the oppression to which black people had been subjected; they were not used to reading the analyses, theory, and philosophy of black writers. James also criticizes James Allen's 1937 study, *Reconstruction,* in which Allen accuses Du Bois of "failing to grasp the fundamental bourgeois character of the revolution" represented by the Civil War and its aftermath (qtd. in RM 189). Though James faults certain of Du Bois's conclusions, he felt that Allen had missed the real strength of the book, that Du Bois, as did James in *The Black Jacobins,* "recognized that the Negroes *in particular* had tried to carry out ideas that went beyond the prevailing conceptions of bourgeois democracy" (RM 189).

Along these same lines, James finds that Herbert Aptheker's works, including *The Negro in the Abolitionist Movement* and *Negro Slave Revolts,* fail to recognize the extent to which the actions of free blacks and insurrectionary slaves were the driving force behind nineteenth-century abolitionism. Aptheker speaks of slave revolts having pricked the consciences of Jefferson and Madison, and of their inspiring and stimulating the white abolitionists (RM 193), but, in James's opinion, Aptheker is unable, perhaps even unwilling, to analyze the revolutionary forces at work among the black people themselves. In sum, James's criticism of Aptheker is that "there is not the slightest hint that the Negro was anything more than an appendage, a very valuable appendage, to what Aptheker considers the abolitionist movement to have been. His whole conception is that the abolitionist movement was predominantly white, and Negroes joined it" (RM 196). Aptheker, like some historians who followed in his wake, is able to think of the Abolitionist movement as predominantly white because he is thinking of the movement in terms of its public expression in legal and above-ground political organizations dominated by white activists. What he tends to give less attention to is the existence of the vital national Negro convention movements, movements that were a proving ground for subsequent black political action. James, on the other hand, sees the white public institutions as a surface manifestation of a much larger revolutionary movement that had seized the imagination of the black people themselves. For James, Aptheker's view of the Abolitionist movement is uncomfortably close to William Lloyd Garrison's opposition to the formation of autonomous black organizations and publications. Again, James may somewhat exaggerate the flaws in Aptheker's texts, but he has located a remarkable paradox that Aptheker is slow to acknowledge. The mode of historiography practiced by Aptheker reenacts that curious logic of America's racial politics whereby the limiting of black intellectuals to black issues serves to repress rather than to encourage independent black actions. James argues, against Aptheker's view of Frederick Douglass, that Douglass "was the voice of the American revolution" and that it was "precisely when the bourgeoisie took over that Douglass became primarily a leader of the Negroes" (RM 204), an effective distinction even though it seems to raise questions about when the bourgeoisie "took over." In the same way, historians who now view Douglass chiefly as a voice of black America at the same time render the independent voices of black insurrection mute. "What is important," James concludes, is this maneuver's "logical identity with the hostility to Negro radicalism and independent Negro politics which has appeared in Aptheker's work from the very beginning up to this climax" (RM 208). In other words, just as the same Communist Party that spoke of self-determination for the black belt South ruthlessly suppressed independent black thinkers within its own ranks, some of the very historians who sought to revise the dominant view of black emancipation in America created histories that too often subordinated independent black social movements. James would advise that readers contrast that mode of historiography to the works of such writers as J. R. Johnson, J. Meyer, and, as he once described himself humorously to Constance Webb, "C. L. R. James, that British Negro" (SD 59).

II. HISTORIES OF PAN-AFRICAN REVOLT

The only place where Negroes did not revolt is in the pages of capitalist historians.

C. L. R. James, *C. L. R. James and Revolutionary Marxism*

Mine too a small
cell in the Jura,
the snow strengthens the small cell with
white bars
the snow is a white
gaoler who stands guard
in front of a prison
This man is mine
a man alone, imprisoned by
whiteness
a man alone defying the white
cries of a white death
(TOUSSAINT, TOUSSAINT
LOUVERTURE)
a man who fascinates the white
sparrow-hawk of white death
a man alone in the terrible sea
of white sand

Aimé Césaire, *Return to My Native Land*

When *The Black Jacobins* appeared in 1938 its publishers, Secker and Warburg, a leftist concern that also published George Orwell, placed great emphasis upon the book's qualities as a literary work, as, indeed, a good read. In advertising that appeared in such journals as *Fact* and the *New Statesman and Nation*, Secker and Warburg promised that readers would encounter "the romance of a great career and the drama of revolutionary history" in a book they characterized as a "biography of Toussaint Louverture, leader of the only successful slave revolt in history." Such advertising falls into exactly the errors James warned of in his later essays on historiography by eliminating from view what James believed was a narrative equally as compelling as the life of L'Ouverture, "The transformation of slaves, trembling in hundreds before a single white man, into a people able to organize themselves and defeat the most powerful European nations of their day" (BJ ix). If James's publishers downplayed one of the main points of his book in their efforts to promote it to a British audience, they did at least recognize the skill with which their author had made of his materials not only a scholarly contribution of lasting merit but a work of literature whose narrative structure and eloquence can compare to much of the best fiction of the time. The book itself was a carefully prepared commodity, with a frontispiece signature portrait of Toussaint L'Ouverture and a foldout map of Haiti to "illustrate the war of independence." In later American printings of the book, the map was reduced in size and moved to the front of the volume, while the portrait of L'Ouverture was first recopied in a color version on the cover and subsequently removed all together. Also absent from later printings are the first edition's prints portraying Christophe, Dessalines, and the Abbé Grégoire. An absence felt even more keenly, perhaps, is that of a series of prints in the first edition whose progress and portent are unmistakable. One shows a set of scenes depicting slaves, free Negroes, and mulattoes in prerevolutionary times. Another reproduces prints published in Paris in celebration of the abolition of slavery, prints in which a black man and a black woman, depicted with none of the usual stereotypical features, pronounce their own freedom. A second print honoring the abolition and published in 1794 depicts Britain offering money to the French colonies, an offer that is rejected "through love of liberty." Climaxing the political evolution traced in this series of illustrations is a portrait of E. V. Mentor, the Negro Deputy from San Domingo to the Council of Five Hundred in Paris. These prints show a movement arising among the masses of Africans in the colony and culminating in new forms of relationship with the revolutionary government of France, and they are paralleled by the prints honoring the heroic leaders of the revolution in the colony, the leaders, like L'Ouverture, thrust forward by the developing movement toward freedom and the building of a nation among the island's population.

A great deal of romance and drama permeates this narrative, and James applied his novelist's skills to its telling. There was from the beginning, though, a contemporary political point to James's historical narration, and while the later printings fail to reproduce the important illustrations from the first edition, the appendix that James added to the second edition serves to foreground the political significance of his 1938 edition that, as he has testified, even he had not at first fully understood. Those subsequent understandings are mostly a matter of following out implications of already astute analyses. "From the outset," according to Anuradha Needham, "James conceived *Jacobins* as part of, even a stimulant for, revolutionary action and thought that accompanied the projects of decolonization, first in Africa and then in the West Indies" (289). That James knew *The Black Jacobins* represented a significant new direction in historiography is evident from his retrospective remarks about the text. In the first place, as he indicated in his 1970 interview with the *Black Scholar*, previous writers from the West Indies had shown some reluctance to make West Indian society (or even contemporary European society) their subject (38). More important, James saw that the theses of his study would disrupt existing modes of thought about the past of slavery and colonialism. For one thing, though the triangle trade "is an instance of programmed accumulation of wealth such as the world has rarely seen," any number of earlier historians had managed not to see that "seemingly inescapable fact" (41). Further, James had recognized that "to give the slave his actual historical due is to alter one's notion about the course of civilization itself" (41).

That James's theses were disruptive is evident from some of the critical reactions to his book. Flora Grierson, writing in the October 8, 1938, issue of the *New Statesman and Nation*, conceded many of the facts brought forward by James but caviled at several of his conclusions. Her political bias against his form of Marxism leads her to accuse James of writing out of political bias. "The intelligent historian should at least aim at impartiality," she writes; "the fanatic cannot" (536). Grierson accepts James's documentation for the horrors of slavery but remarks that "because he is a Communist, he wants to show us the worst." This leads to a rather breathtaking bit of rhetorical shiftiness as she concludes her review of James: "Careful and well-documented as this history is, one's faith in Mr. James's intelligence and acumen is badly shaken by sentences such as this: 'the science of history was not what it is today and no man living then could foresee, as we can foresee to-day, the coming upheavals.' The star had not yet risen in the East." Of course, one need not be a Marxist to recognize that few historians of the late eighteenth century could have predicted the revolution of the slaves of San Domingo and its ultimate success, just as one needn't have been a Marxist historian in 1938 to have foreseen coming upheavals. Grierson seemingly cannot imagine that the star to the East was one of the sources of James's grave concern for the immediate future, but this is in part because she is so intent upon forcing James into a template more readily recognizable (she actually describes him as one whose heart bleeds [536]) that she is unable to weigh his arguments about the applicability of lessons learned from the revolutionary past to the revolutionary present.

Other contemporary reviewers, however, were considerably more positive. In the United States, the black press took great interest in this novel work of history. Writing in the August 1939 issue of the *Crisis,* James W. Ivy neatly summarized the events narrated by James and called the book a "brilliantly written and conceived history" (251). Ivy easily grasped James's argument that "the San Domingo revolt was an integral part, though often obscured in problems of race and color, of the great French Revolution," and seemed to have found particular resonance as an American writer in James's observation that radical leadership often comes from "those who have profited most from the very culture and system that they are seeking to overthrow" (251). Historian Rayford Logan had registered more disagreements with James in his review some months earlier for *Opportunity,* but he concluded that *The Black Jacobins* was a book that should be displayed during Negro History Week (60), and he felt that James's application of the concept of class struggle to his investigations of the slaves' insurrection was accomplished with "infinitely more historical accuracy" than in the work of earlier writers (58). Logan wished that James had made still greater use of primary documents available in France, though he did credit James's "skillful use of the sources that he consulted" (58). Among his other criticisms, Logan expressed his regret that James's book did not include a "fuller development of the diplomacy of the United States and of Great Britain in the latter period," and he questions "the applicability of the term 'Jacobins' to the slaves of Saint Domingue" (58). On the other hand, this North American historian agrees largely with James's interpretations of questions of race and class, concluding that "*The Black Jacobins* is a notable contribution to the history of the Caribbean and of class struggle" and that James is "an historian from whom other authoritative monographs may be expected" (58).

"It is impossible to recollect historical emotions in that tranquillity which a great English writer, too narrowly, associated with poetry alone" (BJ xi), muses C. L. R. James in his preface to the first edition of *The Black Jacobins,* alluding to a favorite work of Romanticist literary criticism that he frequently recommended to his friends and students. Writing at the onset of a second world war, and at a time when colonized populations around the world were becoming increasingly radical in their opposition to European domination, James sought to indicate the extent to which the social and political imperatives of his own time had formed the narrative he had written of the revolution on San Domingo nearly a century and a half before: "It was in the stillness of a seaside suburb that could be heard most clearly and insistently the booming of Franco's heavy artillery, the rattle of Stalin's firing squads and the fierce shrill turmoil of the revolutionary movement striving for clarity and influence. Such is our age and this book is of it, with something of the fever and the fret" (BJ xi). When Cedric Robinson remarks that "James had conflated within *The Black Jacobins* (1938), the Haitian slaves with the modern proletariat" ("World System" 248), he refers to just this tendency in James's work to view the past from the perspective of contemporary struggles. But James argues that events in San Domingo were integral to the production of the current world system, that the Haitian slaves had been among the first to confront the problems faced by a modern proletariat, and that anticolonial revolutionaries in the twentieth century have a great deal to learn from the failures and successes of Toussaint L'Ouverture and the rebels who overthrew the most brutal of repressive regimes. The first thing to be learned is that such successes are possible. In his preface to the 1962 edition of his book, James explains that he has retained the final chapter's "concluding pages which envisage and were intended to stimulate the coming emancipation of Africa [because they] are a part of the history of our time" (BJ vii). As is so often the case in James's texts, this statement carries doubled weight, for James recognizes that his book has become a part of the history of our time to the extent that it has indeed stimulated emancipatory political movements from Ghana to South Africa.

Still, when the second edition of *The Black Jacobins* appeared, much of the African continent remained under colonial rule, thus he might hope his study of the Haitian revolution's success would continue to inspire liberation movements, while some of the African nations had now to contend with the dangers and uncertainties of neocolonial repression and domination, and thus James might hope his analyses of Toussaint's errors would assist new African and West Indian leaders in forming radically democratic political structures. James was able to recognize so clearly that his own writing of history was an event in history because, early in his career as a writer, he had recognized reading as an often revolutionary action in history. In the first chapter of *The Black Jacobins* he recalls one literary opponent of slavery, the Abbé Raynal, who, nearly a decade prior to the storming of the Bastille, had called openly for a slave insurrection. The book in which he issued that call, James records, "came into the hands of the slave most fitted to make use of it, Toussaint L'Ouverture" (BJ 25). In *The Eighteenth Brumaire of Louis Bonaparte,* Marx states that "men make their own history, but not of their own free will; not under circumstances they themselves have chosen but under the given and inherited circumstances with which they are directly confronted" (*Surveys* 146). It is important that we recall in our turn, as we read James's apt paraphrase of Marx at the beginning of *The Black Jacobins* (BJ x), that among the historical circumstances James speaks of which we must confront are our reading and our writing.

Toussaint L'Ouverture, like James after him, read first in the text spread before him in the daily cultural practices and political aspirations of the masses of the people among whom he lived and worked. As the "privileged" property of a prosperous planter, Toussaint of Bréda had a greater freedom of movement, more opportunities to acquire learning, and better living conditions than the vast majority of Africans in the French colonies of the Caribbean, which placed him at the nexus of rapidly developing social movements. James had noted how often the men who lead revolutions are those who have benefited from the very cultural apparatus of the order they attack, and he held that "the San Domingo revolution was no exception to this rule" (BJ 19). The very opportunities that had placed Toussaint in this position also made him at first reluctant to alter his situation as the often unpredictable waves of insurrection passed through the population. But even as L'Ouverture pondered the revolutionary ideology he encountered in such texts as came to hand as the Abbé Raynal's *Philosophical and Political History of the Establishments and Commerce of the Europeans in the West Indies,* the daily lessons offered by the actions of the masses of the workers increasingly pressed his thinking in ever more radical directions.

As had Abolitionist writers of the nineteenth century, James details the terrors visited upon the captured Africans. He describes the horrors of the Middle Passage, the death rates among both slaves and "free" sailors, the enormity of punishments meted out to black workers, and the turn to suicide among those of the slaves who thought the afterlife had to be better. Much more than this, though, James's interest is in correcting the mendacious extant histories of colonial slavery and in narrating the coming to revolutionary consciousness of groups of workers who had not previously had reason to think of themselves as a common class of people. Against the arguments of those European and American historians who had advanced claims that slaveowners would not have abused what, after all, was valuable property, a significant capital investment, James adduces the reports, confirmed by the slaveowners themselves, of the short lifespan of most slaves in the West Indies and of the documented brutality against them. Precisely because the Africans were possessed of intelligence and the desire for freedom, the planters felt compelled to inhuman measures to keep the slaves in the fields and at work. "It is this," James writes with the air of one imparting the most common of sense, "that explains the unusual spectacle of property-owners apparently careless of preserving their property: they had first to ensure their own safety" (BJ 12).

James looks past earlier arguments among white writers regarding the intellectual capacities of Africans to the intellectual lives of the Africans themselves, as they built communities and cultures out of what remained to them of their African past and what was available at hand in their New World present. He records the lyrics of a song long associated with the syncretic practice of New World black religion, a song he translates as a commitment to destroy the existing order that enslaves the singer. Like the seemingly untranslatable lyric W. E. B. Du Bois remembers from his childhood and inscribes in *The Souls of Black Folk,* this lyric survives centuries of white efforts to erase it, survives as a self-replicating strain of cultural intelligence. At every step of his history, James links such intelligence to contemporary struggles against colonialism. He likens the singing of this song in earlier centuries to the twentieth-century Bantu singing their banned "national anthem of Africa." In the same way, he shows that attempts to deny black intelligence in the past, like those in his own day, betray a deep-seated fear of the reality of black intellect: "It was this intelligence which refused to be crushed, these latent possibilities, that frightened the colonists, as it frightens the whites in Africa today" (BJ 18).

The African masses do not begin by thinking of themselves as African masses. In their desire to attain the freedom to exercise their own intellects and to reach for their own ambitions, they do not at first perceive themselves as a class. James, despite his ideals, does not, as Cedric Robinson fears, truly idealize the slaves of centuries past in terms of the industrial present. Though he sees the West Indians as facing the conditions of the modern proletariat, as Robin D. G. Kelley comments, James is "careful not to reduce the masses to either sponges soaking up Enlightenment notions of freedom or an idealized proletariat responding to social or economic stimuli" ("World" 113). Initially, many rebels sought only their own freedom. It was in the process of struggle itself that the New World Africans began to view themselves as joined in a common class. Their movement toward recognition of themselves as a people begins in their shared experiences of abduction and labor, and proceeds in spurts, through setbacks, toward what James describes as an internationalist perspective, a perspective he urges upon his contemporary readers. In his appendix to the second edition, James advances his belief that "West Indians first became aware of themselves as a people in the Haitian revolution" (BJ 391). In their maintaining of African cultural practices, in their labor together in the fields, and in their insurrection against the white planters and colonial officials, James demonstrates, the masses of the laborers in the colonies came to a comprehension of the powers latent in their own modes of cultural organization. In the struggle of revolution they came to recognize that political power over the territory in which they lived was essential to assuring that slavery would not once more be imposed upon them. As the slave rebels built themselves into a nation, they realized, in the course of seizing the power to act as arbiters of their own fate, their political relationship to the populations of other Caribbean islands and to Africa. The most farsighted among them, thinkers like L'Ouverture, began to envision what would have to be termed a form of Pan-African or diasporic movement. James says of L'Ouverture that "he cherished a project of sailing to Africa with arms, ammunition and a thousand of his best soldiers, and there conquering vast tracts of country, putting an end to the slave-trade, and making millions of blacks 'free and French,' as his constitution had made the blacks of San Domingo. It was no dream. He had sent millions of francs to America to wait for the day when he would be ready" (BJ 265). (Incidentally, one of the many valuable contributions James made to revising the standard version of this history, several years prior to his first trip to North America, was his careful delineation of the active role played by the United States in all phases of Haitian history, and of the importance of Haiti to American history generally, points that would not have been lost upon one of James's favorite American novelists, William Faulkner.)

Still, Toussaint L'Ouverture did not appear at the outbreak of the final great surge toward revolution to be a revolutionary. Forty-five years old and the trusted servant of his owner, Bayou de Libertas, he in fact protected his master's property and family from the first waves of destruction. He soon saw, however, the necessity of committing himself to the revolution as it became clear to him that it was far larger and more far-reaching than earlier revolts that had erupted only to be put down vengefully. In one of his more quotable asides James observes, "The masses of the people learn much during a revolution, far more a man like Toussaint" (BJ 91). Possessed of a remarkable intelligence, L'Ouverture had, in his position at Bréda, learned from his own adroit negotiations with whites, mulattoes, and blacks to read acutely the shifting balances of power within his evolving culture. Further, he had read such European master texts of political history as Caesar's *Commentaries* and had studied, in the writings of the Abbé Raynal, the economic and political development of Europe's colonies. L'Ouverture's reading was a constituent part of the social preparation that allowed him to make the history that he was to make.

"The slaves had rebelled because they wanted to be free" (BJ 95), James states matter-of-factly, pointing out at the same time the lengths to which reactionary political leaders and later historians had gone in order to avoid admitting this fact. "As usual the strength of the mass movement dragged in its wake revolutionary sections of those classes nearest to it. Free blacks joined them" (BJ 89). As the mulattoes witnessed the spread of the revolution among the masses, they increasingly joined in the struggle (though for many among them this was the most contingent of coalitions, to be betrayed at first opportunity). The same social forces that had prepared the slaves for mass insurrection, including their knowledge of earlier, failed attempts, prepared Toussaint of Bréda to join the rebellion, and his self-preparation through study and reflection prepared him to lead the masses to an understanding of the international import of their actions that would eventually conclude, under later leaders, in the formation of a new nation.

Wendell Phillips had written of the revolutionary moment in Haiti seven decades before James, describing how news of the French Revolution had burst over the population of San Domingo: "The first words which reached the island were the motto of the Jacobin Club—'Liberty, Equality.' The white man heard them aghast. He had read of the streets of Paris running blood. The slave heard them with indifference; it was a quarrel in the upper air, between other races, which did not concern him. The mulatto heard them with a welcome which no dread of other classes could quell" (165–66). James, in the early passages of his history, sketches the political realignments among white landowners, mulattoes, free blacks, and slaves as the varied classes of the population heard of and responded to events in Paris. James, though, also imagines the response of the slaves differently than does Phillips, for James knew that the slaves were much concerned with signs and portents in the upper air. Each writer portrays the slaves as recasting the news in familiar terms, but James's researches and his experience of the colonial Caribbean produced a considerably less passive version of the text of black response: "They had heard of the revolution and had construed it in their own image: the white slaves in France had risen, and killed their masters, and were now enjoying the fruits of the earth. It was gravely inaccurate in fact, but they had caught the spirit of the thing. Liberty, Equality, Fraternity. Before the end of 1789 there were risings in Guadaloupe and Martinique. As early as October, in Fort Dauphin, one of the future centres of the San Domingo insurrection, the slaves were stirring and holding mass meetings in the forests at night" (BJ 82).

The direction of James's revision of earlier histories and the direction of his difference from Phillips in imagining the slaves' responses to the news of revolution in France are the same. In both instances James underscores the responsibility of the Africans for their own decisions and actions. Because the Africans seized responsibility for themselves they were able to transform themselves from those huddled groups James describes trembling before a white master into a force capably organized and powerful enough to defeat the efforts of the greatest military powers sent against them. This is the great epic that James wishes to narrate and to reproduce in the present. This, too, is what nearly eludes Phillips in his paean to Toussaint. Phillips cleverly contrasts L'Ouverture to a figure of history well-known to his nineteenth-century audience, Oliver Cromwell. Cromwell manufactured an army, according to Phillips, out of middle-class Englishmen to conquer other Englishmen. Like a Puritan divine developing his sermon, Phillips then turns to his application. Speaking of L'Ouverture, Phillips asks his audience, "This man manufactured his army out of what? Out of what you call the despicable race of Negroes, debased, demoralized by two hundred years of slavery, one hundred thousand of them imported into the island within four years, unable to speak a dialect intelligible even to each other. Yet out of this mixed, and, as you say, despicable mass, he forged a thunderbolt and hurled it at what? At the proudest blood in Europe" (172). James, himself a proficient rhetorician, admires Phillips's atmospheric tropes, but he was intent upon moving his readers to an understanding of the fact that Toussaint was only able to accomplish this tremendous feat of organization because the African laborers had already begun to move beyond the boundaries of the organizational units forced upon them by their masters, to organize themselves to war against their oppression.

One of the truly great ironies recorded by James also represents a major revision to accepted narratives of the abolition of slavery. If it is true that the wealth generated from New World slave labor did much to fuel the remarkable capitalist expansion of European economies and that the altered social relationships created in Europe by these new sources of wealth and power did much to instigate new modes of political thought, then, James concludes, "The slave-trade and slavery were the economic basis of the French Revolution" (BJ 47). He cites the French historian Juarès's remark that it was the fortunes created by the slave trade that "gave to the bourgeoisie that pride which needed liberty and contributed to human emancipation" (BJ 47). Though later scholars have contested the estimates of James and of his former student Eric Williams regarding the exact extent to which the changing economics of the slave systems in colonial production influenced the political agenda of Abolition, James is clearly right to argue that the labors of the New World Africans created not only plantation wealth but much of the historical circumstances enabling the rise to prominence of the ideals of liberty, equality, and fraternity, and the ending by violence of the old regime. This is one of those truths about Abolition that James believes "a venal race of scholars, profiteering panders to national vanity, have conspired to obscure" (BJ 51).

James charts the rise of the national bourgeoisie in Britain and France and describes the inevitable political conflicts that arose between newer industrial interests and colonial agricultural interests. In Britain the new capitalist classes increasingly worked against agricultural monopoly, leading to the repeal of the Corn Laws in 1846. Pitt and others came to fear that continuation of the British slave trade served to strengthen French colonial production, and by 1786 Pitt was encouraging Wilberforce to campaign against the Atlantic slave trade. While the French government acted to delay the end of Europe's commerce in African slaves, French liberals, many of them future leaders of the early stages of the French Revolution, began to agitate for Abolition. But it was to require a large social movement before the ideal of Abolition could become a significant political force. "It was the French Revolution," James asserts, "which, with unexpected swiftness, would drag these eloquent Frenchmen out of the stimulating excitement of philanthropic propaganda and put them face to face with economic reality" (BJ 54). Similarly, though the history of the colony of San Domingo was filled with instances of slave resistance and uprisings, it was the altered circumstances wrought by the Revolution on the continent that brought a new impetus and direction to Caribbean insurrection. James notes that "it was the quarrel between bourgeoisie and monarchy that brought the Paris masses on the political stage"; but, radically revising Wendell Phillips's theses about the effect of the French Revolution on whites, mulattoes, and blacks in Haiti, James goes on to claim that "it was the quarrel between whites and Mulattoes that woke the sleeping slaves" (BJ 73). As the slaves witnessed the fight for control of the colonies among those who supported and those who opposed the principles of revolutionary Paris, their natural desire for freedom and their individual modes of resistance were radicalized and given political shape yet more effectively than they had been already by the circulation of revolutionary literature among the literate few.

In James's portrayal, Toussaint of Bréda was a man driven to ever more radical positions by the motions of human history. Early in the struggle he showed a willingness to make peace with the colonists if only four hundred of the leaders of the rebellion were freed and amnestied. He subsequently lowered his demand to fewer than a hundred of the leadership to be freed, yet even this was too much for the colonists to contemplate. "Then and only then," James concludes, "Toussaint came to an unalterable decision from which he never wavered and for which he died. Complete liberty for all, to be attained and held by their own strength" (BJ 107). In the interest of securing freedom from slavery for his followers, Toussaint aligned himself with the Spanish crown and fought against French forces in the colonies. When the revolutionary movement in France abolished slavery at last, L'Ouverture and his forces just as effectively fought on the side of the Republic, retaking much of the territory they had once conquered for Spain. At the front of his armies, Toussaint personified his people's determination to be free: "Leader of a backward and ignorant mass, he was yet in the forefront of the great historical movement of his time. The blacks were taking their part in the destruction of European feudalism begun by the French Revolution, and liberty and equality, the slogans of the revolution, meant far more to them than to any Frenchman" (BJ 198). Abolition resolved Toussaint at the last to identify his struggle with that of the new Republic, and the threat of the French counterrevolution to reimpose slavery caused Toussaint to set his country on a course that would, under different leadership, lead to complete independence from France. The cause of Abolition also brought Toussaint to war with the British forces, battles that significantly affected England's ability to contest the French Republic in Europe: "It was the decree of abolition, the bravery of the blacks, and the ability of their leaders that had done it. The great gesture of the French working people towards the black slaves, against their own white ruling class, had helped to save their revolution from reactionary Europe" (BJ 214).

It is easy to read in James's account of Toussaint's career a traditional Aristotelian tragedy, with Toussaint as the flawed tragic hero, and given

James's love of the classics and of canonical Western narrative such a reading might not be unexpected. When read against the background of James's other writings, though, *The Black Jacobins* appears to put forward one more of James's meditations upon the limits of leadership and the radically democratic aspirations of the masses. James sees the army as Toussaint's instrument, almost a mode of his personal political expression, but "the masses were its foundation and his power grew with his influence over them" (BJ 151). James addresses directly the distinction he would draw between the tragic flaw of Aristotelian theory and the tragedy of Toussaint's flawed thinking. What brought down Toussaint "was not a moral weakness. It was a specific error, a total miscalculation of the constituent events" (BJ 291). Toussaint L'Ouverture, who spoke so eloquently in his letters to the French Directory of his readiness to sacrifice personal happiness to ensure the safety of San Domingo and of his unwillingness to see his people thrust back down into slavery, who, on his own initiative, undertook diplomatic dealings with the United States, who spoke to the people of his island as a representative of the highest ideals of the new Republic while at the same time taking steps to solidify his power against the encroaching counterrevolution, came to neglect his relationship with the masses of the people who had brought him into the revolution in the first place. Though he made errors in his dealings with France and with Bonaparte, these, in James's analysis, were not his greatest errors. His fatal mistake was that he did not give the time and care to open discussions with his people that he was giving to his large strategic visions. The former slaves who were to form the citizenry of Republican San Domingo were confused by L'Ouverture's actions and became increasingly suspicious of his motives. Like too many leaders of too many revolutionary movements, Toussaint was by then so certain of the rightness of his course that he failed to subject it to the scrutiny of those on whose behalf he acted; he did not subject himself to the judgment of his people. James describes a Toussaint who, "shut up within himself, immersed in diplomacy, went his tortuous way, overconfident that he had only to speak and the masses would follow" (BJ 240).

But Bonaparte, too, misread the situation before him in the West Indies. Napoleon was enough of a strategist to conceal the true nature of his plans for the troublesome colony, but he was foolish enough to believe that removing L'Ouverture from the people of San Domingo would be a fatal blow to their resistance to the reimposition of direct French authority. James adamantly disputes the sort of exceptionalist thesis to which Bonaparte fell prey. Toussaint L'Ouverture was not a man fated to be great born to a backward island outpost. Rather, "the same forces which moulded his genius had helped to create his black and mulatto generals and officials" (BJ 256). Napoleon's brother-in-law, Leclerc, warned against just such a miscalculation. Fearing that the island's population would learn of Napoleon's plans for a return to slavery, Leclerc cautioned, "It is not enough to have taken away Toussaint, there are 2,000 leaders to be taken away" (BJ 346). Toussaint himself had said as much as he boarded the ship that was to transport him to France and, eventually, his death: "In overthrowing me, you have cut down in San Domingo only the trunk of the tree of liberty. It will spring up again by the roots for they are numerous and deep" (BJ 334).

With Toussaint removed from the scene, though, it was those already possessed of power within the emerging nation who were able to seize the initiative and lead San Domingo at once to both independence and political disaster. Alex Dupuy, in his reappraisal of James's history, holds that "James underemphasized the significance of an emerging new class of property owners within the ranks of Louverture's army . . . appropriating properties from former white planters who emigrated from the colony" (112). While there is some truth to Dupuy's assessment, James did recognize and analyze the effects of the rise of these newly propertied classes upon the direction taken by postindependence Haiti. Despite the fact that Toussaint L'Ouverture's documents of governance left little room for the representatives of the French state, Toussaint maintained the semblance of an allegiance to France. Like Robespierre, though, Toussaint "destroyed his own Left-wing, and with it sealed his own doom" (BJ 286), at the same time, in James's construction of events, leaving the path clear for those very classes identified by Dupuy. It was Dessalines, Christophe, and Clairveaux who first declared independence from France, and it was Dessalines who, in October 1804, crowned himself emperor of the new nation of Haiti.

Separation from France was inevitable if the former slaves were to remain free, but the ascension of Dessalines to a new throne marked the accession to power of property in new hands, still following old imperatives. "The Negro monarch entered into his inheritance," James declares in telling terms, "tailored and valeted by English and American capitalists, supported on the one side by the King of England and on the other by the President of the United States" (BJ 370). There followed in 1805 the slaughter, ordered by Dessalines, of Haiti's remaining white nationals. This was a selective massacre, not wholly racial, for Dessalines preserved the lives of whites he found necessary to his plans, the British and Americans and skilled workers. These actions signify for James the reactionary path that Dessalines set Haiti upon, a politics announcing itself as racially nationalist rather than one that sought freedom and democracy for black people. James believes that Haiti's people did not want the massacre; "all they wanted was freedom, and independence seemed to promise that" (BJ 373–74). The transformation of revolutionary mass action into a revenge drama was the great tragedy of Haiti's history for James. He writes that there is "no need to waste one tear or one drop of ink" (BJ 373) over the deaths of former slaveowners who had themselves perpetrated even greater savagery, but the tragedy for Haiti was that these reprisals degraded and brutalized the population. The British and the Americans, their own interests strangely served by this bloodletting, did not intervene. Haiti suffered the consequences of this first act of newly propertied power for generations, for "the unfortunate country, ruined economically, its population lacking in social culture, had its inevitable difficulties doubled by this massacre. That the new nation survived at all is forever to its credit for if the Haitians thought that imperialism was finished with them, they were mistaken" (BJ 374).

James ends his book with this cautionary note and with a plea for future anticolonial efforts in Africa. As always, James looks to "the creative capacity of the African people" (BJ 377), confident that they will learn from the mistakes of their predecessors and that they will find their own leadership within their movement for freedom. To the last, James was unsparing in his criticism of those who, like Dessalines, would pervert the creative energies of the masses of the working people and build from what the people gave them a platform from which to organize the subordination of the people to the powers of property and wealth. In the course of his eightieth birthday lectures, held in London in 1981, James said of the state structures of his own Caribbean region that they are, for the most part, "the most reactionary, some of them are the most counter-revolutionary that we have experienced. They have no sympathy at all for the ordinary black people" (BL 53). Addressing himself particularly to the young activists in his audience, he said, "please make it clear that in the world at large you are expecting equal or even greater changes in the Third World countries, as much as you expect them in the advanced countries: those governments have won independence, but that is all they have got" (BL 53). For all its romance and drama, *The Black Jacobins* is a narrative more open-ended than many other histories. At its end, Haiti remains an isolated nation with an uncertain future. Turning his attention again to the independence struggles of Africa and the West Indies, James seems to suggest that the same sort of revolutionary upsurge required to seize self-determination from the colonial powers is also what will be demanded if Haiti is to move beyond independence to democracy and social justice. Imperialism was not yet finished with Haiti, and from this the independence parties growing in Africa should take the lesson that far more than severance of colonial ties would be required to put an end to colonialism.

In preparing the second edition of *The Black Jacobins* James added an appendix that, like his later book *Beyond a Boundary,* defies assignment to any traditional literary genre. Equal parts historical analysis, literary criticism, and political tract, James's appendix is an example of its author's panoramic view of culture and politics. Written in the wake of Fidel Castro's revolution in Cuba, the appendix once more attempts to posit the possibility of a West Indian body politic and to place it in relationship to an internationalist struggle for African freedom. James insists that throughout their history, the West Indies developed a social identity that was formed around the material facts of sugar production and African slave labor. He repeats his thesis of the inherent modernity of that social identity. The labor system that evolved on the plantations "required that the slaves live together in a social relation far closer than any proletariat of the time" (BJ 392), and the twinned requirements for the import of slave labor and the export of sugar placed the Caribbean colonies at the crux of an emergent modern world trade system. As James sees it, the Cuban revolution is the most recent manifestation of the same "inherent movement" (BJ 391) toward a Pan-Caribbean identity that came into such sharp focus at the time of the revolution in San Domingo.

James provides a quick summation of West Indian political history, but just as he held that the great literary artists are those who give us a vision of future social realities through the creation of new forms of character, here James presents a series of representative men, political activists, and artists who contributed to the delineation of forms of diasporic consciousness. There is an inescapable dialectical movement, James believes, that leads from the conception in struggle of a Caribbean awareness of common social identity to an increasingly Pan-African cultural politics. James mentions particularly the work accomplished by the Jamaican Marcus Garvey and James's own childhood friend from Trinidad, George Padmore. Though Garvey was given to mystification, the rise of his Universal Negro Improvement

Association galvanized black people throughout the world around slogans of self-determination and brought New World blacks more and more to think of themselves in relation to Africa. Garvey's "achievement remains one of the propagandistic miracles of the century" (BJ 396) in James's judgment, and Garvey contributed greatly to incipient anticolonial philosophy in Africa itself. Unlike many mainstream historians at the time, James saw that Garvey had had a tremendous influence upon North American political history as well. In *A History of Negro Revolt* James credits Garvey with having built "proportionately the most powerful mass movement in America" (NR 52).

Garvey's great personal weakness, far more of a flaw than any reputed chicanery, was the lack of a rigorously thought-out political program, which drove him to a series of inconsistent positions that could only confuse his followers and strengthen his enemies' hand. In contrast, George Padmore elaborated from his Marxist studies a Pan-African politics that he was able to bring to bear on independence struggles around the world. Padmore's early work with the Communist International placed him in contact with the international anticolonial Left. Following his principled break with the Comintern over its 1935 reconfiguring of its policy with regard to "democratic imperialisms" such as Britain and France, the very imperialist powers that most oppressed Africa at the time, Padmore continued his efforts through such agencies as the African Bureau, which helped to develop the early political strategies of Jomo Kenyatta and Kwame Nkrumah.

Characteristically, James moves in his listing of great Pan-African political leaders from the West Indies to Africa, rather than the other way around. He argues that the earliest international movements for the emancipation of Africa were dominated by intellectuals from the West Indies, because their historical experience had brought them to a diasporic worldview. As his earlier quotation of a song lyric from an African language that had been preserved among the people indicates, West Indian blacks had created a New World culture built upon remnant cultural practices from Africa. It was, in his reading of it, a Western culture, but it was a black Western culture. In time, West Indian intellectuals came to celebrate the "Africanism of their peasants" (BJ 395) as an identifying national characteristic, and thus the movements for Caribbean independence continually reconstructed Africa as a linking cultural source. In turn, young African intellectuals in Europe and America were tremendously influenced by the Pan-Africanist politics they encountered there. Kwame Nkrumah, who James met while Nkrumah was attending university classes in Pennsylvania, subsequently contacted

Padmore, with an introduction from James, in England, where the two men "worked at the doctrines and premises of Pan-Africanism" (BJ 398). When independence was secured for Ghana, Padmore and James came to Africa to greet the new era. Padmore stayed on in Ghana, at Nkrumah's invitation working to further the cause of African liberation and organizing one of the first international conferences of independent African states.

In examining the importance of Africa in the development of West Indian national consciousness, and the importance of West Indian intellectuals to the emergence of Pan-Africanism as an organized political movement, James gives what might in other historians seem a surprising amount of space to considerations of literary artists. A significant portion of his appendix is devoted to surveys of the works of such now-familiar authors as Aimé Césaire, Vic Reid, V. S. Naipaul, and Wilson Harris, and this is because James finds it impossible to discuss the question of national identity without turning to the political aesthetics of cultural production. It is indeed odd that James so frequently speaks of the national identity of places that had not yet become official nations. National identity, for James, is never truly fixed, nor is it confined to national borders. It is recognized among the people themselves as somehow characteristic *of* themselves, though it appears that this recognition becomes strongest in the midst of struggle to become a nation.

James makes much of the fact that Césaire's *Return to My Native Land* appeared in Paris just one year after *The Black Jacobins* was published in London. He reads Césaire's poem as an epic of national cultural discovery, and he reads his own historical text as engaged in the same revolutionary poetic enterprise. Both James and Césaire go abroad to ask themselves the questions of Caribbean national consciousness, and both consciously explore the signifying power of Africa while they are in Europe. In this, their imaginative constructions of political identity mirror what James claims is the cultural experience of the whole Caribbean. James sees the Caribbean experience as differing from other colonial histories in that it is for the most part not a matter of "clearly distinguished economic and political relationships between two cultures" (BJ 405). It is possible to concede that no colonial history is likely to have been solely a matter of clearly distinguished relations between two cultures and still see that James is pointing to a fact that, while experienced differently in the several islands, is actually common to them all. The original Amerindian populations were nearly destroyed everywhere, though they left their mark on the populations that supplanted them. "The people of the West Indies were born in the seventeenth century, in a Westernized productive and social system" (BJ 407); this James insists upon throughout his career. Still, for him and for Césaire alike, "The road to West Indian national identity lay through Africa" (BJ 402). Given this history, it is impossible to assert an essentially racial identity for the Caribbean, but it remains clear to James that all that is essential within the Caribbean bears an African inflection. Thus, while "the West Indian national community constantly evades racial categorization" (BJ 402), Césaire's "negritude" can continue to be of use as a model, for it metaphorically names "what one race brings to the common rendezvous."

That is to say, while such master terms as "national identity" and "negritude" would seem to suggest an inescapable essentialism, James sees them as tropes, metaphors with which people give names to that which they are in the process of producing. In this, James is repeating a strategy spelled out in a series of Pan-African conferences that began in 1919. As George Padmore later summarized the broad principles of Pan-African political philosophy, he made it evident that the movement was never a monoracial or strictly identitarian one. The first goal of the congresses was, of course, to promote the unity and freedom of all peoples of African descent (and how many white people in 1919 were ready to think that this number might include all humans?). However, as an internationalist radical movement for liberation, Pan-Africanism demanded the self-determination of African peoples "and other subject races"; it sought black civil rights and "the total abolition of all forms of racial discrimination"; and it was dedicated to fostering cooperation between "African peoples and others who share our aspirations" (Padmore 127–28). James, addressing himself to the question of national identity for a multiethnic society that was not yet a discrete nation, argues that "in dance, in the innovation in musical instruments, in popular ballad singing unrivalled anywhere in the world, the mass of the people are not seeking a national identity, they are expressing one" (BJ 417). In the very next, seemingly contradictory sentence, however, James suggests that the expressed identity is that of a people "concerned with the discovery of themselves, determined to discover themselves." At a time when modern nations were pursuing the politics of the "fatherland" and of racial purity, James's *Black Jacobins* explored the paradoxical motions of discovery *as* expression, the process whereby nations come into being as the result of the masses of the people expressing themselves in the struggle to determine a common fate. At a time when the entire world appeared torn into violently opposed spheres of cold war influence, James's appendix to *The Black Jacobins,* in the very act of recontextualizing Castro's revolution out of the violently conflictual split of anti-Soviet ideology and back into the procession of Caribbean struggles for independence, describes the West Indies as determined to discover themselves "without hatred or malice against the foreigner, even the bitter imperialist past" (BJ 417). Though that struggle continues and, as in the case of Grenada, continues to cost lives, James remains hopeful: "To be welcomed into the comity of nations a new nation must bring something new. Otherwise it is a mere administrative convenience or necessity. The West Indies have brought something new" (BJ 417).

Itself practically an appendix to *The Black Jacobins, A History of Negro Revolt* was published in the same year as James's history of the revolution in San Domingo. Appearing under the auspices of the Independent Labour Party in the *Fact* monographs series, this second work's rapid historical summary gives an empirical basis to the optimism James expressed at the conclusion to *Jacobins* and again two decades later at the conclusion to its appendix. James saw this short text as both history and tool, and its publication history demonstrates that others shared his utilitarian view of the work. An expanded version of the text was published in 1969 by the short-lived Drum and Spear Press in Washington, D.C. (In that same year, Haskell House Publishers of New York issued a photographic reproduction of the 1938 *Fact* magazine edition, but this version received little circulation.) Drum and Spear also opened a bookstore and sponsored discussion groups. Founded by political activists, some of whom had been members of the Student Nonviolent Coordinating Committee, Drum and Spear, as Marvin Holloway explained in his preface to the new edition, hoped with this first publication to begin a series in response to the black people throughout the world who were "clamouring" for self-knowledge. The suspicion that many in the New Left of black political movements felt toward European-derived philosophies is evident in the back cover copy of the second edition, which remarks that "despite his socialist convictions" James had helped to organize the International African Service Bureau. The changing times were also reflected in a changed title for the book. The Drum and Spear edition is titled *A History of Pan-African Revolt.* The third edition of the book honors the historical context of the text by returning James's original title. Still, this publication of the work remains very much a political action undertaken by a determined organization, the *Race Today* Collective. Their brief introduction claims canonical status for James's book, and their remark that it has stood the test of time is directed both to the original text and to the additional chapter James had added in 1969. The publishers express their hope that *A History of Negro Revolt* will, in 1985 as it had in 1938, lead to informed and critical political actions in a way that, in their reading, few other histories have.

The fact that two subsequent generations of activists in the African diaspora have taken up one of James's more fugitive texts and recirculated it demonstrates the rightness of James's belief that he had provided the kind of "usable past" that had not been available in documentary form to his generation. In his assessment of the career of Guyanese historian and political worker Walter Rodney, James posits his own publications as one of the defining features differentiating the tasks faced by his and Rodney's generations. Speaking of himself, Césaire, Padmore, and Du Bois, James, now in his eighties, said:

> As we grew up and went along, we had to fight the doctrines of the imperialist powers in order to establish some Caribbean foundation or foundations for the underdeveloped peoples. *Walter did not have to do that.* The aforementioned works were written before he was born. Walter grew up in an atmosphere where for the first time a generation of West Indian intellectuals was able, not only to study the revolutionary and creative works that had been created in Europe, but also to benefit from and be master of what had been done in the same tradition in direct reference to the Caribbean. (QP 4)

Writing at a time prior to the widespread postmodern suspicions of metanarrative, James seeks out a metaphorical eminence from which he might spy the embracing logic that unites the varied tributaries of the current of history (NR 65). In the text that results he has three linked goals: to demonstrate the fact of continuous black resistance to oppression both in Africa and in the diaspora, to underscore the need for a truly revolutionary and internationalist struggle if this resistance is to lead to a final end to the oppressions of black people, and to point up the universal relevance of the issues that black people confront. In closing the 1938 edition James wrote, "The African bruises and breaks himself against his bars in the interests of freedoms wider than his own" (NR 65).

The book opens with the one black revolt that had succeeded to that date, the revolution that culminated in the creation of the state of Haiti, and James offers what amounts to a precis of *The Black Jacobins*. This time James points particularly to Toussaint L'Ouverture's skill at manipulating "imperialist contradictions" when the revolution in France was no longer offering even the sustenance of an example to the Haitian rebels. This is followed by two short chapters on North America in which James draws out the incredible importance of the Haitian events to both blacks and whites in the United States, something that many American historians at the time were in the process of forgetting. Another neglected element identified by James is the small but significant participation of radical whites in black struggles from the very beginning. However, while individual groups of rebels seized upon the opportunities offered by periods of social ferment, James believes these constant acts of insurrection were doomed to defeat without the broader support of revolutionary elements in the country and abroad. That development would only come at "the climax of a gradual transformation of world economy" (NR 24). As he had argued in *Jacobins* against prevailing views of British Abolitionist politics, here James argues that this international economic transformation created the grounds of possibility for emancipation far more than "that sudden change in the conscience of mankind so beloved of romantic and reactionary historians" (NJ 24). Like Du Bois, James perceives in the Civil War and Reconstruction the gathering forces of a revolutionary social metamorphosis, ultimately thwarted with the Hayes-Tilden election's marking of national withdrawal of support for black political equality. "Only a revolution in which the poor were the driving force would have held out its hand to the blacks and made common cause of its own objectives and land for the blacks," James writes. "There was no such revolution in America" (NR 27). Instead, the birth of a nation's monopoly capitalism defeated both the working-class whites of the North and the landless blacks of the South. Again resembling Du Bois in *Black Reconstruction,* James points to that brief period in which black Americans were able to participate in the governing of their own country as the high-water mark of progressive legislation, again advancing his argument that black revolt in the Americas was a radically democratic phenomenon, a movement for human rights and dignity in the broadest sense.

James then moves to the continent of Africa, outlining a continuous succession of revolts against European imperialism. The railroad strikes in Sierra Leone, the women's revolt in Nigeria, the 1915 uprising in Nyasaland, the Port Elizabeth strike of 1920—James adroitly details the particulars of each, showing the evolution from resistance to immediate local oppressions, what James terms "the instinctive revolt of primitive tribes," to the "militant action of the proletariat in the towns" (NR 44). James's terminology here is surely to be questioned and proceeds obviously from his Marxist view of history as progressive and teleological, but unlike many other commentaries, James's recognizes, and asks readers to recognize, the importance of modes of rebellion that do not seek their expression strictly in terms of class struggle. As Robin D. G. Kelley observes in his introduction to the most recent edition of the text, James's analysis is unique for its time in its "claim that revolutionary mass movements take forms that are often cultural and religious rather than explicitly political" (15). For example, James gives considerable attention to episodes such as the Chilembwe rising of 1915 and the revolt led by Simon Kimbangu in the Belgian Congo six years later. These mass movements, like Nat Turner's rebellion in North America, derived their impetus from religious visionaries. Though the leadership formed their movements as mass expressions of religious belief, James translates these actions into secular terms. Speaking, for one instance, of Kimbangu's call to his fellow Africans to come out of the mission churches and to establish independent African institutions, James writes that "to every African such a movement is an instinctive step towards independence and away from the perpetual control of Europeans" (NR 38). Still, with the increasing industrialization of the colonies and the growth of urban areas, James sees African campaigns of resistance increasingly taking on the cast of "modern" labor struggles. Perhaps James's best example of this is the rapid growth of Clements Kadalie's Industrial and Commercial Workers' Union of South Africa, a union that began with but twenty-four members and rapidly expanded to a membership of 100,000 with representatives even in many of the outlying rural villages. For James, "the real parallel to this movement is the mass uprising in San Domingo. There is the same instinctive capacity for organization, the same throwing-up of gifted leaders from among the masses. But whereas there was a French Revolution in 1794 rooting out the old order in France, needing the black revolution, and sending out encouragement, organizers and arms, there was nothing like that in Britain. Seen in that historical perspective, the Kadalie movement can be understood for the profoundly important thing it was" (NR 47).

Following a short survey of the Garvey movement in North America, James rounds out his 1938 text with a summary of "Negro Movements in Recent Years." Commencing with a series of strikes in the Gold Coast and Ashanti District, James then moves back to his starting point, the Caribbean, carefully explaining the distinctive social and political contexts that differentiate similar struggles in Africa, the West Indies, and North America.

As in *The Black Jacobins,* James shows an awareness of the importance of radical writing and its circulation to the increasingly industrialized masses in rebellion. He points to "the clamour for literature" (the term picked up by the editors of the 1969 edition in their preface) among West Indian workers anxious for news of movements abroad. He writes that his own "study was already in proof when the Jamaica revolt forced the appointment of a Royal Commission" (NR 61), and thus his own study becomes a part of the historical context against which the report of the Royal Commission will be received by those who are the subjects of the report. Though James concludes this chapter with the same note of optimism found at the end of *The Black Jacobins,* he remains a realist. He says of the acts of resistance of millions of Africans, "They know what they want, but they do not know what to do" (NR 64).

This last is a strategic question. For James, such questions demand a rigorously tested political philosophy. That is what he sought all his life to develop, and that is what, at the end of his 1969 update to *A History of Negro Revolt,* he thought he had located in the vision of Julius Nyerere. James held that there were two major questions that had to be addressed by those struggling for the liberation of black people. The first was the question of how to seize power. It was this point, he believed, that marked the tragic failure of Walter Rodney. Time and again in the islands and coastal countries of the Caribbean basin the masses had taken to the streets in rebellion seeking redress of their grievances. Power was in the streets but the radical leadership did not know what to do with it. In Rodney's case, in contrast, James felt that the younger revolutionary had attempted to move ahead of and without the masses. James knew that the greatest of errors was for those who thought they could lead the masses to take for granted that they would be followed. The second great question was how, having seized state power, to continue the revolutionary movement of the people through to the construction of a truly democratic society. In 1969, when many of the nations of Africa and the Caribbean that had been under colonial domination when James first wrote had achieved at least nominal independence, it was this second question that marked the failure of so many of the postindependence leaders, a failure that has increasingly left many nations open to what Anna Everett has described as the recolonizing of Africa (10).

In his 1969 addendum to *A History of Negro Revolt* James takes Ghana and Kenya as his primary examples. He analyzes the steps by which the

Ghanaian masses organized themselves for action, the emergence of Kwame Nkrumah in his role of leadership, and the success of the movement's nonviolent campaigns in bringing about that day when Nkrumah went straight from a British jail to government office. In the case of Kenya, James explains that, British mythology to the contrary, the Mau Mau "was an ad hoc body of beliefs, oaths, disciplines newly created for the specific purpose of gathering and strengthening the struggle against British imperialism" (NR 72). This armed resistance eventually rendered the colony ungovernable, or at least ungovernable at a price that the British were willing to pay, and ultimately, as in Ghana, the leadership moved from the prison yard to the state house. But the state apparatus taken over by the new independence leaders was of European construction and was intimately imbricated with the economic interests that had just abandoned nominal political title to the territory. In one cogent sentence James describes a history that has been repeated in nation after nation: "Nationalist political leaders built a following, they or their opponents gained support among the African civil servants who had administered the imperialist state and the newly independent African state was little more than the old imperialist state only now administered and controlled by black nationalists" (NR 74). Even in those newly liberated nations that spoke so boldly of "African socialism" James finds this deadly pattern too often played out, for the revolution for independence had not been accompanied by a revolution in the social and economic ordering of the society. New elites had simply taken the reins of government and a share of the proceeds, while property continued to prevail over the working masses of the people (a pattern being further strengthened by "privatization" in many economies today).

This cautionary note lingers in the air as James goes on to review renewed signs of militancy in South Africa, the West Indies and the United States. Plainly part of his message is the warning of the lesson learned once more with great difficulty by many in the 1960s and 1970s, the lesson that cultural nationalism will not in itself suffice as a revolutionary program. James, as always, finds much ground for optimism still. He predicts the collapse, "sooner rather than later" (NR 77), of the apartheid regime of the Nationalist Party in South Africa, he watches with great interest in the United States as the New Left begins to "take shape as a direct result of the black students turning from protests by asking for reforms to protests by revolutionary action" (NR 79), and he continues to believe, heartened by Castro's overthrow of the Batista dictatorship, that "small as they are, their historical origin and development have been such that these Caribbean islands can make highly significant contributions to the economics and politics of a world in torment" (NR 82). One of the chief sources of James's hope in a world of torment in 1969 was the appearance of the 1967 Arusha Declaration prepared by Julius Nyerere's Tanzanian government. To James this document represents the kind of social revolution required if Africa is ever to be freed of neocolonial exploitation and nationalist tyranny. The declaration proposes regulations that would prevent "90 percent of those who govern and administer in other parts of the world" (NR 83–84) from taking office, that would prohibit government officials from holding shares in any company and would thoroughly reconstruct the systems of education. James hails Nyerere's proposals, most specially his proposals in the field of education, as perhaps the most significant socialist thought since Lenin, and argues that "its depth, range and the repercussions which flow from it, go far beyond the Africa which gave it birth" (NR 89). James himself did much to carry the ideals of Nyerere's writings beyond Africa. In addition to calling attention to them in his reissued book, he spoke frequently of them at lectures around the world and made them part of the curriculum of his college courses. In the Arusha Declaration James truly believed he had seen the convergence of the diasporic revolutionary histories he had studied with the international socialist philosophy he had done so much to advance.

His faith, it proved, was not entirely well placed, and there have been those who have sharply criticized James for failing to subject the Tanzanian state to the same sort of thorough critique he had so often advanced in the past. Robin D. G. Kelley, for one, has expressed puzzlement that "even after sharp criticisms of the TANU government were leveled by radical intellectuals within Tanzania, James apparently never responded or corrected his earlier assessments—at least not in print" (Introduction 26). But by that time C. L. R. James was well into his seventh decade. Given his earlier analyses of Nkrumah's success and later failure, eventually published in a separate volume as *Nkrumah and the Ghana Revolution*, who could doubt that James, were he still possessed of his full physical powers, would have led the way in calling Tanzania to account for the distance between its promise and its performance? In class discussions with his students he often explored the available news accounts out of Tanzania. Already, though, in *The Black Jacobins* and *A History of Negro Revolt*, James had offered frameworks with which younger scholars and activists could analyze the workings of a new generation of African political leadership, and even earlier, James had published a book that charted in enormous detail the patterns by which revolutions are betrayed, a book that he composed as "a history of principles, their origin, when and why they were departed from, the necessity for their regeneration" (WR 15). Like his other historical works of the 1930s, that book had much to teach later readers about the rise of oppressive national bureaucracies operating under the guise of socialism.

III. WORLD REVOLUTION

> *Philosophical method and dialectical logic are receiving my closest personal attention. If I were in charge of a party, I would publish such studies* for the general reader. *Lenin begged the academicians of 1921 to do the same. How is it possible to* underestimate *literature, literary criticism, the elaboration of a profoundly new method, and taking this to the masses as one day, God willing, we shall take every God damn thing we are doing to the masses. Let them reject it. We will not assume that they will in advance.*
>
> C. L. R. James, *Special Delivery: The Letters of C. L. R. James to Constance Webb, 1939–1948*

C. L. R. James's first major volume of political history, *World Revolution*, was for most of his career known primarily by reputation, for unlike *The Black Jacobins* that earlier volume remained virtually inaccessible from the time that the original 1937 edition passed from the scene till after James's death. There was a Hyperion Press reprint published in very small numbers in 1973, and there had been talk of producing a second edition from time to time, but most who have read this text in the past encountered it on a library shelf, turned it up in a used book store, or had it loaned to them by a friend. (For many years I made use of a xerox copy of the text that James had permitted me to make). Fugitive as the text may have been for so many decades, readers did find it, even in Colonial India, where it had been banned by the Imperial authorities.

James purported to have completed initial composition of *World Revolution* in an astonishing three months. In his preface to the volume he explains that his task was "chiefly one of selection and coordination" (WR xxvi), indicating his intellectual debt to scholars in France, China, America, Germany, and Russia whose works he had drawn upon in his research.

In effect, James found in the Marxist texts he collected while working on his history a circle of distant collaborators, as he would in later years gather together a more intimate circle of collaborators in America while he hammered out his political philosophy. His greatest debt, he writes, is to Trotsky, and that debt dates to James's first studies of Marxism in the early 1930s. Robert Hill quotes from an unpublished reminiscence of James's in which it can be seen that James drew upon Trotsky as a model for his writing as much as he benefited from Trotsky's work in political thought: "Trotsky referred not only to historical events and personalities, but he made references to literature as expressing a social reality and social change. *The History of the Russian Revolution* gave me a sense of historical movement: the relation of historical periods to one another" (AC 297).

World Revolution also resembles *The Black Jacobins* in that James wrote his history not only to establish the facts of the past as he saw them, but also to convey his sense of historical movement at a particular moment of crisis, to establish the relationship of the present, in which the nations of Europe were rushing toward war, to the preceding periods of crises and consolidation. James also hoped to counter the narrative being expounded by the writers of the Communist Party. In 1936, the Left Book Club had published R. Palme Dutt's *World Politics: 1918–1936,* an apology for the Soviet policies of the moment, and James felt strongly that a critical work written from a Marxist perspective to counter the Communist dogma was sorely needed. James approached the leftist publisher Frederick Warburg with his proposal and then went to Brighton to write the text. (During the same time he was actively campaigning for the Independent Labour Party and working in the struggle against the Italian invasion of Abyssinia.) James had joined forces with a small organization of Trotsky's followers who had broken with Britain's Communist League in 1934 and had begun to operate as a faction within the Independent Labour Party (Richardson xi). James's book bears a dedication to this small band of activist intellectuals.

The book met with the sort of mixed response that James surely anticipated. Communist Party writers were uniformly hostile, no less hostile were the reactions of English reactionaries, and intellectuals somewhat closer to James's own political views were not entirely approving. Trotsky himself admired the work but pointed out in later conversations with James what he took to be its failures in the application of the dialectical method. Typical of the mixed reception of *World Revolution* is Raymond Postgate's review in the *New Statesman and Nation* for May 3, 1937. Postgate opens by acknowledging the need for such a volume and predicting that James's work is "likely to excite more anger than anything yet published this year" (776). Though the force of James's rhetoric is still readily apparent to readers nearly fifty years after he wrote the book, the particular mode of praise delivered by Postgate may puzzle readers today. Remarking the evident prejudice of earlier studies of the period written by adherents of the second and third Communist Internationals, Postgate avers that "this is the first book to be written by a propagandist who despises both sides, and has the clearsightedness that comes from universal hatred" (776). This in turn leads the reviewer to deride what he terms James's "verbal violence and verbosity" (776), charges that will strike some readers now as overstated but that communicate some sense of the great heat generated by these political debates of the mid-1930s. Postgate credits James for having made "no serious error of fact in any place" (776), but he does argue with some of James's conclusions. For example, reviewing James's narrative of events following the rise of Stalin, Postgate writes, "Mr. James seems to regard his record as proving criminal wickedness; it seems rather to suggest stupidity and hysteria. Certainly, the violent change that was made in 1935 by Stalin was not so much wicked as made with insensate disregard for the beliefs of all the dependent parties" (778). Certainly in the wake of subsequent and still surfacing revelations about the Soviet regime, few today would agree that stupidity and hysteria, though present in abundance, sufficiently explain the Gulag or the Moscow show trials.

In subsequent years critics have debated some of James's positions in this study. Al Richardson has questioned James's acceptance of production figures for the first Soviet five-year plan, and Pierre Broué has raised doubts about "James's view that Stalin was responsible for holding back the German Communist Party" (Richardson xvi-xvii). Paul Buhle, in *C. L. R. James: The Artist as Revolutionary,* acknowledges *World Revolution*'s status as "the first comprehensive anti-Stalinist study of the Comintern and the only one, for many years, not based in a comfortable reassurance of capitalism's many virtues" (57). He also, however, judges this to be "James's least original major work" (51). (It would seem that each of James's major critics has identified one text as being James's weakest and that there is little agreement among them on this point.)

One of the greatest areas of disagreement among readers of *World Revolution* has been the relationship of this text to Trotskyism. James himself frequently made clear his indebtedness to Trotsky's work, both as a model of historical narrative and as the primary developer of a valuable critique of communism from the left. But James's was never an uncritical acceptance of Trotsky's philosophy. Al Richardson goes so far as to identify as "the distinctive position of *World Revolution*" the possibility that "its author was already in the process of rejecting Trotskyism" (xv). It was certainly a prolonged rejection. James had not yet had his legendary discussions with Trotsky in Mexico, and many years were to pass before the Marxist scholar from Trinidad made his final and complete break with the old Soviet revolutionary. As late as September 1940, James published one of his most extensive and deeply moving appreciations, "Trotsky's Place in History," in the *New International*. Here James makes far-reaching claims for Trotsky's importance, seeing even the style of Trotsky's writing as giving expression to the deepest social transformations of his age. "The bourgeois critic will explain it in terms of personal ability," James predicts. This James views as "a patent and far-reaching error. The style is the man, and men like Hitler and Trotsky speak for a social order. An age, a class, a political system expresses itself through its great books" (RM 117). Surely this note embodies some of James's own ambitions for his writing as well as his retrospective assessment of Trotsky's.

If James was not yet ready for a final break with Trotsky in 1937, neither did he shy away from discussions that revealed his disagreements with that imposing figure. As one who held to the principle "of the Leninist United Front . . . that never under any circumstances must the right of criticism be abrogated" (WR 173), James would not have wished to work within a political leadership whose founding figures were beyond criticism. That sort of organization was, for James, identified with the Communist Party, who seemed to him to operate under two unchanging rules: "The first law of Stalinism is to praise Stalin. The second is to abuse Trotsky" (WR 353). James in 1937 feels at liberty to outline what he feels to be Trotsky's past errors, while still following Trotsky's example as a Marxist theoretician, historian, and activist.

The particular form taken by the errors that James discerns in Trotsky's actions indicates that James was, in fact, already moving in the direction that leads eventually to his irreversible break with the Trotskyite parties. Each of the mistakes identified by James has to do with the relationship of the leadership to the party, and of the party to the masses. James points to Trotsky's lengthy struggle against Lenin's methods of organization and democratic centralism. Trotsky's advocacy for a much broader party organization prior to the taking of power arose from what James takes to be a mistaken approach. Lenin argued that theirs was the party of a class and that it would be a grievous error to believe that the party, still functioning under capitalism, could educate the entire proletariat to an advanced level of class consciousness. "Trotsky was wrong," James declares with no trace of uncertainty. "Yet from this false approach the specific criticisms he levelled against Lenin's principles as they worked out in practice cannot be dismissed, least of all today" (WR 50). This passage seems in retrospect to be a seed from which much of James's later political philosophy would spring. Rejecting Trotsky's approach in the argument with Lenin, James nonetheless sees the cogency of some of Trotsky's specific criticisms of democratic centralism as practiced by the party and by the International. Eventually these same criticisms, that the central leadership substitutes itself for the party and that the party substitutes itself for the people, will form the core of James's own objections, not just against the Communist Party, but against the Trotskyist International as well. As he held that Trotsky's errors in his approach to these issues did not truly shake "Trotsky's fundamental intellectual integrity" (WR 51), James's own lifelong commitment to Lenin's thought was unshaken by James's own criticism of the Leninist concept of the political vanguard.

A second critique of Trotsky's actions grows directly from this first. James outlines Trotsky's theory of permanent revolution in part to outline its substantial antagonism toward principles adhered to by the Mensheviks. Trotsky believed that the waves of revolution that had begun in 1905 by moving to secure the rights of the bourgeoisie would culminate in the dictatorship of the proletariat, that the proletariat in power "would be compelled to begin the long transformation of Russian capitalism into Socialism" (WR 61), and that these events would lead at last to proletarian revolution throughout Europe "and the permanent economic revolution in Capitalist society." The Mensheviks tended to view Russian capitalism as a national phenomenon and urged support for the liberal bourgeoisie. Prefiguring criticisms that would in later years be targeted at James himself, James here mocks the Menshevik faith that "the revolution would be 'spontaneously' accomplished somehow" (WR 61). Against Lenin's proclivities, Trotsky urged unification with the Mensheviks. James believes that "it was one of the fundamental weaknesses of Trotsky as a revolutionary leader that he could produce this masterly theory of the Permanent Revolution, driving ahead so far beyond Lenin, and yet at the same time advocated organizational fusion with the Mensheviks" (WR 62). Lenin's approach in the crisis of 1905 was to close the door yet more firmly against the liberal bourgeoisie and to bring more workers into the movement's local committees. It was the same strategy that James was to applaud so vigorously in Nyerere's "Arusha Declaration" thirty years after the writing of *World Revolution*.

A third serious error James attributes to Trotsky recalls the failing that James lays at the feet of Toussaint L'Ouverture. Trotsky had a great appeal to a broad sector of the Russian public. His oratory was renowned throughout Europe, and his writings, most especially his pamphlets, "appealed equally to professors and peasants" (WR 145). This gave Trotsky the potential for great power among the people, but it was a potential that he failed to actualize in the greatest moments of crisis. James describes Trotsky as a man possessed of a certain imperiousness of character that made it difficult for him to work with others who were his equals within the party hierarchy but who were, in his estimation at least, his intellectual inferiors. Given the fact that some of the old Bolsheviks viewed him as an interloper, this created a dangerous mixture of resentments and misunderstandings made to order for such a master manipulator of petty jealousies as Stalin proved to be. While Stalin, Zinoviev, and Kamenev consolidated their powers over the party apparatus, increasingly bureaucratizing decision making and moving real power farther and farther away from the rank and file of the workers, Trotsky relied too much upon the powers of his rhetoric and reputation in contending with those who were bent upon his destruction. At similar moments of party divisiveness in the past, Lenin had relied upon the force of the workers to carry the day. In this crisis, in contrast, "the masses played little part, and Trotsky either could not or dared not bring the masses into it, as Lenin would infallibly have done sooner rather than later" (WR 147).

World Revolution, 1917–1936, is, though, a history of *The Rise and Fall of the Communist International*, not simply a critique of Trotsky, and James's concerns could not have been more immediate than in this instance, which in part explains the rapidity of his work on the project. James saw before him in Europe a world driving itself toward the paroxysms of war, and he saw the Communist International poised to betray the internationalist interests of the workers, aligning itself with the national interests of reaction and conquest. In James's view this echoed the betrayals committed by the Second International. In his 1960 series of lectures in Trinidad, published under the title *Modern Politics*, James reminded his audience that in 1914, when war came over Europe, the Marxist International had abandoned its basic adherence to a global united front in resistance to capitalist rule and had broken into national factions: "They led the workers into the war. But the vitality of the Marxist movement was proved by the fact that the moment it had become clear to one of them, Lenin, that the International had broken away from the principles and policies that it had proclaimed, he set out at once to lay the foundation of the Third International" (MP 41).

As he sets out upon the work of *World Revolution,* James finds in front of him a similar landscape. The bourgeois politicians, those liberals and Social Democrats he describes as "the comedians of the modern political world" (WR 419), are playing a deadly game. "If Beelzebub stood on the Treasury Bench without troubling to disguise his horns and tail in coat and topper," James writes caustically, "and swore to them that this coming war would be a war fought for Christianity, they would rush to support it, to bewail after that they were deceived" (WR 419). At the same time, the Communist International, repeating the folly of their predecessors in World War I, were committed to Stalin's myth of "Socialism in a single country" and from this concession to nationalism their policies once more gave the revolutionary aspirations of the proletariat up to the most venal of territorial desires and reactionary oppressions. James writes to show how Marxist principles were abandoned and "the necessity for their regeneration" (WR 15). He writes to expose the treachery of the Third International and to convince readers that the only hope is to succeed in the building of a fourth. The real importance of the Russian Revolution for James is that it was an attempt to found a "Socialist society, resting on an economy in which private ownership was abolished" (WR 414). Stalin had perverted that movement, and James was proposing the Fourth International, a Marxist organization dedicated to "permanent revolution," as a solution to the problems of organizing worldwide for continuing the attempt made by the Russian workers, the problem that for James represented "the biggest question mark of our generation" (WR 414).

In the early stages of *World Revolution* James draws out many of the same theses that he was to explore at length in *The Black Jacobins* and to which he would return decades later in *Nkrumah and the Ghana Revolution.* He observes that the people of Russia did not rise up initially out of a formulated plan to overthrow the Tsars or to institute socialism. "They revolt against intolerable conditions or for some concrete issue, as the peasantry for land or against a war or to stop Fascism" (WR 98). So much depends upon the nature of the leadership that emerges through struggle and the vision in whose name they enlist the powerful forces that have underwritten their leadership. The initial revolution in Russia brought to state power a bourgeois leadership. Because these political figures were bound entirely to the financial interests of Europe, they could not give to the masses the land, the bread, and the freedom that the people wanted; neither could they end Russian participation in the Great War. What James says of the Russian bourgeoisie had been true of many in the French Revolution as well: "as soon as the Liberals saw the workmen in the streets they would see not only the enemies of Tsarism, but their own enemies, and would of necessity rush to compromise with the reaction" (WR 57).

Lenin proved a yet cagier political manipulator than Toussaint L'Ouverture, frequently outflanking his opponents both within and without the party. According to James, Lenin always had his eye upon the masses (though some now might argue about the true purpose of his watchfulness), and he took great "care that the masses should understand" (WR 88) his shifting positions that somehow always advanced toward his unchanging goal. Lenin believed in the creative abilities of the masses of the working people, and he believed that in the organizational form that they had invented for themselves, the Soviets, the workers had modeled the new society that should arise in Russia. By removing wealthy owners from access to political power, the new state would ensure that the majority of the population would be able to enact their will. By establishing a free press among the proletariat, the new state would ensure that the party and the state institutions were answerable directly to the workers. By arming the workers in a national militia, the proletariat would assure themselves that they would no longer live in fear of the police powers of the government. That each aspect of this vision was savagely turned against the workers of Russia by the Communist Party that governed in their name was, for James writing in 1937, evidence of the powers of reaction. Even in James's account Lenin bears a portion of the responsibility for this tragedy. Lenin hoped that the party itself could be made the most effective weapon to fight encroaching bureaucracy and corruption. "His great error—and he saw it too late," James judges, "was to have taken too lightly that filching of their power from the people in the Soviets" (WR 130).

The bulk of *World Revolution* is dedicated to a broadly ranging narrative that details the steps by which power was effectively removed from the masses of the people and consolidated against them. At several points in the text James cautions his readers that what his book offers is "not a complete history, but a thesis" (WR 107). It may be true that *World*

Revolution does not attempt to be encyclopedic in its account of the rise and fall of the Communist International, but the book is certainly a thick description resting upon a solid foundation of detail and document. It is also a most carefully composed narrative, rhetorically effective and novel-like in its symmetrical construction. For example, as James moves from his history of Stalin's destruction of the Soviet revolution to his accounts of Stalin's role in thwarting international revolutionary movements, he follows a similar narrative structure in his writing. The chapters on the interference in the Chinese Revolution and the subversion of the German revolutionary movements are placed in parallel with James's discussions of the International's policies in Germany in the years leading up to World War II; each of these chapters climaxes with an analytical section titled "The Ebb Mistaken for the Flow," sections in which James ably demonstrates the gross political misjudgments enforced by the International.

It is important to recall that James is writing a history of an international, not just a history of Stalin's crimes. Though it was to be nearly another decade before James would fully work through a theoretical explanation of the historical forces that brought Stalin to the head of the international labor movement, the theories that would be set out most explicitly in *Notes on Dialectics,* James was, even in 1937, determined to prove that Stalinism was the product of complex social movements, not merely the product of a singularly demented individual. Stalin was able to gain and consolidate power because he was able to make use of weaknesses and contradictions within the workers' parties, and because his mode of socialist tyranny was a dialectical response within the revolutionary organizations themselves. Once again, James was demonstrating Marx's tenet that men make only that history which it is possible for them to make.

"Whenever [Lenin] was in difficulties he looked below" (WR 161), James repeats. Stalin, too, kept a keen eye on the masses, not, however, to discern their aspirations and their political will, but with an eye to forcing their political behavior into accord with his own will. That he had in this effort the active collaboration of so many who had proclaimed themselves proletarian revolutionaries is a testament to the power of self-interest and property. Instead of building a social structure in which the armed power of the workers prevents private accumulations of great wealth and political influence, the Communist International came to be dominated by a politics bent on the defense of state power and wealth against the workers themselves. For James, a key moment in this evolution is the triumph of the Stalinist slogan of socialism in a single country. Lenin began with the assumption that capitalism and socialism could not coexist. Forced to a series of compromises by Russia's inescapable imbrication in the world economy, Lenin still held to a vision of worldwide revolution and international socialism. What Lenin did not know as he neared the end of his life in 1923, what James believes nobody could have known then, was that the defeat of the German revolution that year "heralded the death of international Socialism in his party, its creed of twenty-five years" (WR 140). Stalin, ever the revisionist, marked his accomplishment of that transformation with a telling alteration of his own texts. In April of the next year, "in his own book, *Problems of Leninism,* he had written that the organization of Socialist production in the Soviet Union was impossible. For that the assistance of several of the most advanced countries was needed. In October he published a new edition of the book in which the passage was changed to exactly the opposite" (WR 157).

From that point forward, the actions of the Communist International were increasingly organized around the national interests of the Soviet Union. State ownership of the means of production became Communism's end goal, and hence the state was a self-perpetuating political body that would never willingly contemplate its own "withering away." Once Stalin had embedded the principle of socialism in a single country in the Communist Party dogma the defense of that single country came to be the primary objective of the international communist movement, and defense of that single country always expressed itself as defense of the positions of Stalin and his party. This is the common thread that runs through all the narratives of betrayal that follow in *World Revolution,* and this in turn leads inexorably to the situation James describes wherein the Third International is poised to replicate the national allegiances of the Second and to align the workers with national states racing towards war.

Thus, in a letter Stalin wrote to Zinoviev and Bucharin, a letter James reproduces, Stalin expresses his opinion that the revolutionaries in Germany "must be curbed and not spurred on" (WR 181). James holds that the collapse of the revolution in Germany in 1923 locked in Stalin's victory in Russia and that ever after "the Russian bureaucracy under Stalin has wanted only to be left in peace, and will risk every working-class movement in Europe going down to defeat rather than face the complications of a proletarian revolution" (WR 187). The betrayal in Europe was followed by betrayals in Asia. James thinks that Stalin sincerely desired a revolution in China "but he had no belief in the capacity of the Chinese masses to make one" (WR 267). Each of Stalin's actions regarding China is traced back to this essential lack of faith in the creative powers of the masses of the Chinese to see and to make their own future. Stalin, Borodin, and their associates strengthened the Right in China, hobbled the Left, and took positions that led to the deaths of thousands of workers and peasants. "This man of steel, fierce Bolshevik, etc.," James judges to be "first and foremost a bureaucrat," and under Stalin's leadership international communism relinquished that which had made it the first representative of the world's workers rather than just an assemblage of competing national interests. "Henceforward the International had one exclusive purpose—the defence of the U.S.S.R." (WR 267).

James meticulously recalls the now much better-known means by which the Stalinist party suppressed its own people, pressing for national industrialization (which Stalin had earlier opposed) and purging the nation of dissenting voices. Where in the past peasants were shot for stealing from their masters, the landlords, now they would be shot for stealing from their master, the state. Defense of the revolution *became* counterrevolution, and the policies and methods used within the Soviet Union were extended to the Communist International. The expulsion of oppositional voices from the International engineered by the Stalinists set the stage for the suicidal policies adopted in the years leading up to James's writing. It appeared, prefiguring the Hitler-Stalin nonaggression pact, that Stalin preferred that Nazism come to power in Germany rather than the Social Democrats. In a frequently reprinted chapter titled "After Hitler Our Turn," James describes how the International adopted the policy reflected in that impossible slogan. The party's official prognostication was that once the Nazis had attained power, inflation and financial crisis would follow, and in the ensuing crisis the proletarian victory would be assured. As late as 1934 Stalin was pointing to the fact that the Soviet Union had successfully established relationships with the Fascist government of Italy as analogous to the relationship sought with Germany. What mattered was that Italy and Germany opposed France and Britain. (This would all change later, of course, and men like George Padmore would be asked to go easy on such colonial powers as Britain while Germany was defeated.) What mattered to Stalin more than the fact that German and Italian people suffered under the Fascist regimes was that those same Fascists opposed his international enemies. The safety of the national regime was of greater importance in Stalin's calculations than the safety of the international workers' movement. That movement was to have its day after Hitler. "After Hitler, our turn," James observes quite rightly, "is the concentrated expression of bureaucratic inertia and short-sightedness" (WR 338). But there was no room remaining in the revolutionary international for a revolutionary to make that point.

In the Soviet Union the Party had abolished both the Society of Old Worker Bolsheviks and the Communist Academy. The great avant-garde Russian arts of the Revolutionary years were replaced by retrograde socialist realism, and "Shostakovitch, the brilliant young modernist composer, was disgraced for writing 'leftist' music" (WR 370). Stalin now feared his own population as deeply as must any dictator abroad, and those same fears led to the demolition of all democratic possibilities within the Third International. James felt that an international Marxist coalition was still required if the workers were to save themselves from the holocaust their masters intended for them. He concludes his polemic with a plea for a Fourth International, an organization dedicated to the theory of permanent revolution and one that would be as openly democratic as the Third International was now monolithically intolerant. "It is a sea of blood and strife that faces us all, and shrinking from it only makes it worse" (WR 421), James writes in the last paragraph of his history.

James's determination in this conclusion is accompanied by that same optimism with which he seems to end all his histories. His is never an uncritical assessment. He believes, for instance, that "Leninism is the only solution to the problems of the modern world. It might have saved us another world-war on the scale of the one which approaches. But there was too much need of Lenin in both the planning and execution of Leninism" (WR 188). In later years James might well have been tempted to say the same thing about the Trotskyist movement to which he had given such a significant portion of his life. Both Lenin and Trotsky were critical historians and unstinting activists, and James took them as his models in so much that he attempted. In his writing of history James often reaches the highest goals he has set himself after reading those earlier revolutionary scholars. It could well be said of *The Black Jacobins* and *World Revolution* that readers of these books will find that in James's telling "workers' power emerged half-way from books, became something that they could touch and see, a concrete alternative to the old slavery" (James, "Red" 177). James always believed that there must be an alternative to the old slaveries, and he believed, even on the brink of holocaust, that the dialectical motions of human history would bring that alternative out of the pages of books and into the mutual material circumference of human existence. He had faith that his own writings would become a part of that movement, that his own faith in the creativity of working and thinking people would be translated from the page and onto the stage of history in the self-activity of peoples moving irreversibly toward their own freedom. He was himself an untiring critic of the revolution. He was, most measurably in his works as an historian, the kind of revolutionary intellectual described by the Uruguayan novelist Mario Beneditti in 1968. James was a writer who was never "a simple amanuensis of the man of action" but rather the man of action as writer, one whose seemingly natural role within revolution "is to be a vigilant conscience, its imaginative interpreter, its critic" (qtd. in Salkey 126).

3

The Future
in the Present

> *In the middle of the Twentieth Century a spectre is haunting Marxism, keeping it within what is already a graveyard, and when it attempts to come out in the open, ready at the slightest sign of faltering, to show it the way back.*
>
> C. L. R. James, Grace Lee, and Cornelius Castoriadis,
> *Facing Reality*

I. NOTES ON DIALECTICS

It is only appropriate that one should read Jacques Derrida's *Spectres of Marx* with a certain sense of déjà vu, as that is precisely the first sense of the uncanny that marks Derrida's "hauntology," as it must mark any encounter with a ghost, the ghost of Marx especially; for it is that unwonted sense of reencountering that which one thought never again to face that is the defining trait of the ghostly. Whose ghost this is, though, that we meet on the battlements at century's end, is not so clear. If we return to a reading of the most spectral passage in *Facing Reality*, the 1958 text coauthored by C. L. R. James, Grace Lee, and Cornelius Castoriadis, we find that Marxism had long ago been seen entering a graveyard, ushered in and guarded over by its own spectral other. Derrida, too, has seen this ghost, and he has seen it in the company of Marx himself. In *The Eighteenth Brumaire of Louis Bonaparte*, a text that C. L. R. James taught from frequently in his classes at Federal City College, Marx warns that "the revolution paralyzes its own representatives and endows only its opponents with passion and forcefulness. The 'red spectre' is continually conjured up and exorcised by the counter-revolutionaries; when it finally appears it is not with the Phrygian cap of anarchy on its head, but in the uniform of order, in *red breeches*" (*Surveys* 171). As Derrida reminds us, this red specter is summoned forth in the context of Marx's meditation upon a history "painted grey on grey," in which both men *and* events appear "as Schlemihls in reverse, as shadows which have become detached from their bodies" (*Surveys* 171). Derrida hastens to point out that this is not the philosopher's "night in which all cows are black, but grey on grey because red on red" (*Specters* 117).

In *The Eighteenth Brumaire* Marx writes as one who has seen a ghost, and in his own readings of Marx, C. L. R. James writes as one attempting to differentiate the varied grey shades cast upon the wall before him. His concern with the spectral precedes *Facing Reality*'s remarkable comment on the specter haunting Marxism by more than two decades. In his 1937 history *World Revolution, 1917–1936: The Rise and Fall of the Communist International*, he produces a displacement of *The Communist Manifesto*'s most often cited spook. On the first page of his introduction, written in the shadow of the approaching world war, James states simply that "communism is no longer a specter" (9). This, in James's view even then, is not entirely a good thing. At the opening of their manifesto, Marx and Engels propose to make manifest the reality of communism as a European power, and so, by appearing in the open, to dispel the "nursery tale of the Spectre of Communism with a manifesto of the party itself" (*Revolutions* 67). This, in turn, echoes in a curious way a passage from Marx's earlier "Critique of Hegelian Philosophy" among *The Economic and Philosophic Manuscripts of 1844*, texts that C. L. R. James's political group circulated in English translation long before they became generally available to readers in that language. The very first significance Marx attributes to "the surmounting of the object of consciousness" is "that the object as such presents itself to consciousness as something vanishing" (179), perhaps suggesting that the beginning of communism's vanishing act was the making manifest of itself as party written by Marx and Engels in 1848. Engels, introducing the *Manifesto* in his "Preface to the English Edition of 1888," adds that prior to 1848 the Communist League had been "unavoidably a secret society" (62). James, who lived unavoidably in the shadow of a pseudonym for many of his years in America, suggests that an unavoidable consequence of communism's coming out of the grey shadows of secrecy was that it would appear accompanied by a specter, followed, as it were, by a detached shadow of itself. At the conclusion of *World Revolution* James pictures Stalin as a communist haunted by shades of Marxism. In James's estimation, Stalin was trailed everywhere by "the specter which haunts him at home, the return to Leninism, which he calls Trotskyism" (WR 418). Two decades later, having broken with Trotsky, James and his colleagues see Marxism as having been, from its secret origins, haunted by its own shadow, the red specter of ordering communism.

In *Specters of Marx*, Derrida derides certain "readers-consumers" for their ahistorical thinking that they are the first to face the end (14). Wondering at the "jubilation of youthful enthusiasm" evident in the most recent celebrations of Marxism's end, Derrida is struck by the lack of a certain sense of déjà vu in the writings of Francis Fukuyama and of those literary journalists who received his book with such unconstrained joy. To Derrida's eye, "they look like latecomers, a little as if it were possible to take still the last train after the last train—and still be late to an end of history" (15). Derrida, being well read and of a certain age, remembers that period of the 1950s when eschatological themes were "bread of apocalypse in our mouths naturally, already," and he offers as a possible canon for consideration by late defenders of canonicity this reading list "of the modern apocalypse (end of History, end of Man, end of Philosophy, Hegel, Marx, Nietzsche, Heidegger, with their Kojevian codicil and the codicils of Kojéve himself)" (15). Fukuyama has placed himself in the lineage of Kojéve and purports to have read a certain Marx, but one wonders if Francis Fukuyama, author of *The End of History and the Last Man*, remembers that Marx closes one portion of his 1844 manuscripts with the observation that "industry, both in the form of monopoly and in that of competition had to ruin itself so as to learn to believe in man" (105). Man, here, appears as the ghost in Fukuyama's machine, the specter haunting humanism and late twentieth-century celebrations of the triumph of capital.

To Derrida's canon of modern apocalypse we can again add C. L. R. James and the coauthors of *Facing Reality* (a book that Paul Berman has hailed as an "underground classic" of the American left [211]), and in this conjunction we might also begin to track a series of genealogies leading into the poststructuralist moment. By 1958, James, now deported from the United States, was writing under his own name, as was Grace Lee, his longtime collaborator. The third name on the title page of *Facing Reality* in its original publication was Pierre Chaulieu, but this was a pseudonym for Cornelius Castoriadis, a founder of the group *Socialisme ou Barbarie*. That gathering of radical intellectuals is now well-known among students of French intellectual history, for it included among its associates Jean Baudrillard and Jean-François Lyotard. It also attracted the man who later was to author *The Society of the Spectacle*, Guy Debord, producing a tantalizing if unexpected connection between the American Marxists of James's group and Debord's Situationist International. (This was typical of the internationalist intellectual movements of James's group. James's close colleague Raya Dunayevskaya had held conversations with Roman Jakobson, and the James group were also in contact with the Frankfurt School. They were in correspondence with Herbert Marcuse, and, according to Paul Buhle, James also had discussions with Theodore Adorno [*Artist* 106].) Cornelius Castoriadis was aware of James as early as 1947. Raya Dunayevskaya had gone to Paris to attend the conference of the Fourth International, and while there she established contacts between the *Socialisme ou Barbarie* group and the political tendency she had organized with James, sending detailed reports back to her American colleagues. The following year Grace Lee visited Paris and further developed the contact between the two groups. Castoriadis learned from Lee in the course of her four-month stay in Paris that what had come to be known as the Johnson-Forest Tendency, after the pseudonyms used by James and Dunayevskaya in the course of their years of organizing in America, shared with the members of *Socialisme ou Barbarie* an interest in "the self-activity of the working class" (Castoriadis 283). There followed a series of exchanges between Castoriadis and James in London in the period 1954–1955, and in 1955 James met in France with the larger group, a series of discussions that led to issue 20 of the journal *Socialisme ou Barbarie*. The appendix to *Facing Reality* offers a canon of its own, recommended readings in publications of James's and Castoriadis's groups. But *Facing Reality* does more than simply supply a missing American link to the Derridean context. Edward Said has written that new social formations that are "international or paranational in nature . . . have tended to be avant-garde formations in the metropolitan center" (29). Speaking specifically of C. L. R. James and other intellectuals from colonial regions writing in "imperial" languages, Said notes that "these figures address the metropolis using the techniques, the discourses, the very weapons of scholarship and criticism once reserved exclusively for the European, now adapted either for insurgency or revisionism at the very heart of the Western center" (29). James, then, was one of those colonial subjects writing in an imperial language who appeared in France in the 1950s, using the weapons of Western philosophy to forge an avant-garde formation, one of those contributing to that eschatological moment encountered and reencountered by Jacques Derrida, a colonial Jew from Algeria writing in his mother tongue, French.

Facing Reality is one of those spectral texts of the 1950s that almost vanished, that attempts to place a gravestone over the body of the reigning ideologies of the West. In a chapter titled "End of a Philosophy," the authors state plainly, "Philosophy as such has come to an end" (65). Rejecting with equal vehemence continental existentialism and Anglo-American analytic modes descending from Wittgenstein and Austin, the *Facing Reality* authors present themselves as champions of a form of working-class praxis. "The development of science and industry," they argue, "has brought men face to face with the need to make reasonable their daily existence, not to seek in philosophical systems for the harmony that eludes them in life" (66). (To their employers, such workers must ever appear as Bartlebies who would prefer "not to be a little reasonable.") Derrida, looking back at the last end of history from the vantage point of the most recent end of history and the last man, feels obliged "to wonder if the end of history is but the end of a *certain* concept of history" (15). But there must already have been a certain sense of déjà vu to this always premature burial, for when James and his coauthors come to bury a certain philosophy, they are revisiting a grave that Marx had visited before them. Marx, too, had declared the end of philosophy as such, and had begun to look for the truth of philosophy from another source. In a 1944 essay on "Germany and European Civilization," James had written that "Marx was speaking the simplest truth when he said that with Hegel philosophy had come to an end. But he went on to say that the German proletariat was the heir to the classical philosophy of Germany, that the truth of philosophy was in the proletariat and the truth of the proletariat was in philosophy" (358). James, Castoriadis, and Lee, in declaring the death of philosophy *as such,* make their announcement under the chapter heading "End of a Philosophy," and it now becomes clear that those philosophies they wish to see ended are those certain views of thought which have presented themselves in the West as philosophy *as such,* those philosophies that have denied that philosophy existed before the Greeks, or in Africa, or among contemporary working people. Though James is patently not a "deconstructionist," and here I have to disagree with the position of Paul Buhle and Paget Henry in their otherwise instructive essay "Caliban as Deconstructionist" (Buhle and Henry 130), it is equally clear that James's analyses in *Facing Reality* and elsewhere are part of an international theoretical development that brings us to the threshold of poststructuralist, post-Marxist, and postcolonial critiques.

At several points in his writings James can be seen to be moving in the directions that eventually lead to Derrida *and* Spivak, to Lyotard *and* Paul Gilroy, points at which the grey shades of two critical motions meet. This comes most fully into view in James's *Notes on Dialectics,* an informal text in which James locates his opposition to communist parties and his support of Marxism in a return to the texts of Hegel, the same Hegel who had positioned Africa, the land of James's ancestors, outside history as such. But in the same way that Marx attempts to turn Hegel on his head, James's rereading of Hegel is a movement by way of Hegelian dialectic away from Hegelianism. ("Let him have his World-Spirit," James comments wryly at one point [171].) James appears to read both Marx and Hegel by his own lights, and James's turn to Hegel is easily distinguished from the approach of Louis Althusser, who attempts a form of exorcism in the course of his *For Marx* a dozen years after James's *Notes.* For Althusser, "one phantom is more especially crucial than any other today: the shade of Hegel. To drive this phantom back into the night we need *a little more light on Marx,* or what is the same thing, *a little more Marxist light on Hegel himself* " (116).

Warning his readers that "simple, abstract identity is a fiction, a deadly trap for *thinkers*" (85), James, writing in 1948, sounds as if he has been reading Saussure's lecture notes, but it is his reading of Hegel that leads him to the paradox that "identity . . . can only exist on the basis of difference" (84). James undertakes his review of Hegel under the influence of Lenin's prior readings, and it is in one of Lenin's notes on Hegel's larger *Logic* that James locates a neo-Derridean sense of the trace. Lenin's note concerns the transformation of the ideal into the real. This leads James to identify the infinite as the other of the finite, but this is an other discernable *in* the finite: "The infinite is *not* something in general that is beyond what we know as actual. It is the fact that what is beyond the finite comes back, and accomplishes a return to the finite and keeps on doing this, that makes it a true infinity" (102). Already, in James's insistence upon the importance of repetition as the defining feature of the infinite, we can see the link emerging between the idea of identity being based upon difference and the essentiality of repetition to difference. Next we see James grappling with the trace of the infinite in the finite: "The beyond, the infinite, is not *abstract* or *indeterminate* Being, something we know nothing about, our old monster, Nothing. It, the infinite, the beyond, is self-related Being, because to come into existence at all the infinite is going to have to negate the finite. It is thus a negating force. And whatever negates is something present" (102). Because

James is a Marxist, committed to historical materialism and to the telos of the inevitable proletarian revolution, we will not find in *Notes on Dialectics* any of the poststructuralist suspicion of metanarrative so closely associated with Lyotard in his later years (and it would have been surprising indeed if the author of books such as *Black Jacobins* and *World Revolution* would ever have developed such a suspicion of metanarrative). But we can, in passages such as these, see that James's return to Hegel and his rejection of abstract identity is part of a larger developing logic of post-Cartesian critique directed against dominant assumptions about human subjectivity and agency. James is historically posthumanist already in 1947. His essay on "Dialectical Materialism and the Fate of Humanity" (JR 170) describes humanism as "the substitution of a liberal culture" for the self-expression desired by the masses of the people. It is, of course, that very liberal culture that Fukuyama now declares our legacy at the end of history. In James's view humanism was a means by which "the concrete objective protection of wealth" was supplemented "by abstract subjective claims of being the arbiter of justice" (JR 170). This, though, serves to sharpen still further the contradictions inherent in such a supplement. "Humanism had dragged universality from heaven down to earth and had by that made the contradiction between the real and ideal an intolerable antagonism" (JR 170).

All this might seem somewhat removed from James's immediate task as he began his *Notes on Dialectics,* which was to consolidate the political and philosophical work he and his associates in the Johnson-Forest tendency had carried out through the 1940s, providing a larger framework for the group's thesis of state capitalism, the specter that they saw haunting Marxism at midcentury. Following his group's break with Trotsky's analysis of the nature of the communist state in Russia, James, Dunayevskaya, Lee, and the others felt compelled to produce a sound theoretical apparatus to justify their double heresy. One of the many ghosts of Marxisms past stirred up by Derrida's *Specters of Marx* is the corpse of Marxist internecine factionalism. "There was a moment," Derrida remembers, "in the history of European (and, of course, American) politics, when it was a reactionary gesture to call for the end of the party" (103), and yet this is just what James did call for, seeing the party finally as the embodiment of the specter pushing Marx ever backwards into the grave. What seems so clear to post-New Left radicals at century's end was not so clear to earlier generations, as Derrida's comments remind us. One has only to review the vituperative attacks upon the Johnson-Forest tendency by Communist Party types and

Trostkyites alike to get a sense of the violent emotion with which these battles were then engaged. (Irving Howe seems to have developed a "life-long resentment" [Buhle, *Artist* 81] of James following the Johnson-Forest group's departure from the Trotskyite Workers Party.) By the late 1940s, however, it had become evident to James that "if the party does not wither away, the state never will" (ND 176), and that understanding led him to what at the time must have appeared sheer madness to most other Marxists, the assertion that "the party must organize itself for no other purpose than to propagate the destruction of bureaucracy" (224).

James posits this as an inevitable conclusion of Marxism, the very telos of dialectical materialism. Again, James follows Lenin and Marx back to Hegel's texts for a clearer comprehension of the roots of the Johnson-Forest theses. His eye falls across a word that has long troubled English discussions of Marxism. (And continues to do so—at the conference to which Derrida delivered his address on *Specters of Marx,* Gayatri Spivak felt compelled in the course of discussions with the audience to reassert this very point.) James notes that "for the word abolition, *aufhebung*, Marx went again to Hegel." In his April 1943 essay "Production for the Sake of Production," James explains that "*aufhebung* does not mean mere non-existence, or abolition as you abolish a hot dog or wipe some chalk off a board. As Hegel explains at length, it means for him transcendence, raising of one moment or active factor from its subordinate position in the dialectical contradiction to its rightful and predestined place, superseding the opposite moment with which it is interpenetrate, i.e. inseparably united" (9). Similarly, James annotates a passage in volume three of *Capital* in which Marx revises his theses on profit. In 1858 Marx had written to Engels that he had "thrown over the whole doctrine of profit as it has existed up to now," and, as James quotes from the letter, Marx specifically credits his rereading of Hegel's *Logic* for his methodology ("Production" 7). In reexamining profit, Marx was able to recognize that "*capital* appears *as a relation to itself*" (3: 48). James here portrays Marx as a sort of linguistic grave robber. In discussing the self-developing value of capitalist society, Marx uses a term that James then unfolds: "*verselfstandigung,* a term lifted bodily from Hegel. The prefix *ver* in Hegel always means a transformation at the root, something that transcends itself from its own inherent (and thereby contradictory) nature" (7).

When James makes his own return to Hegel in the company of Marx, it is in an attempt to understand how it is that Marxism comes into being accompanied by its spectral other, state capitalism, and how dialectical critique might unveil "the future in the present," the traces within contemporary social formations of the still inevitable *aufhebung* of the state. In his introduction to the first book publication of *Notes on Dialectics*, which did not appear till 1980, more than three decades after its first circulation in manuscript form, James gives some indications of the book's genesis. He had long been familiar with Lenin's 1915 essay "On the Question of Dialectics," but only recently had James gained access to the texts he would require for a fuller examination of his subjects. In addition to the translations of early Marx, members of his political group, primarily Grace Lee and Raya Dunayevskaya, provided James with translations of "all that Lenin had written on *Capital*, on philosophy and on the Russian state; and . . . all of Hegel and Marx in German on philosophy and political economy" (ND 7). In the process of their lengthy discussions, the group concluded that they needed "a fundamental investigation . . . on Hegel's *Science of Logic*" as well as a study of Hegel's smaller *Logic* (ND 7). Raya Dunayevskaya, former secretary to Trotsky and a formidable proponent of Marxist theory, brought her knowledge of Russian and her experience in political economy to the group's interpretive tasks. Grace Lee, who had participated in the "March on Washington Movement" which prompted Roosevelt to move against segregation in defense plant hiring, had completed graduate studies in philosophy and could translate German. She remembers days in the early 1940s when she and James "spent hours reading passages of *Capital* in German side-by-side with passages from Hegel's *Science of Logic*" ("Thinking" 39).

Though many of the texts tracing the evolution of James's thought through the 1940s and 1950s were collaboratively produced, including *Facing Reality, The Invading Socialist Society,* and *State Capitalism and World Revolution,* James did the actual writing of *Notes on Dialectics* alone, drawing on the invaluable contributions of his colleagues in the Johnson-Forest group. Much obfuscation has surrounded the history of the group's interactions during this period, much of it attributable directly to the bitterness surrounding their eventual parting of the ways. In many published texts, Dunayevskaya and members of her later *News and Letters* organization have sought to diminish James's contributions to the state capitalist thesis and to misrepresent James's theoretical positions. A few judiciously decontextualized quotations from James's writings have been deployed over and over again in an effort to downplay the importance of his work in *Notes on Dialectics* and later works. As late as 1987, Dunayevskaya can still be seen dragging an aged hobbyhorse through her *Philosophic Moment of Marxist-*

Humanism. As she did for more than three decades, she characterized her break with James in the 1950s as a principled stand upon her interpretations of Hegel's Absolute Idea. She argues in her "Presentation on Dialectics of Organization and Philosophy," as she had argued so many times previously, that James had not properly grasped this aspect of Hegel's thought, in part because he was unable to get anything out of Hegel's *Philosophy of Mind*. In explaining what she portrays as her breakthrough on the subject of the Absolute Idea, and why in her May 20, 1953, letter to Grace Lee (included in *The Philosophic Moment*) she "suddenly [speaks] on the *Philosophy of Mind*," Dunayevskaya repeats three times in three pages that "when James said that he looked into *Philosophy of Mind*, he concluded that he found nothing there 'for us' " (9, 10, 11). She explains that by "for us" James meant the Johnson-Forest tendency, but readers should wonder at the fact that only two words are actually quoted from James's statement. The footnote Dunayevskaya offers refers to James's own letter to Grace Lee dated May 20, 1949, and included in the published *Raya Dunayevskaya Collection*.

Lou Turner, a colleague of Dunayevskaya's while she was still alive, and managing editor of the *News and Letters* paper, returns to this same point in the correspondence among James, Lee, and Dunayevskaya in his attempts to clarify the theoretical differences that eventually drove the group apart. Turner agrees that a philosophical breakthrough was anticipated by the work that James, Lee, and Dunayevskaya undertook at midcentury, but he argues that James, unlike Dunayevskaya, never accomplished the breakthrough (198). Twice in three pages, Turner again cites that same James letter of May 20, 1949, reporting that James "had looked at Hegel's *Philosophy of Mind* and got nothing from it" (200, 202). (As he presented this essay at the conference *C. L. R. James: His Intellectual Legacies* at Wellesley College in 1991, Turner underscored his reference to the correspondence by flourishing a bound copy of the massive file before his audience, as if to indicate the concrete availability of the text.) Central to Turner's version of James's inadequacies is his contention that while the "explanatory method" employed by James in *Notes on Dialectics* "reduces the subject (proletariat) to substance (the mass party) for the purposes (end) of displacing the absolute substance (bureaucracy), this purpose is only further determined by the notion of the proletariat 'taking over' the absolute substance of the state rather than abolishing it" (195). As Turner presents *Notes on Dialectics*, James's dialectics of the party constitute an original insight that at the same time represents "the theoretical limits of his excursion into the dialectic"

(197). Both Dunayevskaya and Turner severely limit their actual quotations of James, and a checking of the quotations indicates that they don't really attribute words to him that do not appear in his texts, but the abyssal elisions in their citations are breathtaking. When a reader follows the invitation of Dunayevskaya's footnote into the microfilmed records of the correspondence she cites, it turns out that this is what C. L. R. James actually wrote to Grace Lee in May of 1949: "I have not been doing much but I went over Mat'm and Empirico-C [Lenin's *Materialism and Empirio Criticism*]; and had a good look at the Philosophy of Mind. I got nothing from the second—for our task now, but I have a hunch something is there for us" (*Dunayevskaya Collection* 1612). In the copy of this letter that has been microfilmed for the Dunayevskaya collection, somebody has drawn a circle around the phrase "I got nothing from the second," and has written "NB" in the adjacent margin, thus extracting from James's complete sentence the orphan text that has formed one basis for Dunayevskaya's theoretical attack upon James ever since. James's original sentence patently indicates that James has found nothing of immediate use in the task at hand but that he believes there is something very much there to be returned to for further investigations. Given the import of the actual sentence James wrote, there's really nothing that "sudden" about Dunayevskaya's return to the *Philosophy of Mind* in her 1953 letter to Lee.

The strategy Dunayevskaya and Turner adopt in repeating the charge that James got nothing from *Philosophy of Mind* is an odd one, not only because it seems so quickly contradicted by a reading of the very letter so frequently cited, but because it places such great weight on judgments about the relative importance of various Hegelian texts. James, in fact, continued throughout his career to return to Hegel's most difficult works. A ready example is the text titled "The Gathering Forces," a document that was to serve as a major statement of James's group in the years after the breakup of the Johnson-Forest Tendency. Coauthored with Martin Glaberman, William Gorman, and George Rawick, "The Gathering Forces" returns to the *Phenomenology of Mind*. The James group brings Hegel's text into their discussions as part of the theoretical preparation for their positions on "The Third World: The Peasantry," specifically drawing readers' attention to Hegel's meditations upon the master and the slave. James and his collaborators devote several pages to a running commentary on extracts from *Phenomenology of Mind*, drawing in the end the lesson that "if we penetrate this bit of Hegel, we can come to understand the bitter but inevitable nature of the struggles that go on in the world . . . The life and death struggle that Hegel talks of appears in the bitter character of peasant wars" (26–27). For the James group as it existed in 1967, despite what we might gather from Dunayevskaya with regard to James's abilities to make use of Hegel, "What Hegel expostulated as philosophy for the individual thinker Marx proceeded to advance as the movement of social bodies" (27). Lou Turner, in turn, seems to be following the same exigetical practice employed by Dunayevskaya as he quotes from *Notes on Dialectics,* for far from advancing the "notion" that the proletariat take over the "absolute substance of the state rather than abolishing it," what James actually writes in his *Notes* is that "the coming of age of the proletariat means the abolition of the party" (176), and that this means "*the disappearance of the state*" (176).

The correspondence among the three Johnson-Forest collaborators in this period, as well as internal evidence in the publications, makes it evident that James's is the organizing editorial hand, setting tasks for the group and revising the project when the investigations indicate the need. Not only do the letters he exchanged with Lee and Dunayevskaya show the participants carrying out their tasks with relish and carefully reading and criticizing the work of the others, but we can see from these letters how democratic the relationship was. In his letter to Grace Lee of June 19, 1949, James writes: "Within this circle I can polemicize against Grace. One step out of it and I wouldn't. I also invited you to polemicize against me—you didn't take it. I have spent the last three weeks thinking about what you told me about quantity and Leibnitz. I am an infinitely wiser man. I know now what you were talking about in your letters to Nevada. I knew something was missing" (*Dunayevskaya Collection* 1630). Within the text of the *Notes* themselves we find indications of how lines of investigation would lead to new areas of historical and philosophic research. Giving an example of how his applications of dialectics to history sometimes brought him to hunches about the past (like the hunch about the future usefulness of the *Philosophy of Mind*), James informs his readers: "I remember telling Rae [Dunayevskaya] one day, 'Go and read Populism and search for an independent Negro movement. It ought to be there.' She found it in a few hours, over a million Negroes, buried and forgotten. Over and over again I have to look for an important missing link or links. If I cannot find them, I have to give up the theses and try another" (ND 204). As they crossed the country in their travels, the three principle theorists of the Johnson-Forest group passed drafts, ideas, and research to one another through the mails, keeping up a philosopher's workshop and a writing seminar in their course of correspondence, each responding to the instigations and criticisms of the others.

In retrospect, James claims to have undertaken *Notes on Dialectics* with a degree of reluctance. Scott McLemee has retrieved a revealing statement that was included in the 1971 mimeographed edition of James's *Notes*, a statement manifesting James's characteristic combination of complaint and irony. James compares the writing of the *Notes* to his earlier project in *World Revolution*, a job he felt someone else should already have done. Having departed from England, he says:

> I come here [the United States] and have to take up dialectic. I am no philosopher. That was a job for a *trained academic* who had embraced Bolshevism. Luckily Grace [Lee] was there to help. I then found myself writing [like] hell about (1) American politics. That was not my job either . . . But (2) I next find myself up to the eyes in the analysis of internal party politics in the U. S. That was not *my* job either. *This should have been the job of a trained dialectician,* to whom the experiences were familiar . . . I *know* that where I could work most concretely would have been *British* politics; the literature, the traditions of Britain are in my bones. I grew up on them. This work forced upon me has been valuable. I . . . have worked through from the start the chief spheres of our movement's theory. (qtd. in McLemee 226)

There are, of course, other instigations at work as James begins to work through his *Notes;* it is probably not the case that his primary reason for writing the book was that nobody else would do it. At least one part of his motivation in undertaking this daunting task may date to his earlier meetings with Trotsky himself. In April 1939, Trotsky, meeting with James in Mexico, had greeted James's proposals for a position on what was still in those days termed "The Negro Question" with real interest and enthusiasm. But there was one criticism the older revolutionary offered that must have rankled still eleven years later when James wrote his work on dialectics. Trotsky's praise for James's work was mixed with a teacherly note of correction: "In parts the manuscript is very perspicacious, but I have noticed here the same fault that I have noticed in *World Revolution*—a very good book—and that is a lack of dialectical approach. Anglo-Saxon empiricism, and formalism which is only the reverse of empiricism" (FP 60).

By the time he had completed his notes, James had satisfied himself that it was Trotsky who had failed to apply the dialectical method with sufficient rigor. There is a more fundamental sense in which Trotsky inspired the work that led James to his *Notes,* however, one having to do with his group's mission to adapt Bolshevism to the American context. In their 1947 *Balance Sheet*, in which the Johnson-Forest group rehearse the history of their movement into and out of the Workers Party, they report that "in Trotsky's view, 'It was absolutely necessary to explain why the American "radical" intellectuals accept Marxism without the dialectic (a clock without a spring). The secret is simple. In no other country has there been such a rejection of the class struggle as in the land of unlimited "opportunity" ' " (2). The *Balance Sheet* also clearly delineates the way that the Johnson-Forest writers parceled out the tasks to be accomplished. Following the 1941 Workers Party conference, James's group were concerned about the relative superficiality of the party's theoretical positions. They decided to commence a joint project: "[Dunayevskaya] was given the task of working on the Russian question . . . [James] was to complete the theoretical study of political economy as applied to the contemporary world and to take up the question of dialectical materialism. . . . [Lee], with an academic training in philosophy, eased the road to the fundamental grasp of the principles of the Hegelian dialectic and their application to Marxian economics, sociology and politics" (8).

The critical response to *Notes on Dialectics* has been as mixed as was Trotsky's informal review of *World Revolution*. Cedric Robinson, writing in his monumental study *Black Marxism: The Making of the Black Radical Tradition*, has said that "Ten years after *Jacobins*, James wrote a second masterpiece" (389), *Notes on Dialectics*. In sharpest contrast, Alex Callinicos has written that "in fact, the odd brilliant *apercu* aside, the book is philosophically uninteresting, consisting largely of lengthy extracts from Hegel which James then expounds and seeks to illustrate by applying to debates within the [Fourth International]" (63). Paul Buhle, an admirer of the book, says, "Rarely, at least until the structuralist documents of the 1970s, has so difficult a text been presented to the American Marxist reader" (*Artist* 92), but Ivar Oxaal, reviewing the republication of *Notes* in book form, feels to the contrary that James's style in this work directly informs the text's reception. "*Notes on Dialectics*," in his judgment, "is a work written in a populist style but despite of this—or as James might quickly interject, *precisely because of* that style—it is a serious Marxist contribution to technical philosophical analysis" (132).

Scott McLemee has identified James's study of Melville, *Mariners, Renegades and Castaways*, as "perhaps the oddest volume James published" (227), but *Notes on Dialectics* not only has an odd publication history, it is a formally odd text as well. *Notes* first circulated among members of the Johnson-

Forest tendency as a set of carbon copies of a typescript in progress, and was known to those first readers by the name of its geographical point of origin, as "The Nevada Document." James wrote the text while living in Nevada briefly, working as a gardener and handyman by day and carrying out a major theoretical investigation in his "off" hours. The *Notes* truly are notes, and to the difficulties of the materials James is working with is added James's series of ironic and sometimes hectoring addresses to his readers. One wonders, for instance, how a member of the Johnson-Forest Tendency trying to make out the type on the eighth carbon of part one might have reacted when James wrote: "I reread this passage. I know where I am going. The question is: do *you* know? As a matter of fact I am attempting the impossible" (30). We know from later writings by his contemporaries of the excitement James's colleagues felt as they received the installments. Martin Glaberman opens his 1981 review of the republished texts by recollecting:

> I can still remember when I saw the first draft of *Notes on Dialectics*. I was drilling holes in crankshafts at the Buick Division of General Motors in Flint, Michigan. . . . The impact was unbelievable. Rereading it over thirty years later, it still makes a powerful impression. On the days that a section of the document came in the mail we would sit up late into the night reading and discussing it. Each day we would wait for the mail to see if another section had come. That was pretty remarkable for a book that was difficult then and is difficult now (although it is not as difficult as taking Hegel neat). (97)

The book's difficulties are not to be denied. In a 1949 letter to Dunayevskaya, James made a telling remark on matters of style and substance. "Strive to be understood," he advises his collaborator, "but you cannot write a serious theoretical study on the assumption that your reader knows nothing" (*Dunayevskaya Collection* 1646).

The many playful touches in *Notes on Dialectics* include James's placing of a headstone at the close of part one, marking a resting place for both Hegel and the reader at the end of James's reflections upon the preface to *The Science of Logic:*

Here lies
G. W. F. Hegel
R. I. P.
He deserves it
---

(66)

James, however, immediately tips over the headstone he has just erected. He then disinters the Hegelian logic on the facing page as he takes up "the Doctrine of Being." Appropriately for one taking up the logic of the dead, James tells his readers that he feels "a slight chill" (67) as he proposes an approach to the larger *Logic*. Throughout his *Notes* James reminds us of the informal nature of these discussions. He wonders to himself how Grace Lee may be reacting as she reads one of his figures of speech. Looking at Hegel's disquisitions on Absolute Ground and Determined Ground, James asks rhetorically, "What the hell can we do with that?" (83). Working his way into "Leninism and the Notion," James remarks, "I am writing *en famille* and as these ideas strike me, I put them down" (135).

As fond as Walter Benjamin of citation, James introduces a lengthy quotation from the *Logic* by telling his readers, "It is very long. But this is in its way an anthology and I would like it in" (73). Benjamin, commenting upon his own process of composition by accumulation, said of the method that "everything that comes to mind has at all costs to be incorporated into the project one is working on at the time" ("N" 43). Also like Benjamin is James's fascination with the leaps of dialectical thought (a fascination that spread quickly among his correspondents during these years). In the *Arcades Project*, Benjamin says of the constellation of the Then (*das Gewesene*) and the Now (*das Jetzt*) that "while the relation of the present to the past is a purely temporal, continuous one, the relation of the Then to the Now is dialectical—not development but image[,] leaping forth (*Sprunghaft*)" ("N" 49). Tracking Lenin's progress through the thickets of Hegelian dialectic, James comes across a related constellation. James copies into his notes the excited earlier notes made by Lenin as he studied Quality in the Doctrine of Being:

> LEAP
> LEAP
> LEAP
> LEAP
> (ND 99)

Again, the trace of the new thing leaps from its position already in the existent. Lenin notes at the core of Hegelian thought "Movement and 'self-movement' (NB this. An independent (*eigenmachtige*) spontaneous, internally necessary movement)" (ND 101). According to James, "every single one" of Hegel's "transitions involves a *leap*" (100). The German word for "proposition," *satz*, as Samuel Weber has recently reminded me, is also the word meaning "leap," and Lenin must have had in mind at the time he transcribed Hegel's leaps into his notes the preface to the *Phenomenology*. In discussing these passages of Lenin's *Philosophical Notebooks*, Kevin Anderson argues that Lenin's stress on Hegelian leaps and discontinuities is a means of separating "himself a bit from Plekhanov's more evolutionist interpretation" (42). James, finally, remains closer to Lenin and the Hegelian model of dialectic than to Benjamin, but for both the transitional leap, the kicking free of the traces, is already there as a structure of possibility *in* the proposition.

If, then, the possibility of proletarian revolution is already present within the structures of capital, then Marxism's spectral other, state capitalism, must also arise from within the contradictory motions of capital. James is always careful to demonstrate that he is following out a thesis with its roots in the founding texts of Marxist dialectic. Dunayevskaya and James had arrived at the state capitalist thesis independently of one another early in their work, but neither claimed to have originated it. Their original contribution to the thesis was their application of it to capitalist formations as well as to explanations of the Soviet state. In *The Invading Socialist Society*, a text the two of them coauthored with Grace Lee, we find cited Lenin's 1918 article on state capitalism, in which Lenin argues that "from petty-bourgeois capitalism it is *one and the same road* that leads . . . to large-scale state-capitalism and to socialism" (IS 23). Marx had written of state capitalism in volume two of *Capital*, where he addresses government securities as "outstanding claims on the annual product of a nation" (353) and he also examines the modes by which the state performs "the functions of industrial capitalists" (100). In 1878, Engels made what James considers to be "a statement of the most profound significance for the modern world." In his essay on "The Russian Question," James summarizes Engels's proposition: "The growing socialization of production would compel the capitalists to treat the productive forces as social forces, *so far as that was possible within the framework of capitalist* relations" (25). Zinoviev, as early as 1921, had denounced Russia as a state capitalist formation, and Bukharin wrote a series of articles on the subject in 1928 (ND 36). In the Johnson-Forest publication *State Capitalism and World Revolution*, James and his colleagues rush to point out what they share with those earlier theorists: "We have never said that the economy of the United States is the *same* as the economy of Russia. What we have said is that, however great the differences, the fundamental laws of capitalism operate" (SC 49). This, in James's estimation, is what Trotsky had never entirely grasped, and what Trotsky's continued commitment to the belief that a workers' state equals nationalized property prevented him from grasping (ND 33). Imprisoned by inflexible categories of thought, Trotsky persisted in seeing the Soviet Union as a decayed workers' state, and was thus proved as wrong in his predictions as Stalin was terrifyingly right. Trotsky predicted, incorrectly, that Stalin would restore private property. James, reexamining Marxism and rereading Lenin, offers the hypothesis that Stalinism "comes out of the contradictions of Menshevism," and that "this thing comes . . . from capitalism" (ND 204).

James here portrays himself as continuing the earlier methodology of Marx's analyses of capital to an inevitable conclusion. In his 1941 "Resolution on the Russian Question," James reminded his colleagues of the constructed nature of the model that appears in the first two volumes of *Capital:*

> To deduce the laws of capitalist production, Marx constructed a capitalism such as never existed and never could exist. In it labor, like every other commodity, was always sold at its value, the capitalist found on the market whatever he wished, consumption was always equated to production, fluctuations of prices there were none, no single capitalist enterprise advanced in front of the other in organic composition, unemployment and crisis were absent, all was in complete equilibrium; no capitalist could construct for himself a more ideal haven of peaceful accumulation. Yet this is the capitalism from which Marx drew his laws of motion, and even this capitalism Marx proved, was bound to collapse. (20)

In his own analyses of the motions of capitalism, James observes the presumptively capitalist and presumably communist societies following a predictable inner logic. A significant feature of the logic of capital, as James sees it, is that it survives "the abolition of the traditionally free capitalist market" ("Russia" 20). In fact, James argues that "it is . . . the law of capitalist production to abolish the private character of capital" (20–21). In the same way that Marx saw the joint-stock company as the abolition of private property that did not truly alter the boundaries of capitalist production, James argues that "the capitalists abolish the free market and shape circulation as far as possible to their own purposes, rationing every commodity including labor power" ("Russia" 26). These laws of motion become the chief subject of the James group's 1947 text *The Invading Socialist Society,* which draws its title from a phrase of Engels's. James had pursued this concept as early as 1941, when he wrote that "more and more capitalist society, in Engels's phrase, will capitulate to the necessity for planning of the invading socialist society. We must be prepared for strange transformations" ("Russia" 26). James was obviously closer to the target with this last premonition than with his 1940s era speculations about the readiness of American workers to form soviets. Grace Lee, now Grace Lee Boggs, the philosophy scholar who used to work through the German texts of Hegel and Marx with James, has lived long enough to witness some of these strange transformations wrought by late capitalism. Speaking of the profound alterations in the American economy since the time of her meetings with James, she remarks icily that "instead of labor being liberated from capital, capital is being liberated from labor" ("Thinking" 43). To paraphrase Derrida paraphrasing Marx, who analyzed so astutely the spectral qualities of money, the shadow of capital is detaching itself from the body of labor.

In the Soviet sphere, where a form of proletarian revolution, or at least a revolution in the name of the proletariat, had occurred, the laws of capitalist motion had produced the phenomenon of the Stalinist state. In *Notes on Dialectics,* James advances the thesis that "the conflict of the proletariat is between itself as object and itself as consciousness, its party" (61), and he argues further that "the party has a dialectical development of its own. The solution of the conflict is the fundamental abolition of this division" (61). (Here it is important to remind ourselves again that James means "abolition" in the Hegelian sense of *aufhebung,* not simply disappearance.) *State Capitalism and World Revolution* offers the clearest statement of James's position on the Communist Party, that is, what we once called the "actually existing" Communist Party. The Johnson-Forest tendency took the position that "as the Social-Democrats were the labor bureaucracy of monopoly capitalism, the Stalinists are the labor bureaucracy of the period of 'vast state-capitalist trusts and syndicates'" (7). The Communists are, as successive American administrations always held them to be, deadly enemies of private property. However, as James describes it, "Theirs is a last desperate attempt under the guise of 'socialism' and 'planned economy' to reorganize the means of production without releasing the proletariat from wage-slavery" (7). Thus, within a few years of the Bolshevik seizure of power in Russia, the party that was to be the consciousness of the proletariat has become the capitalist subject continuing the oppression of the proletariat as object.

Beginning shortly after Lenin's death and accelerating with the recent release of long secret Kremlin files, we have seen analyses claiming that Leninist thought was inherently totalitarian and that it inevitably led to Stalinist oppression. It was never enough simply to dismiss such assertions as misreadings of Lenin's texts. Even during the period of his work within Trotskyite parties, James had struggled with this argument. Disputing the Worker's Party's reliance upon Lenin's "What Is to Be Done" as their justification for belief in their own role as a vanguard political leadership, James railed against the presumption that only party intellectuals can bring socialist consciousness to the masses. In the *Balance Sheet* that he and his colleagues prepared in August 1947, James points out that "Trotsky took care in his last book to expose Lenin's error, and showed that Lenin himself admitted it" (18). But there remains a further stage of critique on this point. As Derrida has argued that we must produce readings of Nietzsche that will account for both the Nazi and the antifascist readings of Nietzsche, James wants to produce readings of Lenin that locate the inevitability of Stalinism in the ineluctable structures of the history Lenin studied and made rather than within the Leninist texts themselves. Indeed, it was the Stalinists, as James reminds his readers, who were most bent upon situating their self-justifications within the texts of Marx and Lenin. It was never enough to have the corpse of Lenin in one's possession, his ghost must be made to speak on one's behalf. Characterizing Stalinist theory, James and his collaborators stitch together a remarkable trope. "Its theory," they write, "is the result and expression of empiricism and then a search in the closet of Marxism for something that will fit. If nothing is found, a new garment is created, and the Marxist label attached" (SC 61).

The 1950 *State Capitalism* text rehearses the historical record of labor modes in Russia from the time of the October 1917 revolution, detailing the move from the orientation to workers' power in the Soviets on to the consolidation of Stalinist control and the horrors of the Gulag; from Lenin's ideal state wherein every cook can govern, set forth in the 1918 Declaration of the Rights of Toilers, through the state's use of the GPU to organize production as "creative labor." James points to the bureaucratization of the production conferences associated with the first five-year plan during the transition period of 1924–1928 as the beginning of "the alienation of mass activity to conform to specified quantities of *abstract labor* demanded by the plan to 'catch up with capitalism' " (SC 45). This leads to Stakhanovism, to the Stalinist constitution of 1936–1937, to increased measures of Fordism and Taylorism in Soviet production. Finally, "whereas in 1936 we had the singling out of a ruling class, a 'simple' division between mental and physical work, we now have the *stratification* of mental and physical labor" (SC 47). This, in turn, requires ever-increasing measures to discipline the working classes, ever more oppressive constraints both inside and outside the party. As soon as 1937, James had recognized the absolute contradiction between the interests of the Communist Parties and the workers' aspirations toward free activity. In his appendix to *World Revolution* he asks quite starkly, "What sort of Socialism is this that does not allow itself even to be discussed?" (WR 425).

James's *Notes on Dialectics* place Trotsky's inability to comprehend what had taken place in the Soviet Union in the context of the dialectical motions of history. Trotsky held that Stalinism was a deception perpetrated upon the workers, but James and his group find that diagnosis both simplistic and condescending. James holds that the concrete existence of Stalinism "requires that you take it as an impulse from below and incorporate it into your categories and drive *them* forward" (ND 29). This Trotsky could not do. Unable to *know* whether the Stalinist parties were defenders of private property and the national state or not, Trotskyism ended by perpetuating rather than destroying the social supports of counterrevolution (ND 157). James begins the work of *Notes on Dialectics* by asserting that Stalinism is an "inevitable . . . form of development of the labor movement," and works to reorganize his categories "to fit this phenomenon" (ND 30). This seems contradictory to the position he had taken in his "Resolution on the International Situation," written for the conference of the Fourth International just two years earlier (21–22), but undoubtedly the progress of James's thought on these issues had much to do with his group's split from the Workers Party in 1947, and from the Socialist Workers Party after that.

James posits Stalinism and Trotskyism as two offshoots of an "arrested" Leninism. Both were developments which bore the traces of the Leninism from which they sprang. Stalinism converts Leninism to counterrevolution; Trotskyism takes Leninism "as Understanding" and develops "itself as inevitably as Leninism did" (NF 151). James's own tendency is a dialectical movement out of Trotskyism, a mode of contending with the new in ways that Trotsky himself could not countenance. James writes that his ideas "come out of Trotskyism; *as ideas they could have come from nowhere else*" (ND 151).

One error shared by Trotskyism and Stalinism is the substitution of the consciousness of the party as subject for the party *as* consciousness of the workers as subject, an error they derive in their differing ways from their common origins in Leninism. In the Soviet Union, the Stalinist apparatus declares that class struggle has ended because antagonistic classes have been abolished. Henceforth, as Zhdanov claims, criticism and self-criticism impel the development formerly growing out of class struggle. Nevertheless, James comments succinctly about a seemingly unending process of social terror: "The proletariat's role in the struggle for socialism is to work harder and harder, while the leadership and organization are left to the 'criticism and self-criticism' of the elite, the bureaucracy, the party" (ND 124–25). The Trotskyist modality of this same error is its unwillingness to relinquish its view of itself as a vanguard. This vanguardism propels itself invariably to narrow sectarianism, endless "party-building" activities, and, despite all that building of the party and preparing of the working classes for revolution under the party's leadership, continual splitting into smaller and smaller "groupuscules," as the history of the Johnson-Forest group and their movements from the Workers Party to the Socialist Workers Party and finally into an orbit of their own (where they would split still further into smaller subtendencies) confirms. Even without their analyses of the Fourth International's declining influence, their own experiences taught them harsh lessons about the results of considering oneself an advanced element, a vanguard leadership *for* rather than *of* the masses. In the pages James and his colleagues produced from Cornelius Castoriadis's contribution to *Facing Reality* he drives this lesson home: "On every occasion 'the vanguard' has found itself far behind in relation to the action and ideas of the masses in the revolution; on every occasion, instead of showing the road, they have dragged lamentably in the rear, trying with great difficulty to adapt themselves to events; on every occasion it is the most exploited elements, the most 'backward,' the most humble, who have been the most audacious, the most creative, the ones who have carried the movement forward" (FR 92–93). His own historical researches had brought James to similar conclusions about the relationships of leadership to revolutionary masses in widely divergent contexts. From his study of Toussaint L'Ouverture's development in the course of the revolutions in San Domingo to his critique of Eric Williams's leadership in Trinidad in *Party Politics in the West Indies,* James discovered examples of leaders who were pushed to their most significant decisions, to their most revolutionary positions, often reluctantly, by pressures arising from the increasingly self-aware masses of the people, and who failed most tragically when they allowed themselves to believe that their judgment was to be followed, rather than formed, by the masses.

This led James and his group to that most heretical position, the one that Derrida says was, at one moment, thought a reactionary gesture. For

Derrida, "to analyze the inadequation of existing parliamentary structures to democracy itself" is no longer reactionary, and neither is it always the case that it is reactionary, at least in the gestural sense, to call for the end of the party. Derrida's hypothesis "is that this mutation has already begun; it is irreversible" (*Spectres* 103). There are many late arrivals who call for the party's end only as it is visibly and irreversibly already breaking up. If such a mutation has already begun, it was called for and predicted by James. In *Notes on Dialectics* James offers his hypothesis that "if the free activity of the proletariat is to emerge," it can emerge only by destroying the communist parties. James quickly adds, however, and this motion is manifested in Derrida's hypothesis as well, that "free activity means not only the end of the communist parties. It means the end of capitalism" (ND 118). Here we see what the Johnson-Forest tendency had in mind when they argued that while American "free market democracy" and Soviet "communism" were not the same economic systems, they both were modes of capitalist social formation. In *Facing Reality*, the James group put forward their thesis that both Stalinist and Trotskyist modes reintroduced the separation of subject and object. "The failure of the world revolution," in their analysis, "reintroduced the old separation between economics and politics" (FR 13). James believed that Western capitalism produced the same results with its differing mode of economy. Writing in his column in the *Militant*, James said, "In bourgeois society there is no continuity for the workers between their economic ties and their political lives. When a worker goes to the polls to vote . . . The man in front of him and the one in back of him he may never see again. After he has cast his vote, he again retires into the shadows of a separate existence" ("The Social Ties" 3). Here, in the United States at midcentury, we again see the construction of Schlemihls in reverse. As Marx predicted, and as Derrida remembers at the end of a certain history, the shadows of a separate existence have become detached from the last man.

II. DIALECTICS AND THE FATE OF HUMANITY

In the end, James felt, the proletariat would be in revolt not just against the state, and not just against the appropriation by capitalism of the value they produced by their labor, but "against value production itself" (IS 13). This obviously leaves James open to criticisms that his philosophy is an idealistic one, and that is a charge that James might ultimately not have wished to evade. That is, he would reject absolutely the imputation that he was an idealist in the sense of one who believes in a transcendent realm of a priori truth, but he was idealistic in the sense that he was persuaded that mankind would inevitably reach a universal, material ideal of social organization that would eliminate economic exploitation and political oppression. In his 1960 series of lectures delivered in Trinidad, the text that the government of Prime Minister Eric Williams impounded, James shared with his appreciative audience his vision of that ideal: "The end towards which mankind is inexorably developing by the constant overcoming of internal antagonisms is *not* the enjoyment, ownership, or use of goods, but self-realization, creativity based upon the incorporation into the individual personality of the whole previous development of humanity. Freedom is creative universality, *not* utility" (MP 115). If James is sometimes criticized for adopting a political philosophy that may lead to quietism and an unrealistic reliance upon spontaneism, this doesn't seem to have troubled James much. As late as 1985 he insisted in one interview: "The leadership is always an imposition on the rank-and-file. The rank-and-file don't need them, don't need them. That's my view. This is rather an unusual view, but I am certain of it as time goes on" (EC 47). This assurance is discomfiting to political activists because it gives them so little prescriptive advice about that always returning Leninist question, "What is to be done?" As James's 1985 conversation with younger radicals from Jackson, Mississippi, proceeds, one can see the interviewers becoming increasingly uneasy with the seeming lack of specificity of the advice they are receiving from James. When asked point-blank what radicals should "*do* if they wanted to promote the revolution," James responds matter-of-factly, "People don't promote the revolution. The revolution takes place because an instinctive mass of the population feels that it can't live as it's been living so it breaks out. And people who are writing or speaking take part in that" (EC 33–34). This is nearly the same answer James and his colleagues had delivered to a dubious audience of intellectuals and activists at midcentury. For James, facing reality meant facing the fact that the Left's internal arguments about the preparedness of the masses, while perhaps raising an important question, have little immediate bearing on the self-activity *of* the masses. "The insurrection will come when it will come," we read in *Facing Reality*. "The world revolution will triumph in the whole world or in part in its own time. This has been and can be a legitimate subject for discussion" (FR 51). On those occasions when James did offer practical suggestions for intervention, he was as direct and specific as anyone might wish. In 1941, the coordinating committee that had led a bus boycott in Harlem turned its attention to protest against hiring discrimination in the colleges of New York City, and James contributed his advice through a column in the newspaper *Labor Action*. When the coordinating committee approached the City College administration, James offered the assistance of the Workers Party, an offer that models as clearly as anything could James's conception of the role of the intellectual in mass movements: "Our theoretical contribution is very simple. It can be summed up in four words. 'Don't play with them.' Our material contribution can be summed up in five words. 'Tell us where to picket' " ("From Jobs" 4).

James was able to exhibit such equanimity about the possibility of revolution, while constantly surveying the world for signs of mass insurrection, because his studies of history and his personal experiences as a revolutionary had taught him that when the masses leap into movement, they thrust forward leadership, good or bad, of their own choosing, leadership that they would just as quickly repudiate if they felt the need. The effectiveness of that leadership could be measured by their abilities to understand and work with the forces loosed by the masses to seize the opportunities presented during the insurrectionary surge. James had seen that the rebellious masses of San Domingo had propelled L'Ouverture onto the world stage. He had made a careful study of Marx's analyses of the Paris Commune, of Lenin's and Trotsky's analyses of the Soviet revolution; he had observed firsthand general strikes on three continents, and he had personally worked with many of the major revolutionary leaders of his time. Lenin, James insisted over and over again, had always kept an eye on the direction of the great masses of the people, and Nkrumah, James recorded in his study of the rise and fall of the first postcolonial head of state in Africa, was "not ashamed of the fact that at every decisive stage the mass drove him on and . . . roughly told him what it wanted" (NG 104).

It was the question of what the masses wanted that led James to his most optimistic conclusions. It was evident to James that the masses were often stirred to action by grievances, by, after long periods of suffering, a final refusal to accept the fate that their oppressors envisioned for them. However, James saw confirmed time and time again the ability of the masses, in their moment of rebellion, to perceive a higher and more revolutionary goal than the amelioration of their immediate suffering. "When workers in a union or in a factory strike," he believed, "they strike for concrete advantages to themselves. The revolutionary struggle, however, is of a higher order of intensity" ("From Jobs" 4). The 1941 actions against hiring discrimination in the City Colleges of New York afforded James an exemplary case study. As he thought about the fifteen hundred demonstrators who turned out in support of the demand for equality of opportunity in faculty hiring, James, who at that point had not yet become a university professor himself, imagined that no more than 5 percent of the crowd were likely to have friends or relatives in a position to benefit directly if the demands were granted. "Yet these Negro people," wrote James, "urged on by a tremendous passion for equality, turned out in numbers and worked for weeks to get a few Negroes jobs driving buses. Now they go further and show they are prepared to fight in order to get teachers at colleges that few of them attend and few of them have any prospect of attending" ("From Jobs" 4).

This was the same revolutionary determination that W. E. B. Du Bois had observed in the masses of ex-slaves as they struggled to build a new mode of life in the America of the Reconstruction era. In his epochal history *Black Reconstruction*, Du Bois had delineated the path taken by the struggling masses of African Americans in search of equality, the path that led inevitably to the ideal of free and universal education as a human right. James was to see this same phenomenon again in the course of the independence movement in Ghana. When the colonial authorities arrested several members of the United Gold Coast Convention, students and teachers in many schools organized strikes in protest. They were expelled. In response, Nkrumah and his compatriots hired a hall and improvised an anticolonial secondary school, with the dismissed faculty as the new school's staff. From this beginning in a rented hall with cast-off odds and ends as classroom furnishings grew the Ghana National Education Movement: "At news of the foundation of the school, requests poured in to Nkrumah from all over the country, and new schools were founded, sometimes within a few days of each other—a dozen schools and colleges, technical schools, elementary schools in the colony, in Ashanti and in Togoland. The people subscribed money. Chiefs appropriated land, teachers taught for small salaries and the consciousness for national self-education was established" (NG 88). This is a prototypically Jamesian narrative. The people require leadership for certain organizational, educational, and technical tasks, but no one needs to teach them a desire for freedom, equality, or knowledge. This much James knew long before reading Marx or Lenin, and this idea is at the core of his theory about, and action in the service of, movements to overthrow colonialism. This concept, furthermore, gave form to his understanding of autonomous movements of peoples in the African diaspora for freedom. For James, these struggles were inseparable ultimately from the self-action of the proletarian masses to free themselves from the imposed necessity to create surplus value for capital—inseparable, but still autonomous.

From the publication of his earliest texts, James shows himself as one committed to collaborative action for the ending of colonial and racist domination. His *Life of Captain Cipriani,* a portion of which was reprinted by Leonard and Virginia Woolf's Hogarth Press under the title *The Case for West Indian Self-Government,* opens with a foreword that pleads for the direct assistance of the reader, for, "in fact anything which would be useful in the effort to rid ourselves of the weight we have carried for so long that some of us scarcely realize that we are carrying it" (LC n.pag.). Equal parts polemic and political biography, this early book finds James advancing arguments very much like those of American abolitionists of the nineteenth century and those of the twentieth-century Civil Rights movement. Since the claim of the British in the early part of the century was that self-government would be granted when the West Indians were "fit for it," James sets forth to call the British bluff. Reproducing the "overwhelming evidence" that the West Indians are fit to govern themselves, James argues that the British have little to lose by keeping their word. This, however, should not be taken as a sign that James had accepted the initial premise of the colonizers that West Indians had once been unfit. James, rather, is employing here the same rhetoric found in so many of the slave narratives, whose authors often cited the whites' claims to Christianity as a means of underscoring the rankest hypocrisies of a society built upon slavery. James's basic principle is given just before his conclusion. It is a principle he held to all his life, that all communities of humans are entitled to political self-determination: "a people like ours should be free to make its own failures and successes, free to gain that political wisdom and political experience which come only from the practice of political affairs" (JR 62).

From this fundamental principle James evolved his later positions on African liberation and the developing struggle for freedom within diasporic African communities, and from this too comes James's bedrock belief in the inextricability of black liberation and proletarian revolution. Beginning with his first publications, James made it clear that for him race was a biological fiction, albeit a social fact with an undeniable history, and that race had been constructed upon the most material of motives. It was manifest to James from his readings of history that traits held by Europeans to typify African peoples were produced by white discourse in the interest of domination and exploitation. In the prologue to *Black Jacobins* he says of the earliest French colonists in San Domingo, "So little did they bring Negroes because these were barbarous or black, that the early laws prescribed similar regulations for both black slaves and white *engagés*" (BJ 5). Race comes into existence as a discursive formation in the service of exploitation, not as a genetic fact; it has a history that continues to exercise its influence in the present. For these reasons James holds that "to think of imperialism in terms of race is disastrous. But to neglect the racial factor as merely incidental [is] an error only less grave than to make it fundamental" (BJ 283). As we have already seen, James proposed a thesis similar to that long advanced by W. E. B. Du Bois, that black people, both in Africa and in the Americas, were among the first to experience historical modernity. In the modes of social organization forced upon them, and in the modes of resistant self-organization that they built for themselves in the shadow of white hegemony, black people confronted the disruptions and alienations of modernity and industrialization at an early stage in the development of international capital. Just two years after James's birth, Du Bois noted of the black workers in the American South that they had come to form "one of the chief figures in a great world-industry" (*Souls* 163). In *Black Reconstruction,* published just three years before James's *Black Jacobins,* Du Bois described the black workers as the "founding stone of a new economic system in the nineteenth century and for the modern world" (15). The centrality of Africans to New World culture as well as industry was remarked by Du Bois often and forms the opening note of his book *John Brown:* "The mystic spell of Africa is and ever was over all America. It has guided her hardest work, inspired her finest literature, and sung her sweetest songs" (15). James's appendix to *Black Jacobins,* published with the second edition of his history, argues that "the Negroes . . . from the very start lived a life that was in its essence a modern life. That is their history—as far as I have been able to discover, a unique history" (BJ 392).

When James undertook his studies of Marxism he discovered, as did Du Bois, consistent confirmation of his earliest insights. He was later to write in his regular column for *Labor Action,* titled *One Tenth of the Nation,* that "it is remarkable but not strange that the great leaders of Marxist thought, Marx, Engels, Lenin and Trotsky, all took the keenest interest in the Negro Question in the United States" (NQ 130). Marx's interest in the subject of slavery is already evident in his writings of the 1840s, and continues through all three volumes of *Capital*. Already in 1850, Marx and Engels were devoting pages of the *Neue Rheinische Zeitung Revue*, a paper that circulated in America as well as in Europe, to considerations of the continuing importance of American slavery to the European economy. Spotting an article in the *Economist* that detailed the importance to the prosperity of Manchester of the treatment of the slaves of the United States, Marx and Engels build to an analogy very much like those James was to construct a hundred years later: "as soon as the free labor of other countries can deliver sufficient supplies of cotton to industry more cheaply than the slave labor of the United States, then American slavery will be broken together with the American cotton monopoly and the slaves will be emancipated, because they will have become useless as slaves. Wage labour will be abolished in Europe in just the same way, as soon as it becomes not only unnecessary for production but in fact a hindrance to it" (*Revolutions* 297). In the first volume of *Capital*, Marx turns briefly to a consideration of the economic workings of slavery, a subject to which he would return frequently. *Capital*'s second volume recounts the fact of slavery's origins in theft, presenting it matter-of-factly as "the actual appropriation of the labour-power of others by direct physical compulsion" (483). The slave, at least in modern American slavery, becomes both laborer and commodity, becomes "himself an element of the annual reproduction" (483). In *Capital*'s third volume, Marx turns his attention to the torturous twists and turns of capitalist ideology. Surveying his sources in American publications, Marx finds examples of the modes of justification advanced for slavery by its defenders, modes that present the slaveowner as reaping his just reward as the owner of capital (385). But Marx unmasks once more the fraudulent nature of such claims and again shows how what is true with regard to slavery is ultimately true of other forms of property:

> the slave-holder considers a Negro, whom he has purchased, as his property . . . because he has acquired him like any other commodity, through sale and purchase. But the title itself is simply transferred, and not created by the sale. . . . What created it in the first place were the production relations. As soon as these have reached a point where they must shed their skin, the material source of the title, justified economically and historically and arising from the process which creates social life, falls by the wayside, along with all transactions based upon it. From the standpoint of a higher economic form of society, private ownership of the globe by single individuals will appear quite as absurd as private ownership of one man by another. (776)

Marx also, in his 1861 articles on the American Civil War, observed the grip that the slaveholding states had held on the national political structure from the time of the Constitution's ratification onward, creating a situation in which "the Union had in fact become the slave of the 300,000 slave-holders who [ruled] the South" (*Surveys* 339).

James located in such scattered notes reinforcement of the theses he was developing all through the 1930s regarding the integral role of slavery in the formation of capital, the importance of economic developments to the eventual abolition of slavery in the Americas, and the importance of black struggles for liberation to the worldwide movement toward liberation from capitalist hegemony. James saw, in his studies of history and in his studies of Marxist and Leninist theory, that the "Negro Question," both in the diaspora and in Africa itself, was central to the revolution against capitalism and imperialism, and this forms the basis for his utter rejection of the positions commonly held by American communists on the "Negro Question." James had little patience with those who would subsume black struggles beneath the supposedly encompassing preparations for proletarian revolution. In James's view, the independent black struggle "is able to exercise a powerful influence upon the revolutionary proletariat, . . . it has got a great contribution to make to the development of the proletariat in the United States, and . . . it is in itself a constituent part of the struggle for socialism" (JR 183).

The prospects for anticolonial revolution certainly did not look promising as James began his lifelong work as a leading theorist and proponent of the struggle. With the exception of Ethiopia, which was shortly to come under attack by Italy, all of Africa and James's English-speaking Caribbean were under colonial administration, and there were few visible signs that the imperial powers had any inclination to leave soon. But leave they would, James felt assured. Aside from his reported attempt to enlist in the army defending Ethiopia, James's efforts were as a writer and a public speaker, but in these realms his powers were formidable. To his fellow activists in the International African Service Bureau, James was able to offer theoretically informed critiques of strategy. To the broader public he offered his vision of the future in the present. Who among that general public might listen to the plea for an end to colonialism was not immediately clear. Du Bois, writing in 1920, had quoted "a great Englishman" to the effect that "there does not exist any real international conscience to which you can appeal," and Du Bois added that there were "no certain signs of abatement" (*Darkwater* 59). Even so, James saw in the 1930s what Du Bois had already recognized, what Cedric Robinson was later to describe as the unusual historical opportunity confronted by peoples who seemed everywhere to be oppressed and despised. "Physically and ideologically," Robinson has written, "and for rather unique historical reasons, African peoples bridge the decline of one world order and the eruption (we may surmise) of another. It is a frightful and uncertain space of being" (450). For James there were few remaining uncertainties. The real question was when and where the greatest opportunities would arise.

The organization of the International African Service Bureau typified much of James's subsequent work. In collaboration with such activists as Jomo Kenyatta, Amy Ashwood Garvey, George Padmore, and Ras Makonnen, James formed a Pan-African nucleus whose influence far exceeded its immediate audience, and whose influence is still felt today. James, as the chief literary talent of this most talented gathering, edited their publication, the *International Journal of African Opinion.* Their motto, "Educate, propagate and agitate" (which James was later to repeat as the title of an important essay), is an apt description of James's entire career. According to John Gaffar LaGuerre, the bureau's organizing principles were "very much the distillation of a long experience by the colonial intelligentsia within metropolitan parties" (94). What this meant, as LaGuerre interprets it, was that James and his colleagues recognized both "the importance of the racial factor in the pursuit of a common strategy by the working class" and "the disadvantages of insertion into the party politics of the metropolis" (95). Already James had realized that the sectarian disputes of the Left, while rooted in the most serious of issues, were a trap for those actively fighting to bring to a conclusion Europe's colonial adventure in Africa and the Caribbean. The eclectic bureau's immediate constituency was small, as Paul Buhle points out in his biography of James, but the bureau's strategists had at this very preliminary stage of their thought established the links between anticolonialism and the labor struggle (Buhle, *Artist* 56). The goals of the bureau are set out in an advertisement they placed in the same issue of the magazine *Fact* that was given over to the publication of James's *History of Negro Revolt.* That September 1938 notice identifies the bureau as "primarily an African organization, run solely by Africans. It serves as a clearing house of information on matters affecting Africans and people of African descent" (95).

In his 1936 article "Abyssinia and the Imperialists," which appeared in the journal of the League of Colored Peoples, James's strategy looks back to Marx and the nineteenth-century abolitionists, and forward to the mass movements of the mid-twentieth century. James again joins the anticolonial movement to the labor struggle, pointing out powerfully that "British imperialism does not govern only the colonies in its own interests. It governs the British people in its own interests also" (JR 66). In his conclusion he argues that what was true of Haiti will be true of Africa as well: "The only thing to save Abyssinia is the efforts of the Abyssinians themselves and action by the great masses of Negroes and sympathetic whites and Indians all over the world" (JR 66).

More than three decades later we see James adopting the identical rhetorical strategies in his studies of the revolution in Ghana. Early in the volume he argues that it is not truly the colonial peoples who are ultimately deceived by the myth-making apparatus of British imperialism. "The real victim of it is the great mass of the British people" (NG 34). Later, after reviewing the contributions of *Black Jacobins* to the politics of African revolution, James reports with considerable satisfaction that "Nkrumah's party was not built one by one. It was a crusade, a revivalist campaign and the villagers joined in the thousands" (NG 84). Trinidad, where blacks constituted the majority under a colonial government, and Ghana, where centuries-old social institutions afforded possibilities for black organization almost unmatched in the Americas, clearly presented a different set of problems from those faced by African peoples in the United States. Nonetheless, James recognized the common need for mass actions, independently responsive both to immediate local issues and to internationalist proletarian movements.

Both Walter Rodney and Anuradha Dingwaney Needham have noted that "James often focuses on little-known or virtually unacknowledged resistances and social movements" (Needham 297), an approach that seems unexceptional in the age of new historicism, cultural studies, and history from the bottom. Still, such strategies were considerably less well established at the time that James first migrated to the United States. What James sought in his readings and in his probing conversations were those signs—such as the New York movement from bus boycott to mass organizing for the integration of the City College faculty, such as the improvisation of a network of liberation schools in Ghana—that indicated the self-chosen direction of independent social movements for black freedom, movements that would one day coalesce with mass movements among the proletariat as a whole to shake the foundations of capitalist society. In his 1948 "Revolutionary Answer to the Negro Problem in the United States," a document prepared for the Socialist Workers Conference, James, who opposed arguments for American exceptionalism among radical theorists, advanced his own thesis regarding the exceptional revolutionary consciousness of black people. "The hatred of bourgeois society," James held, "and the readiness to destroy it when the opportunity should present itself, rests among them to a degree greater than in any other section of the population in the United States" (JR 189). This had been James's message since *Black Jacobins* and *A History of Negro Revolt*. James found again and again in published histories and in his own primary researches episodes of self-organization and mass resistance within the African diaspora. James knew in 1948, as few of his white associates knew, "that the independent Negro movement that we see today and which we see growing before our eyes is nothing strange. It is nothing new. *It is something that has always appeared in the American movement at the first sign of social crisis*" (JR 187). In "Revolution and the Negro," James observes acidly that "the only place where Negroes did not revolt is in the pages of capitalist historians" (RM 77). James agreed with Du Bois that American Reconstruction represented a moment when black and white workers together might have forced the birth of a truly democratic nation, had not the counterrevolution used racial politics so adroitly. The Populist movement appeared as another of these great lost opportunities. Each episode was followed by a period of the most vicious racist violence. James, in 1948, saw the magnificent promise and the enormous peril of the post-World War II social ferment: "The independent Negro movement, which is boiling and moving, must find its way to the proletariat. If the proletariat is not able to support it, the repression of past times when the revolutionary forces failed the Negroes will be infinitely, I repeat infinitely more terrible today" (JR 187). For James, the sort of proletarian support offered by the Communist Party was plainly inadequate. While the party was often usefully supportive of individual defense committees and some black workers, that support often came with a price attached, and the black movements were generally seen as an opportunity for the party, rather than as movements that might make use of the party in reaching for their own vision of their destinies.

In what might appear to some readers as a great understatement, John LaGuerre remarks that when James "entered the ranks of American Trotskyites in 1938, there had already been a voluminous, if confused, discussion as to what the approach to the Negro problem in the U.S.A. should be" (105). Truly, the root of much confusion was attributable directly to the modes of relationships between white activists and African-American people. Almost two decades prior to James's arrival on the American scene, Du Bois had caustically noted that "in Germany and America 'international' Socialists had all but read yellow and black men out of the kingdom of industrial justice" (*Darkwater* 47). Speaking of his own Caribbean in *Party Politics in the West Indies,* James argued that "the white people have to reorient themselves and make a positive and independent contact with the masses of the people. It has been done before, many times. But you have to aim consciously at doing it" (PP 155). In the United States, where blacks made up a large but marginalized minority, few whites had devoted very much imagination to forging new modes of independent contact with their black brethren. When Trotsky and James met in Mexico in 1939 to discuss the position of the Fourth International on African-American struggles, Trotsky's lack of familiarity with black America, despite his widespread contacts with Americans, gives the conversation an occasionally unreal air. Trotsky believes that James, though insufficiently dialectical, is "realistic" on the Negro question, but, again, he charges James with being "a *little* opportunistic on the Negro question" (RV 63).

To the contrary, James meticulously aligns his current position with his earlier work, specifically referencing the International African Service Bureau's support for self-determination of the black populations in Africa and in the West Indies. In America, though, James contends that the historical dynamics have produced a different array of imperatives. James is certain that Garvey's "Back to Africa" slogan was effective because blacks were seeking militant directions, not because they intended to return in large numbers to Africa. James held that it was important to investigate black responses to calls for a separate state in the black belt South, but he believed in the end that this was a radical's red herring. As he explains to Trotsky, "for us to propose that the Negro have this black state for himself is asking too much from the white workers, especially when the Negro himself is not making the same demand. The slogans of abolition of debts, confiscation of large properties, etc., are quite sufficient to lead them both to fight together and on the basis of economic struggle to make a united fight for the abolition of social discrimination" (RV 35). What James has in mind is a popular struggle like that envisioned by Du Bois during the period of Reconstruction, and like that which James had seen as a tantalizing possibility in the Populist era. Nevertheless, and this is characteristic of James, he holds that should the black masses of their own volition express themselves as desiring a separate state, then the parties should mobilize in support of that goal.

James believed that what the black masses really desired was self-determination within their own political movements and within their own lives. James told Trotsky that 79 percent of the black members of the New York State Communist Party had left the organization. James had spoken personally with many of these people and had found that they had no wish to move into the Fourth International. Rather, they were interested in the formation of an independent Negro organization (RV 40–41). James says of his meetings with American blacks upon his arrival in the country that they "hated the Communist Party, agreed entirely with the programme put forward by the International African Service Bureau, and were extremely interested in the journal *International African Opinion*" (RV 40). This observation leads directly to James's recommended plan of action. The very first thing he advises is publication of a pamphlet that, in outline, closely resembles his own *History of Negro Revolt*. Alongside that pamphlet for general distribution, James calls for the preparation of a theoretical study of the permanent revolution and of its meaning for African peoples worldwide. Further, James proposes a series of weekly pamphlets and papers *of* the Negro organization itself, followed by the enlarging of *International African Opinion*. James anticipates a larger black organization growing from the bureau's international nucleus. His practical program centers on unrelenting demands for racial justice. He proposes a national campaign bringing together a united front to end trade union discrimination. He calls for the creation of a nationwide organization around the issue of housing for African Americans, "attempting to draw the women in for militant action" (RV 44). In addition, James's program includes organized campaigns against discrimination in restaurants, against black unemployment, and against the oppression of southern sharecroppers. He wants to organize domestic servants nationally, and he proposes that the Negro organizations should be at the fore of all actions against fascism. James offers a series of quite practical steps for the Trotskyite groups to take toward realizing these most ambitious goals, including arranging an American tour for a South African militant speaker (RV 47).

Trotsky appears to accept much of James's program (and the transcripts of these discussions are included to this day in the Pathfinder Press volume *Leon Trotsky on Black Nationalism and Self-Determination*). As the conversations approach their end, Trotsky expresses his great faith in James's value as an organizer, advising that James perform underground political work "in order to avoid attracting too much attention from the authorities" (RV 47). At the end of six months, Trotsky believes, enough of a base will have been established that both an independent black organization and an interracial nucleus of revolutionary activists could continue the work even if James were forced to leave the United States. By the time James and his colleagues in the Johnson-Forest tendency broke with the Trotskyite parties, they were no longer convinced that these parties were capable of following through on the program outlined in the late 1930s in Coyoacan, and they were certain that the parties were not going to make serious strides toward a mass movement of American blacks. Still, James's strategies for black revolution, to the extent that they did alter in subsequent years, continued along the path set out in those early years.

In his 1945 "Resolution of the Minority" on the Negro Question, published in the *New International,* James has become, if anything, more insistent that "*it is utterly false to draw the conclusion that the independent struggle of the Negro masses for their democratic rights is to be looked upon merely as a preliminary stage to a recognition by the Negroes that the real struggle is the struggle for socialism*" (NQ 74), and James is equally adamant that the alliance with organized labor is "for the specific purpose, first of all, of gaining their own democratic demands" (NQ 80). James's insistence upon the autonomous development of black liberation struggles presaged the rise of the Black Power movement decades later, but James also prefigured the antiessentialist analyses of many activists and critics following the Black Power era. In that same minority resolution of 1945, James argues that African Americans are not a nation but rather a national minority. Sounding much like the critical race theorists of a later era, some of whom have been profoundly influenced by James's more readily available texts, James concludes that "the Negro question is a part of the national and not of the 'national' question. This national minority is most easily distinguishable from the rest of the community by its racial characteristics. Thus the Negro question is a question of race and not of 'race' " (NQ 71).

That statement exactly parallels the often cited remarks in *Black Jacobins* warning of the perils attendant upon either overestimating or underestimating the role of race in the battle against capital. Similarly, James's lifelong work as a historian and revolutionary drew him again and again to examples of the same social forces he had discerned in the revolution of San Domingo. In the same way that he had seen the reorganization of African communities into masses of laborers under New World slavery as producing the conditions for modern revolution, James saw replicated in the twentieth century social formations preparing the masses for revolution far more effectively than most party organizing. James's "Resolution of the Minority" includes a remark that might have surprised more moderate proponents of civil rights and racial integration. "To the degree that the Negroes are more integrated into industry and unions," James predicts, "their consciousness of racial oppression and their resentment against it become greater, not less" (NQ 68). In much the same way, James saw that the inclusion of black troops in the United States Army, a goal for which activists from Frederick Douglass to W. E. B. Du Bois had fought, tended to accelerate rather than ameliorate the rising demands for full desegregation of the armed forces and equality for all troops. In fact, the very training given to the black soldiers provided them with the skills to carry forward their demands. The August 11, 1947, installment of James's regular column in the *Militant,* "The Elemental Urge to Socialism," finds James locating among the African-American troops the phenomenon he had earlier detected among the plantation slaves of the previous century: "The Army had given the Negroes organization; and the sense of solidarity and arms in their hands drove them to prodigies of revolutionary action. They fought an unceasing civil war with the Army authorities and with Jim Crow-minded white soldiers" (2).

These analyses were, of course, the most natural extension of Marx's insights regarding the organization of the proletariat by the bourgeoisie under capitalism, but James learned to search out such patterns even in societies, such as nineteenth-century San Domingo, that did not appear to follow the industrial models sketched by Marx. Writing in *Nkrumah and the Ghana Revolution,* James concedes that he had at least implied in *Black Jacobins* that the success of the African revolutions would be contingent upon socialist revolution in capitalist Europe. With the contradictory examples of Ghana and Kenya before him, he is no longer so sure of that contingency, but he is certain that the anticolonial revolution will take specifically localized forms: "Whatever the future of tropical Africa will be, one thing is certain, that it will not be what the colonial powers are trying to make of it. It will be violent and strange, with the most abrupt and unpredictable changes in economic relations, race relations, territorial boundaries and everything else" (69). James's examination of the revolution in Ghana is itself a partial record of those unpredictable crises, including James's repudiation of later decisions taken by his longtime protégé Kwame

Nkrumah. But most evident of all is the acuity of James's observations of the modes of social organization that had prepared the way for what looked to Europeans like the sudden accession to power of Nkrumah's United Gold Coast Convention. James perceives what the British imperial mythology prevented the citizens of the metropolitan nation from seeing, that the revolution would be made by the workers, the women, and the youth, and James is alert to the revolutionary potential of structures whose political significance was not immediately apparent to the colonial administrators. In a virtually premodern region like the Gold Coast, where technologies of communication and transportation were nowhere near the stage of development they had reached in Europe and the United States, James saw the incredible social importance of so simple a phenomenon as the lorry. For James, the rapidly expanding network of lorry traffic is a crucial element in the modernizing of the Gold Coast society. Indeed, James claims that "these did more to prepare Ghana for independence than all the graduates produced in Achimota during the same period. They reunited the common people" (NG 57). Likewise, James discerns in the indigenous marketplaces of West Africa a modernizing and politicizing force more significant for the anticolonial struggle than European observers such as the *Manchester Guardian* could realize. Surely these are not the market forces spoken of in such reverential tones today by those celebrating the final triumph of the "free market," but, as James so rightly indicates, the market has for centuries been the center of African social life: "In reality here was, ready formed, a social organization of immense power, radiating from the centre into every corner and room of the town. Instead of being confined to cooking and washing for their husbands, the market-women met every day . . . these women, although to a large extent illiterate, were a dynamic element in the population, active, well-informed, acute, and always at the very centre of events" (NG 56). According to James, these were the social forces that made the revolution, the conditions that made it possible for great men such as Nkrumah to make such history as they did make. The oppressors' failure to understand these forces of mass organization led them to believe that imprisoning an Nkrumah, or later a Mandela, would be a way of imprisoning the revolution.

In James's studies of revolution in the African diaspora we can see the bringing together of the major themes of his intellectual work. James utterly rejects the biological essentialism of "race" while at the same time recognizing the historical consequences of race. As he explains in a 1970 interview with the American journal *Black Scholar:* "I should like to say that I don't believe in race as a basis for intellectual dissension. But I believe that it is black men, black men who live in the black community, who are connected with it and have the black experience and are sensitive to it, who are best able to do the kind of studies the black race needs. They are not the only ones able to make such studies, but they are best able to do an analysis, not only of black people, but of white people who are concerned with the black experience" (39). While few today would speak comfortably of *the* black experience, or would speak only of black men, James's own casual formulation here implies a multiplicity and openness of the sort routinely practiced by such contemporary critics as Paul Gilroy, bell hooks, and Cornel West.

James would continue to reject all forms of vanguardism, both social and political, even as he continued to champion such cultural and political avant-gardists as Wilson Harris and Angela Davis. Though obviously himself the product of a "middle-class" colonial education, James was never under any illusions about the talented tenth. In 1971, speaking with Patrick Griffith in a *Black World* interview, James said of the American Civil Rights movement that "the middle-class, that few, small percentage of Blacks who were educated in universities and had jobs with the Government, they were not ready to take to the streets and to lead a mass movement" (7). Only when the gathering forces of the people, drawn together by a cadre of vulnerable middle-class teachers and labor activists, turned to Reverend Martin Luther King to serve as the personal focal point of the mass activities, did the larger number of intellectuals and middle-class blacks go into the streets. James could, as he did in this same interview, express his interest in and support for the dedicated work of a Huey P. Newton and an Angela Davis even as he insisted that "the concept of a vanguard party does not suit the world in which we live" (12). James persisted in his resistance to those who subordinated the black liberation movements to proletarian organization, those who "make the movements subject to the Marxist movement . . . That is not Marxism, not at all" (*Black World* 8). To the contrary, as James argued in his 1969 addendum to *A History of Negro Revolt,* the independent black struggle offered an opportunity to renew Marxist practice throughout the world. "It can," he concluded, "fertilize and reawaken the mortuary that is socialist theory and practice in the advanced countries" (NR 89–90). Further, in a last sentence that simultaneously disposes of "a new category labelled African socialism" (NR 86) and the "Marxist Humanism" of his former colleague Raya Dunayevskaya, James ends his renewed history by showing once more how much the West has to learn from Africans: "'Marxism is a Humanism' is the exact reverse of the truth. The African builders of a humanist society show that today all humanism finds itself in close harmony with the original conceptions and aims of Marxism" (NR 90).

While it is true that James often seems overoptimistic in his predictions and evaluations, it is also true, as is readily seen in such texts as *Black Jacobins, Party Politics in the West Indies,* and *Nkrumah and the Ghana Revolution,* that no critic was more severe in his appraisals of those who betrayed the desire for freedom spoken by the masses. Reviewing James's *The Future in the Present* for *New Society,* Stephen Cumberbatch judged that "virtually all the ideas contained in the subsequent literature" on West Indian independence had been anticipated in James's first book, that the same could be said regarding James's analyses of the rise of Stalinism, and of James's "account of the relationship between the socialist movement and black struggles in the United States" (243). More than for his optimism, James has been taken to task for the reliance his political philosophy appears to place upon concepts of spontaneity. Still, as P. I. Gomes has argued in his essay on *The Marxian Populism of C. L. R. James,* James's insistence upon spontaneity and upon the revolutionary initiative of the masses is a recognition of "an inevitable logical movement on the part of any oppressed individual or group" (25). For James, mass initiative and revolutionary spontaneism are dialectical antitheses to the oppressive bureaucratism of traditional revolutionary organizations. In Gomes's estimation, James is simply following the imperative that "one has to consistently derive dialectical relations among social forces rather than impose fixed categories on the processes of social reality" (26).

James's faith in the spontaneous revolutionary initiative of the masses was confirmed for him in his researches and experiences as often as his lack of faith in self-declared vanguards was confirmed by history. By the time of his death in 1989, James had lived to see his old political nemesis, the Stalinist party, collapsing everywhere under the advancing pressures of the masses, and he had lived to witness the popular revolutions of black people end direct forms of colonial dominance from North Africa to the southernmost bastion of racist apartheid. Neither in his own West Indies nor anywhere else had James seen realized his vision of a society in which every cook could govern. At the end of his essay on "Production for the Sake of Production" in 1943—an article that was preceded upon publication by a disclaimer from the secretariat of the Workers Party denouncing James's essay as abstruse and unintelligible—James responded to the criticisms that held him to be a fantasist. Writing under his pseudonym as J. R. Johnson, James asked rhetorically: "Johnson is cockeyed? Maybe. We shall see. But I offer myself as the sacrificial goat" (12). James, like Du Bois, had predicted that the color line would be the problem of the twentieth century, and also like Du Bois, James dared to dream that black people everywhere might throw off the chains of imperialism and end racist hegemony. Even more than Du Bois, James saw in the revolutionary self-activity of the masses the solution to the problem of his century. Not leaders (though not without them) but the masses of the people would determine the direction of their freedom struggles. Toward the end of his life Du Bois went into the party that James had rejected at the outset of his own career, but James continued to his last years to "take Dr. W. E. B. Du Bois as the basis of the present approach, both to Pan-Africanism and to the Black question inside the United States" (*Black World* 5). At the time of his death, twenty-six years following the death of Du Bois, James's dream of a party that would *be* the entire people, a dream that had to many seemed a matter of "soviets in the sky," was making headway against what had long seemed an immutable Stalinist monolith. Within a few years, the long-banned mass party of South Africa, the African National Congress, had put an end to the apartheid state and established the first nonracial democratic state in South Africa. In Eastern Europe, the forces that brought themselves together in the most massive resistance to Stalinist dictatorship since the Soviet Revolution itself, Solidarity, had gone on to drive ruling parties from power throughout the former Soviet empire. Though James would not have allowed himself any illusions about the terrible consequences of our history that find ever new ways to plague us in the post-Soviet and postapartheid era, he would have insisted that we look again to the revolutionary initiative of the masses, as any good dialectician should, to uncover the motions that would rise in response to our "New World Order." Whether in Europe, Africa, Asia, or the Americas, James assured an audience in 1981, "when the day comes when people feel that those national mobilisations are not doing what they want them to do, there will not be any longer a national mobilisation but there will be a mobilisation of the nation" (RV 272).

In retrospect, it is not at all difficult to see in James's texts precursors of the studies of micromovements, national and ethnic struggles, postcolonial critiques, and poststructuralist political philosophies that have become the common ground for so much debate near the end of the twentieth century, even among those, too many still, who have never read James. So varied and so fecund are James's works of political philosophy that, as Martin Glaberman noted shortly after James's death, "Everyone produces his/her own James. People have, over the years, taken from him what they found useful and imputed to him what they felt necessary" ("Recollection" 80). What all these varied Jameses have in common, after all, is the demand that Marxism be an open book, a text open to the masses rather than a dogma guiding those who would guide the masses. James always had open books strewn all around him. It was typical of James, whether speaking from a podium to huge crowds or speaking from his desk to the students in his classes, even when he worked with no notes whatsoever, that he would wave an open book before his audience, inviting them to a collaborative critique of the texts. There was no book that couldn't be reopened, appended, revised, and there was no book that could not be read with any person who was interested. Theory was, for James, the most democratic of practices. Thus James's *Notes on Dialectics*, composed *en famille*, is an annotated anthology of Hegelian meditation, circulated in carbon copies for comment, mimeographed for ready distribution, only years later reified into a bound book. James's political philosophy is, like those open books he brandished before us, an open invitation for us to take up on our own initiative. At the end of "Production for the Sake of Production," that essay in which James offers his "cockeyed" pseudonymous self as sacrificial goat in the theory wars of Marxism, James declares the haunted house of Marxist philosophy open for tours: "We live our lives in the upper reaches and derivative super structure of Marxism. We are not academicians and must perforce spend most of our time there. But the foundations and the lower floors are huge unexplored buildings which we enter if at all in solitude and leave in silence. They have been shrines too long. We need to throw them open, to ourselves and to our public" (11–12).

4

The Struggle for Happiness

Hegel, Ricardo, Shelley, Beethoven, Savigny, all between 1816–1820, stated the fundamental problems of bourgeois society.

C. L. R. James, *The Raya Dunayevskaya Collection*

Music, great music, will become a possession of the people. It is revolutionary. Why? Because the more the technical discoveries of capitalism bring culture to the masses, the more they resent the degradation and humiliation of their role in production—*the grinding slavery of the machine.*

C. L. R. James, *Special Delivery: The Letters of C. L. R. James to Constance Webb 1939–1948*

The end towards which mankind is inexorably developing by the constant overcoming of internal antagonisms is not *the enjoyment, ownership, or use of goods, but self-realization, creativity based upon the incorporation into the individual personality of the whole previous development of humanity. Freedom is creative universality,* not *utility.*

C. L. R. James, *Modern Politics*

I. POPULAR ARTS AND MODERN SOCIETY

C. L. R. James was a historian who was given to exploring the political significance of the Cuban Revolution by means of an exegesis of the surrealist poetry of Aimé Césaire. While discoursing upon the development of the literary imagination in the United States, he was likely to focus on the political polemics of a small band of radical Abolitionists. When advancing his arguments for the independence of the West Indies from colonial rule he turned to talk of calypso singers and novelists. Writing a column on the sport of cricket, James naturally found himself writing about James Baldwin,

William Wordsworth, and Willie Mays. In a series of lectures on the topic of *Modern Politics* he discussed ancient Greek tragedy, the poetry of Eliot and Pound, the films of Griffith and Chaplin, and the paintings of Picasso. Evidently experience had never taught James that being interdisciplinary is so very hard to do. Today, the few scholars who have directed their attention to James's body of work link his name to those of more widely studied Marxist critics of culture such as Lukács, Gramsci, Adorno, and Benjamin. Even as some students of James attempt to remind the burgeoning cultural studies industry in the American Academy of James's importance to the thinking of those British critics whose model has been so eagerly adapted to cultural studies in the United States, other critics step forward to caution that James's studies of culture may, perhaps should, have a decentering effect upon the enterprise of that emergent field of interpretation. Following the recent republication of much of James's writing, James's value to postcolonial studies throughout the world is made manifest to generations of students who had never before heard of him, but postcolonial studies will itself of necessity be transformed by the introduction of an author who begins a study of colonial resistance with an examination of Saint John, whose status as a colonial activist is little discussed among scholars of the postcolonial. James tells an audience in Trinidad in 1960: "If you want to read about anti-imperialism and anti-colonialism, take the Bible and read the last book, that is the *Revelations of St. John*" (MP 6). James suggests to his attentive audience that if someone in "any ordinary colony" were to write today as Saint John had in his day, that person would be arrested (MP 7). One hesitates to predict how existing modes of postcolonial critique might have to reinvent themselves to accommodate James's epistle on biblical hermeneutics. What is certain is that reading James must unsettle the territory of cultural analyses, for on the one hand, as Robert Hill so aptly points out, "James's view on the radical impulse underlying American popular culture stands in . . . marked contrast to the cultural conservatism of the social critiques of mass culture emanating from the post-Second World War generation of social critics as well as assorted 'New York intellectuals,'" and on the other hand, as Hill also argues, James's "theory of aesthetics becomes a dual theory of cultural autonomy, providing a synthesis of the polar positions advanced by both Benjamin and Adorno" (in AC 360).

Robert Hill had many years earlier joined with C. L. R. James, Andrew Salkey, John La Rose, and other West Indian intellectuals in a delegation to an international congress held in Havana. In the course of that trip Hill was to notice what Andrew Salkey and numerous other friends observed over the years, "C. L. R. James clutching a well-thumbed coffee-table *Michelangelo* which he very rarely leaves behind on long journeys" (Salkey 13). James was as likely to display that well-worn volume to students in his political history courses as he was to insist that his students of dramatic literature read political history. James held that "it is an unspeakable impertinence to arrogate the term 'fine art' to one small section . . . and declare it to be culture. Luckily, the people refuse to be bothered" (BB 209). It was an unspeakable impertinence of which he often spoke. Just as often, he worked to integrate those sections of human existence he believed had been alienated from one another by the modes of social organization that dominated the world in his lifetime. For James there was a continuity of aesthetic perception between the quotidian experiences of the people and the formal presentations of "high" art. Thus, James commences his consideration of Picasso's *Guernica* with an autobiographical appreciation of horse transport:

> A few necessary words about the observer. I am a West Indian who grew up in the West Indies during the important years of my life. During those years there were not many motor cars in the West Indian islands. Most transport was either by rail or, more often, by horse. Chiefly horses. I used to ride, and when I came to England in 1932 I continued to ride. I went to Ireland and regularly rode in Phoenix Park. The horse meant a great deal to me. There were lots of fields and open spaces to be crossed in a Caribbean island in those days, and we were careful always to look for and avoid the fearsome bull. (FP 226)

There is much to remark in this lecture, prepared for a television presentation in 1970. We can see the characteristic, self-reflexive positioning of the critical subject that James had long recognized as both politically necessary and rhetorically effective, a technique now so common among critics delivering lectures as to have become a cliché. It might be well, also, to note the manner in which James's narrative links the colonial experience of two island peoples, the West Indians and the Irish, to his study of the aesthetics of a modernist masterpiece. Our attention inevitably fixes, however, on the way that James's account of his past experience of horses and bulls brings him at last to his contemplation of the formal and symbolic modes of Picasso's painting. James believes that Picasso's work does in fact speak to universal human concerns, but that each viewer of the painting is delivered before it by a specific route, giving the aesthetic experience of that universal symbolism a describable localized inflection.

James held that those same evolving technological and economic instrumentalities that have alienated the aesthetic from the working life for so many in the modern world also pointed the way to reintegration. In the same way that Marx had viewed the modes of industrial production that oppressed workers as simultaneously organizing them for revolution, James viewed the mechanistic constructions that disrupted and commodified aesthetic practices as at the same time repositioning the masses for a new universal. In a talk that he delivered in Paris in 1954, James declared that "our world of the twentieth century is *panoramic*" (JR 247). The social and political circumstances of this declaration proliferate with typically Jamesian ironies. He spoke these words at the headquarters of the journal *Preuves* in the course of a conference on mass culture sponsored by the Congress for Cultural Freedom. Even as he made his remarks he knew that his political positions would be discomfiting to some among the conference sponsors. The Congress for Cultural Freedom included Bertrand Russell, Ignazio Silone, and other "liberal-minded" gentlemen, as James later characterized them, gentlemen who, whatever their other virtues, probably had more in common with the cultural politics of the New York Intellectuals than with James. In his 1960 lectures in Trinidad, which were themselves to be suppressed, James recalls the occasion of his 1954 participation in the Paris conference: "I once wrote an article for one of their papers and I told the Editor, 'You will never publish that article in your paper.' It was a French magazine. He said, 'I will publish. You get it translated.' I got it translated. He paid me the money to get it translated. He paid me twenty pounds for the article, and to this day it has not been published. I said, 'They will never let you publish that.' He said, 'I am the Editor.' I said, 'We will see' " (MP 144).

What James may not have known as he spoke in Paris was just how closely his comments paralleled the thinking of Walter Benjamin as expressed in "Paris, Capital of the Nineteenth Century," a text made more widely available the following year when it appeared in Benjamin's *Schriften*, edited by Theodor and Gretel Adorno. In that text Benjamin, looking at the panoramas of Paris in relationship to the arcades and the changing architecture of the city, argues that the panoramas "declare a revolution in the relation of art to technology" and at the same time represent "an expression of a new feeling about life" (*Reflections* 150). The panoramas mark the point at which painting begins "to outgrow art" (149). Benjamin sees them as an effort to simulate the real in its temporal changefulness, and thus as prefiguring cinema. In this the panoramas are both conservative and revolutionary. They represent "attempts to introduce the countryside into the city" (150), demonstrating an urbane superiority over the rustic details of the real countryside even as they play to the powerful nostalgia for the preindustrial. They re-represent the city's dream of a lost landscape at the same time that they are an instance of modernity's superior ability to manipulate an environment. But the technological skill required to produce such "a perfect imitation of nature" (149) also develops in the city dweller a new perspective, a new point of view. Benjamin notes the rise of a panoramic literature alongside the panoramas themselves, a literature whose anecdotal form and broad informational base correspond to the plastic foreground and painted background of the panorama (149). As a result, this literature is not only formally panoramic but is also "panoramic in a social sense" (150).

James, who came of age contemplating the heroic vistas spread before him as he looked out from his island home, holds that these modern restructurings of the social have imbued the world's population with just such a panoramic social sense: "Contemporary society gives man a sense, on a scale hitherto unknown, of connections, of cause and effect, of the conditions from which an event arises, of other events occurring simultaneously. His world is one of constantly increasing multiplicity of relations between himself, immense mechanical constructions and social organizations of world-wide scope. It is representation of this that demanded the techniques of *flashback, cross-cutting* and a camera of extreme mobility" (JR 247). James perceives in the popular arts of the twentieth century a hostility toward the Romanticist values of the nineteenth. Still, contrasting American modernity to European, James finds an "undefeated buoyancy" (JR 249) that can only be understood as a transmuted Romantic openness and optimism, traits that derived from the fact that the American mass audience "lived in an atmosphere of social freedom and absence of traditional restraints characteristic of the growth of the United States" (JR 248).

It was the newer modes of modern life that "demanded a modern technique, not vice versa" (JR 247), as James has it, finding always a dynamic, symbiotic relationship of base and superstructure rather than a static and monolithic model. The creation of new technologies enabled filmmakers to develop new techniques, but those new technologies grew out of new ways of looking out at the world and had to satisfy the aesthetic and social demands of a popular audience. The industrial corporation was a radical new mode of economic organization, as significant a development as the creation of a large urban proletariat. The cinema was an art form created by modern corporations for mass audiences. "In other words," said James in 1954, "the artists, the medium and the audience, were an organic part of the social structure of their day" (JR 249). While there is much to argue with today in James's organicist views of the social, the dynamic relationship between the mass audience and popular arts as James describes it has much to teach us even now.

In the later 1940s when James drafted his prospectus for a study of *American Civilization,* there were not that many intellectuals who spoke so freely of the social and political significance of soap operas, comic strips, and movies. James was already impatient with traditional boundaries between high and low arts. Though his frequent references to the "vulgarity" of most cinema leave no doubt that his largely Victorian sensibility to aesthetic value remained intact, James never believed that a highly developed aesthetic sense was the peculiar property of the propertied classes. The age of mechanical reproducibility brought about a radical transformation in the accessibility of art. Those same cheap reproductions of the great masterpieces of Western art and mass-produced excerpts from classical symphonies and operas purchased by so many American families and derided so often by public intellectuals were for James an exciting sign of social change. If *Song to Remember* was a vulgar picture, James wrote to Constance Webb in 1944, it was vulgarity accompanied by Chopin. "Imagine people sneering at the Iturbi vulgarizations," he tells his young correspondent, "as if that mattered" (SD 139). What did matter was the way that the masses took the film to their hearts and took possession of the music, enfolding it in their daily lives. The masses could not own *Guernica* (this seems even more true when the people's tax-supported museums hold art in their name), but they could and did own prints of modern art, imbuing them with an aura defining them as art as such. When James spoke of *Guernica* in the course of his lectures on *Modern Politics* at the Trinidad Public Library, he brought a reproduction along to illustrate his points and he arranged to have another copy of the painting sent to the library, one "made in a material which does not reflect the light and is . . . washable" (MP 138). James did not look with such optimism upon the increased availability of the arts in cheap reproduction solely because he felt it would hasten the day of revolution as people measured the distance between their working lives and the life of art; he genuinely believed that great music, art, and literature should be possessed by the people because the people were the ultimate source of the creative powers manifested in the works of the greatest artists. Language, aesthetic form, melody, and harmony are distinctly social phenomena. James's view from beginning to end was that great art, though never merely a reflection of the social, always gives aesthetic form to social movement. Thus in *Guernica*, for example, "In all the chaos and catastrophe of the modern world, Picasso affirms the undying vision of Greek civilization and the power inherent in the mass of mankind" (MP 139), and that undying vision James speaks of from first to last is freedom as creative universality (MP 115).

There remains an additional revolutionary effect of mass reproducibility that excites James tremendously. As he explains to Constance Webb in 1944, "Today an intelligent worker sees the same films, reads the same bestsellers, hears the radio speeches, same newspapers, etc., as the bourgeoisie" (SD 139). However, where other Marxists at the time might have viewed this phenomenon reductively as simply the mechanism by which those who dominate society enforce their cultural hegemony, James found once more the dialectical motions of human history. Capitalism was indeed a tremendous revolution, one that Marx predicted would of necessity create the conditions for its own dissolution. James did not choose to believe that the masses of the people read resistantly at all times, reconstructing bourgeois imagery in the form of revolutionary tropes, nor did he believe that the masses were helplessly interpellated within bourgeois ideology, but he was convinced that the evolution of capitalist culture must inevitably produce contradictions within itself. "Thus we see a great dialectical law," he writes, speaking of films and their fashions, "the capitalist seeking profit or Marlene Dietrich seeking publicity with pants, opens up an avenue through which the masses recognize something and at once appropriate it—with all sorts of distortions but yet a step forward" (SD 140). Again, James's suggestion that there might be an undistorted originary reading of the social text raises problems, but his own reading of the popular audience's appropriations from commodity culture prefigures the identification with putatively resistant fandoms so common in today's cultural studies. James saw the mass audience neither as dupes of capitalism's fantasy apparatus nor as rampant deconstructors. Rather, as an audience member himself, he saw the masses of the people applying their intellects to the search for meaning within the context of mass media arts, and he saw them finding something they could make use of in their understanding of their lives. Their desires were truly mediated and manipulated by those who owned the means of cinematic production, but Hollywood, precisely because it was in the business of producing mass media, did not have an entirely free hand. In 1943 James told Webb: "The movies, even the most absurd Hollywood movies are an expression of life, and being made for people who pay their money, they express what the people *need*—That is what the people miss in their own lives. . . . Like all art, but more than most, the movies are not merely a reflection, but an extension of the actual, but an extension along the lines which people feel are lacking and *possible* in the actual" (SD 73). What interests James is the nature of the exchanges between audience and industry. Capitalism must organize populations in new ways if it is to produce its miracles of multiplication, but it cannot entirely control what the people will do with these new modes of organization. The audience will not buy tickets to any and everything that the culture industry would place before them, but they may only select from among those cultural commodities that are offered them. Such a situation generates the form of ideological dialectic that James sees as key to the future directions of modern society.

If we are to believe James's own testimony, which is often delivered with the most deliberate irony, it was bad health that brought him to this understanding of the revolutionary potential of cinema. He writes to Constance Webb, herself a model and actress in her early years, telling her in 1943: "During the last two years, illness and other difficulties have caused me to spend a certain amount of time at the pictures. I rather despised them—Hollywood I mean. I don't anymore. The rubbish I look at would astonish you. I can sit through almost anything. When it is very bad I see why it is bad. I have, on the other hand, seen Now Voyager 6 times and will see it if necessary 6 times more. . . . And I am learning plenty, I can assure you" (SD 72). Rereading James's early short story "The Star That Would Not Shine" should be convincing evidence that James had learned much from the cinema long before bad health and Bette Davis brought him to a renewed appreciation for the possibilities of popular film. In any event, James took away from his study of and at the movies a belief that this new art form, in addition to organizing audiences in new ways, was "symbolic of a new pattern of art in relation to society" (JR 221), and that it offered "the clearest ideological expression of the sentiments and deepest feelings of the American people and a great window into the future of America and the modern world" (AC 119). I shall have more to say of James's windows later; for now it will suffice to note that in this comment James joins his sense that modern peoples had developed a panoramic view of their world to the panoramic technology of the cinema camera. In a later letter James predicts that future artists, those who "take the people seriously," will "transform these entertainments into works which will satisfy the most exacting" (JR 221). James believed that cinema had approached that level of transformation in its early stages, in the works of such American artists as Chaplin and in the films Eisenstein made before the full effect of the Stalinist freeze became evident. In the cases of both Chaplin and Eisenstein, James portrays these filmmakers as "people who . . . found themselves in circumstances in which they did not write or work for the intellectual public . . . , but found themselves compelled to appeal to the ordinary citizen" (MP 138). Later cinema, of course, was also compelled to appeal to a broad audience of ordinary people, but by then, James is going to argue, there had come another fundamental change in society.

To approach that moment of change, though, it is important to see how James contextualizes film within the universe of the popular arts. In a 1953 letter defending his interest in such phenomena as comic strips, James repeats that his ideas of art and society "are based upon Aristotle and Hegel" (JR 220). But upon that basis James built a new thesis. As he had earlier found a specific early emergence of modernity among the Africans of the colonial slave system, James now posited that the particular problems of culture and social organization in the United States led its population, sooner than most Europeans, to the development of modern mass art forms. Because Americans were, as he saw it, the first to face the problem of "the relation of individualism to democracy as a whole" (AC 50), their popular arts were among the first formed to "the deep social responses . . . in relation to the fate which has overtaken the original concepts of freedom, free individuality, free association, etc." in the late stages of industrial capitalism (AC 199). The technologies of print, radio, and film combined with increasingly broad (but narrowly owned) networks of commercial distribution to bring about these new modes of relationship that Benjamin had theorized. James locates in America's mass art forms that expression of a new feeling about life also theorized by Benjamin. James, though, argued that "a new pattern of art in relation to society" (JR 221) was being worked out earliest and most thoroughly in the United States, and he further argued, in what Robert Hill describes as "a significant theoretical advance," that the popular response in the process of cultural production "was a reflection of the struggle for association and autonomy within the sphere of everyday labor" (Hill in AC 360).

James advised one of his correspondents that his perspective on artistic development in the civilization of the United States was "rooted in comic strips, soap opera, and jazz; the gangster film; the television comedians; and especially the great men of the movies up to 1930" (JR 220). It was his understanding that, following World War II, European culture had reached a dead end, and though he at other times highly praised the works of individual American authors and painters, in the context of his discussions of mass arts he could go so far as to say that "American writers and artists, like the fellows abroad, have nothing to say" (JR 226; like his scattered remarks on Sartre, James's assessments of post-World War II artists are among his least consistent). In his view of much European art as "decadent" (JR 221) James resembles his communist antagonists more than he resembles his own insightful studies of such novelists as Wilson Harris. In his tracing of "the decline in poetry beginning with Baudelaire, through Rimbaud to the bankruptcy of today" (JR 221), James seems almost pre-New Critical (though by the time I met him in the 1970s, he was open to listening with great interest to the works of the new poets I carried with me to his class). In his analyses of popular arts, however, James has moved from the lessons learned in his Victorian education, beyond the boundaries of Arnoldian views of culture and society, to provide both a possible groundwork for contemporary studies of culture and, as Neil Larsen has argued effectively, an implicit critique of the positive investments cultural studies sometimes have made in popular culture's ability to produce transgressive readings. Andrew Ross cautions that it would be an error to celebrate James simply "as a 'celebrant' of popular culture" (78). It would be an easy error to commit, especially in light of such frequently repeated Jamesian predictions as his faith that future historians will regard the great masterpieces of the age, "both in form and in impact upon the generations that they served" (JR 223), to have been not the novels of Joyce and Hemingway but the films of Chaplin and Griffith. Such claims rest rather uneasily upon a whole series of questionable oppositions in James's writing, and may lead more dismissive readers and celebrants alike to give less weight to the fact that James viewed film as a highly complex negotiation of corporate, artistic, and popular interests and desires.

What strikes James most forcefully and most immediately about these art forms is their mass appropriations of individual experience. Recalling in 1953 a soap opera he had listened to religiously, a radio program whose plot closely followed the unfolding events of World War II, James says, "I can imagine that millions listened in as I did, every day, and saw themselves and their family and friends in a form of artistic representation" (JR 221). Even more impressive to James is the phenomenon of a script that moved back and forth from radio to screen, its adaptations and multiplications making it a fascinating form of intermedia serial. *Sorry, Wrong Number,* featuring the voice of Agnes Morehead, was repeated several times on radio broadcast to satisfy the remarkable public response in the wake of its first airing. In 1948 the script was released as a movie starring Barbara Stanwyck, who also appeared in a special broadcast performance in the role. In each of these cases James is struck by the breadth and depth of the public's involvement in the shared experience of familiar plots. In each instance commercial narrative succeeded in gathering an audience of individuals into a community sharing repeatedly in a common experience. The facts of the vehicle, the audience, and the repetitions are as important to James as the actual content of the programs. Serial media such as the comic strip, the soap opera, and episodic film, like the advent of industrial techniques of mass production, reorganize society around new forms of aesthetic experience, and these experiences in turn become the focal point of conversation in the daily lives of the masses. Where the serial novel had once captivated thousands of middle-class readers, the new media aimed at affecting millions, aimed, in fact, at enlisting the entire population in their audience.

The great novelist, the great painter, the great composer, each, according to James, senses underlying currents that portend tremendous shifts in social psychology. The masses, acting both as the medium through which these underlying currents flow and as the originating force of these currents, responds more immediately and more locally than do the artists. James argues often that political responses to immediate outrages, like the New York boycott against racial discrimination in the hiring of bus drivers, leads to broader movements for social justice beyond the sometimes parochial interests of the initiating group. Likewise, the responses of the masses to day-to-day events in their individual lives register the formation of emergent social structures, which may also express themselves in new forms of art. In capitalist society there invariably are those who wish to seize upon these new forms as profit-making ventures. In order to earn a profit at all, the entrepreneur must be at least minimally attuned to the shifting desires of the popular audience; but the commodity form of art must neither threaten basic public acceptance of capitalist modes of organization nor exceed the public's willingness to accept new narratives of American life. "Any success tends to be repeated and squeezed dry, for these people are engaged primarily in making money" (AC 123), yet to make money the commodity must in some way appear to "represent some of the deepest feelings of the masses" (AC 123). Though he does not use the term "hegemony," James does describe the encompassing net of discourse agreements within which the tireless production of familiar novelty must take place. He imagines the social uproar that would ensue should a highly-skilled draughtsman produce a widely circulated comic strip serial that depicted the lives of a black family in the United States, and he concludes that such an artist wouldn't "last two weeks" (JR 226). The broad public "appears to accept the general political ideas, standards, social ethics, etc., of the society which is the natural framework" (AC 123) of these popular art forms, as do the producers of them. But there must, then, be an accounting for the possibility of change in these arts, and James finds that possibility in the relationship between audience and corporate producer. The audience are not merely dupes of the media; James rejects that as a "totally unhistorical" conception (AC 122). Neither do producers of mass art forms "spend their time thinking about how to use [them] in order to maintain capitalist society" (AC 123). The end result of their efforts to develop and expand markets is, still, the maintenance of capitalist society. Narrative forms of mass media such as the soap opera and the movie must be responsive to the altering currents of public mood in the interest of their own reason for existence, the making of money, but James has a thesis, novel in the late 1940s, about the form taken by that media response.

The appearance in 1931 of the *Dick Tracy* comic strip in the *Daily News* is a paradigmatic instance for James. He notes that Chester Gould had attempted unsuccessfully on many occasions to interest publishers in a strip centered on a detective, but it was not until the Depression was well under way that his proposals were accepted, and James underscores the incredible importance of the suggestions made by Gould's editor at the *Daily News* to the immediate popularity of the strip. It is Patterson, the editor, who urges that Dick Tracy should not be a police officer but "an ordinary guy" (AC 120) reacting to a criminal outrage against his own family, a common man who dedicates the remainder of his life to defending all the ordinary people against the criminals. Tracy, though, like the criminals themselves, operates apart from the structures of the law. Further, it was the editor who suggested the new level of realistic violence found in the strip in a phrase that James repeats with fascination: "Show the bullets going right into him" (AC 121).

Tracy was to be a private citizen who got, and disposed of, his man. Thus American newspaper readers found themselves confronted, on October 12, 1931, with the "*first* murder in comic strip history" (AC 121). James does not linger to remark the fact that this date is now known to most Americans as Columbus Day, but he does point out that this is the same year in which Hollywood released *Public Enemy*, starring James Cagney.

Here James locates the great shift that he describes in American cinema history. One might readily disagree with James regarding his estimation of the relative artistic merits of pre-and post-Depression films, but it is crucial that we follow his reasoning as he explains the sea change marked by 1929 and 1931. James holds that early cinema aimed to make money by pleasing the masses, and that this period stands as film's epoch of greatest artistic accomplishment. The great film characters of the period (and we must recall how much emphasis James places upon the creation of new types of character when he is judging literary artists) were individuals who boldly defied reality, and precisely because of the medium in which they appeared they were able to "make the universal appeal *to all classes*" (AC 142). (James believes in universals, but he believes that they are generated out of particular classes and that they may not be eternal, which makes them universals of an odd type.) In the years following the Stock Market Crash, James feels, the modern masses, unable to find in their mass media any serious treatment of their own relationship to their difficulties, "fostered on the one hand an individualistic response to violence, murder, atrocities, crime, sadism; and on the other they . . . pertinaciously fostered and encouraged by their money and interest [the] creation of synthetic characters" (AC 146). Each of these responses within the framework of capitalist ideology deflects democracy's respect for the individual as a thinking member of a society into a mythic creation of the individual distanced from all others. What the gangster and the star have in common is that they exist apart from any ordinary community of aspiration and action, apart from any real possibilities of significant political change generated from among the people themselves.

Benjamin, writing in Europe, had also noted the rising of the star in the cinema. As plots and forms that generated profits were repeated and squeezed dry, now the image of the actor who generated profits was replicated and squeezed dry. Less and less were audiences shown the everyman character who somehow triumphed over adversities, both mechanical and social. More and more audiences found their point of identification in the distant star. Anybody could become a star, they learned from their media, but almost nobody would, they knew in their hearts. Chaplin's "creation was himself" (AC 135), but the new stars were created by others. The people in the audience were the stars that could not shine. Nobody becomes a star without being selected and put forward by the corporate media, but the media are not able to make a star of anyone they choose. The audience "chooses its major stars" (AC 144) from among those offered to them. While one might well discuss the acting skills and creative genius of a Chaplin or a Lloyd, James suggests that the question of the star's acting ability is rather beside the point. Acting is not their true function: "These stars do not exist to interpret plays, to express emotions, ideas, etc. Plays, scripts, etc. are written to give them an opportunity to display the personality. It is realism at its lowest, a complete denial of any serious creative effort on the part of the artist or the audience. It is purely primitive" (AC 144). The star is not merely the product of a cynical industry; he or she is a product of the age, of the social forces operating between industry and the people. The adoration of the individual as star James sees as a perversion of the democratic desires of individuals.

Where more recognized public intellectuals of the period might chide audiences for their philistinism, James charges those critics with a far greater philistinism. James does not accept the idea that the entertainment industry simply gives the people what they want (as measured by ticket sales, ratings, and so forth). Audiences might, given the opportunity, respond favorably to freely created artistic productions addressing the pressing issues (at least, the issues they saw as pressing) of the day. It is not that "the American masses could not understand it inasmuch as they were not 'educated' enough as yet. They would understand it only too well. That is why such things are not written for the film" (AC 158). Philistine intellectuals who blame the public tastes for the sorry state of the cinema are looking to only one side of the equation that produces James's remarkable theses about American popular culture, and the side they choose to focus upon, not surprisingly, tends to strengthen their identification with economic elites in opposition to the masses of the population.

Though James never completely works through these theories, he describes a vortex of contradictory currents out of which emanates America's mass culture. The broader public accepts the doctrines of liberal democracy, the two-party system, the ethics of individual morality, and all the other mores and presuppositions of American capitalism. At the same time, nonetheless, it is perfectly obvious to most of the population that these presuppositions and ethical imperatives are not functioning as they have been led to expect that they should. Individuals work hard and are honest, yet they do not seem to share equally in the rewards that their labors have produced. It is evident to most people most of the time that the ideals of American bourgeois democracy, ideals to which they remain committed, are illusory, and it is equally evident to most that the people are nearly powerless to effect significant political change within the existing party structures of governance. They want to see representations of their lives and problems within their popular arts. James points out that "where millions of individuals make a common response to a social problem, they thereby give proof of a *common collectivized social attitude* to that problem" (AC 136). The producers of mass art cannot afford to ignore completely that collectivized social attitude, and in point of fact their profits are dependent upon appealing to such collectivized attitudes. What they would really like would be to mold that collective response, but they are successful only to a degree: "The industrial magnates, a movie producer so anti-union as DeMille, and great numbers of people in authority would wish nothing better than to employ the finest available talent in order to impose *their* view of the great political and social questions of the day upon the mass. *They dare not do it*" (AC 123).

James has, in effect, drawn out a classic dialectical movement. Out of the contending forces of mass social and political desire and capitalist ideology leaps a strange and exciting synthesis. Popular film operates within a consensus uniting capitalists and the masses of the workers in such a way as to avoid most of the time either outright censorship from above or social explosions from below. The films do, in James's analysis, "represent some of the deepest feelings of the masses," but the key is a phrase with which James qualifies this assertion, "if only negatively" (AC 123). The figure of the detective gives the audience a cathartic focus for their antiauthoritarian impulses that ends by reinscribing authority. The detective shows the police to be useless bumbling obstructions. Yet at the end of the film the detective moves on to the next case, while the police are still very much on the scene where most of us live. The gangster, like the detective, "is the persistent symbol of the national past which now has no meaning—the past in which energy, determination, bravery were certain to get a man somewhere in the line of opportunity. Now the man on the assembly line, the farmer, know that they are there for life; and the gangster who displays all the old heroic qualities in the only way he can display them, is the derisive symbol of the contrast between ideals and reality" (AC 127). Film provides audiences with the image of the freestanding individual able to act in the world to resolve his or her problems. Films and comic strips fill with sadistic violence (as does the evening news in our day) in part because it no longer seems possible to most people to give effective expressive form to the rage that they feel in common at the common impasse to which American capitalism has delivered them. Their desires and frustrations are represented by a mode of displacement in their popular arts, by aesthetic acts of substitution.

James sincerely believes that "an art for the mass openly and directly must come" (AC 157), but he does not believe it likely to come under capitalism. In the years following the advent of the Great Depression, the general social crisis, combined with the increasingly centralized corporate modes of film production and distribution, largely prevented the sort of direct relationship between the audience and the film artists that James thought characterized the earlier period of Chaplin in America and Eisenstein in the Soviet Union. Yet even as film production and circulation became increasingly monopolized by a few corporate giants, that industry, like the comic strips and soap operas, had to offer some form of satisfaction to the masses of the people. The people themselves, though, were no longer the audience that had been entertained by Chaplin's first films (in part because those films now formed part of the critical vernacular of American audiences). Now the individual audience member was "seeking individuality in a mechanized, socialized society, where his life is ordered and structured at every turn, where there is no certainty of employment, far less of being able to rise by energy or Going West as in the old days" (AC 127). That the mass media should respond to these new social imperatives with a mode of political and metaphorical displacement should not surprise us, and was in fact the subject matter of some films of the era. In *Sullivan's Travels,* a film directed by Preston Sturges in 1941, the protagonist is a Hollywood director who is determined, against all advice from his corporate colleagues, to turn from making his highly successful comedic vehicles and to produce an epic social statement. He sets out upon a picaresque journey among the downtrodden, only to learn, in one of the more suspect of 1940s cinematic epiphanies, that the people *need* laughter, that his highly profitable light comedies serve a valuable, indeed universal, social function, and that it was foolish of him to think that a rich Hollywood director had the ability to speak significantly of grave social issues. *Sullivan's Travels* charged admission to teach the masses that laughter is truly the universal medicine, demonstrating in passing that while the rich may be selfish and silly, the ranks of the poor are filled with avaricious bums and thieves, albeit often amusing bums and thieves. This is the "new type of symbolism" that James discerns in film beginning around 1929, "a symbolism that goes to the very heart of the modern age, its denial of personality to the mass and the determination of the mass to realize some form of individuality in however vicarious a form" (AC 142). Few experiences of individuality could be more patently vicarious than the adoration of the media personality, the star (film ads for *Sullivan's Travels* declared, "There's no speed limit and no brake / When Sullivan travels with Veronica Lake!"), nor was there any mistaking the spirit in which such films were placed before the public. Eileen Bowser has said of *Sullivan's Travels* that "it danced on the grave of thirties social cinema" (qtd. in Walker 1034).

American Civilization remained in manuscript form at James's death, and he had never been able to return to his prospectus, first composed around 1949, long enough to flesh out his plan for fuller analyses of these phenomena. As contradictory as his surviving outline may at times appear, however, this much is clear. What James intended to explore was the dialectical motion by which the mass media, providing their public a genuinely popular new symbolism of displacement and substitution, invariably created the contradictions within which the masses could see the future opportunities that they might one day seize. This much was inevitable, though infrequently remarked in the late 1940s. All social expression is by its nature mediated, and all symbolism operates by displacement. What James found himself yearning for, still, as he sat in the dark movie house of America, was the possibility of a cinema in which we might read "the permanent mass needs of the future as outlined in the present" (AC 120). "Until then," James promises, "gangster films and Rita Hayworth" (AC 158).

On March 14, 1950, Raya Dunayevskaya wrote to James reporting, among many other things, one friend's response after reading the prospectus, which was finally published in 1993, for James's study of *American Civilization*. This friend held grave doubts about James's interpretation of Melville but suggested that James "should write up the Melville part separately & circulate it for criticism among specialists" (*Dunayevskaya Collection* 1711). When James did publish a separate work on Melville in 1953, *Mariners, Renegades and Castaways,* the book had very little circulation among Melville specialists or anyone else, though James's political colleagues did see to it that members of congress received copies, just as Melville's own

White Jacket had been delivered to members of congress in the preceding century. Dunayevskaya's friend was even less hopeful about the prospects for James's proposed longer critique of America. He thought "few people 'would have the patience to plod through the overlong prospectus' and hence he could give no further suggestion either to publishers or people with money" (*Dunayevskaya Collection* 1711).

By the time that James wrote his initial prospectus he had been on the American scene over a decade, observing from his nomadic perspective as pseudonymous radical intellectual. During that time he wrote regular columns for such leftist newspapers as *Labor Action, Socialist Appeal,* and the *Militant,* contributed longer political and cultural essays to a number of periodicals, and made frequent speaking tours, sometimes, particularly in the last years of his first American sojourn, appearing in news items in the black popular press. He spoke on such topics as "New Currents in Historical Thinking and Research," "The Negro in the World Crisis," "The American Negro: Touchstone of American Civilization," "Walt Whitman and American Culture," and, in what Robert Hill has described as the capstone of James's career as a public speaker in the United States, James gave a lecture series at Columbia University under the title "The American Vision" (AC 324–25). Out of this sustained working contact with Americans James hoped to synthesize a work for a popular readership, applying Marxist methods to the analysis of American history and culture, that would be as hard-hitting as the books of Richard Wright and as accessible as the daily news. That he had been thinking of such a project for some years is evidenced in a 1944 letter to Constance Webb in which James enthusiastically anticipates the appearance of Wright's *Black Boy.* James complains that neither white nor black America has truly confronted the fundamental significance of "the Negro Question" in the cultural and political life of the nation. Wright, though, had reached a level of understanding James admired. "He has worked at it artistically," says James, "I through history. But our conclusions are identical." Then James resolves himself upon his future work. Having read the advance pages of *Black Boy,* James tells Webb: "I have been wavering about writing a book. But now I shall hesitate no longer. By the time they have recovered from his autobiographical novel I shall hit them across the eyes with a historical study" (SD 190). James proposed a book "written for the average person, in 75,000 words or less" (AC 278), that was to be quite different from the prospectus. Where in the existing manuscript he quotes frequently and at length from various authorities, he hoped in the final version to place materials and quotations derived from "research in the actual lives and opinions of the people" (AC 39) that would establish the same points as those he had made by citing various intellectuals, as if the anticipated work in *American Civilization* were to be something of an oral autocritique of the American people. The extant volume is one of those nearly uncharacterizable texts that James seems to have specialized in producing. Circulated confidentially among a group whose opinions of the text James valued, his manuscript was an attempt to essay a position. "What is written here," James advises, "is not a rough draft of the book. It is not an outline. It is not an abridgement" (AC 39). Indeed, in addition to replacing the current quotations with materials garnered from his contacts with ordinary thinking and working Americans, James proposed that his essay was to be "ruthlessly cut" (AC 278).

Robert Hill has said of the surviving text that "to the best of our knowledge... there does not exist another work of comparable scope produced by a black visitor to the United States" (in AC 299). James himself said of his project: "As a stranger who has lived in the United States for twelve crucial years, I propose to analyze the concepts of liberty, freedom, individuality and the pursuit of happiness as I have observed them and studied them in the past history and casual lives of the American People" (AC 30). But after a dozen years of close contact, even if much of it had been clandestine, James was no more a stranger. He was a visitor who would not leave till he was put out, and he returned in the next decade. James was able to see America as one who had come from the outside, but he saw already that mass popular culture as exportable national product was beginning to Americanize that outside. Conversely, he was able to perceive how important his own Caribbean had been in the intellectual history of the American people, and his life in the United States caused him to see life in Britain and in the Caribbean differently. It was, after all, not only that his American experiences taught him a more visceral understanding of racial prejudice, but also that it was while attending a baseball game in America that he learned something new about class and culture in the Caribbean. For Anna Grimshaw, James's American experience formed the crucible out of which he created his last great major text; for Grimshaw, "*Beyond a Boundary* was made possible only by the work of his American years" (in AC 18). Even as his American years returned him to his West Indian birthplace with a transformed view of his island home, his writing on *American Civilization* and *Mariners, Renegades and Castaways* was a way of textualizing his own Americanness. Out of the crucible of his internment on Ellis Island James created a testament to his own Americanization, a testament he then presents to America as a plea for citizenship; the text he presents in *Mariners* is put forward as the best claim he can make to be a legal American citizen. (This formalization of his plea has been partly or entirely edited out of later editions of the book, but, as James makes plain himself in the last chapter, *Mariners* is from beginning to end a claim to American character.) That same dynamic is at work in the earlier *American Civilization*. Though James introduces himself to a small group of critical first readers—who know him intimately—as a stranger, his text is a testament to the growing intimacy of his relations with America. Andrew Ross has recently argued that "James was therefore writing his way into citizenship both personally and politically. For all of its immigrant past, US intellectual history had provided relatively few good examples of this genre of self-initiation, and none so exhaustive as the hard analysis undertaken by James, in which his conventional 'conversion' from European ways is underpinned by a searching reassessment of American traditions" (76).

What James's analysis revealed to him was the evolution of American politics and culture from the struggles for freedom in the nineteenth century to the arrival of the security state in the era following World War II. He begins where so many others have, by noting that America is known in the rest of the world primarily for two accomplishments, the Declaration of Independence and the full development of methods of mass production. James then moves to a synthesis of these two phenomena, arguing that "in fact, life, liberty, the pursuit of happiness and mass production are today not distinguishable. They form an entity" (AC 27). James notes the missionary zeal with which American men of government and cultural workers alike offer this entity to the world as its "only hope of salvation" (AC 28), and one now might add that this seems just as true of the post-cold war world of mass information industries as it was of the post-World War II era of mass production of consumer goods. As Nixon predicted victory over the Soviet system while standing next to a model kitchen, recent years have witnessed a proliferation of declarations of victory for bourgeois democracy and proclamations of faith in the inherent democracy of electronic media. But James saw that even with victory in war, America was "ridden with conflicts over elementary human relationships, love and marriage, which create a sense of social chaos and fear for the future" (AC 28). As the security state proceeds to transform itself once more, the times have become yet more fearful, and political debates in the America of the 1990s demonstrate that it is still true of America, as James said of it in 1949, that "the greatest power in Western civilization no longer knows what to believe about itself" (AC 28).

The problem as James framed it was an inherent tension between America's dedication to the freedom of the individual and its majoritarian faith in the utilitarian commitment to the greatest good for the greatest number, the same contradictions James's friend Ralph Ellison examines so poetically in his many essays collected in *Shadow and Act* and *Going to the Territory*. In James's historical researches he believed that he had located in the nineteenth-century Abolitionist movement a model of an early effort to synthesize these contradictory commitments, a mass, democratic organization determined to secure the freedom of individuals who had been oppressed as a group. As Du Bois had shown in *Black Reconstruction*, though, the attempt to bring about the political equality of all in America had been defeated, following victory in the Civil War, by a group of men "who in their effort to replace equality with caste and to build inordinate wealth on a foundation of abject poverty have succeeded in killing democracy, art and religion" (707). James saw that tragedy mirrored in the post-World War II cold war society. In the late 1940s, he felt, "the economic and social structure of the United States [had] created so huge an apparatus of economic, social and political institutions that the freedom of the individual except in the most abstract terms does not exist" (AC 106).

In the reorganization of American society following the victory over the Axis powers, James saw cold war politics and postwar economic resurgence reconstituting that tension between individual freedom and the modes of organization required for mass production in the institutions of the modern welfare state. "Caught in this contradiction and under the pressure of the labor organizations, the state actually proposes now no longer freedom but security; security for children; against sickness; better housing" (AC 106). This portion of James's thesis was shared by many other observers, but it is important to note that James finds the same sort of displacement at work in the political arena of postwar America that he finds in the popular entertainment industry after 1929. Labor peace is purchased by capital during the cold war by provision of individual security, which takes the place of true individual freedom. In the years following the Roosevelt era America commits its political structure to the consolidation of a safety net for the majority of its working people, and that safety net becomes synonymous in the minds of many with the freedom it replaces, and it comes to be seen as the inevitable reward for hard work in a democratic society under capitalism. (In later decades, as that safety net is dismantled, it will increasingly be identified in the mass media with the undeserving poor, the alien claiming unearned "entitlements," and the racial minorities.) The workers' own organizations under this dispensation become identified with the preservation of the basic elements of security, which in turn are tied in the popular mind to production. James says of the major unions that "the labor leadership has been forced into this position because, except for the alternative, utopian as it may seem to the ordinary mind, of the workers themselves controlling production, there is nothing else for them to do but to attempt to preserve the interests of the workers as they see them; but this they can do only on the condition that they satisfy not only the industrial leaders but the country at large that they are performing an essential social function" (AC 181). That essential social function is now no longer to act as the vehicle for the self-expression of the workers but rather to maintain both workers' benefits and increasing levels of production. In the wake of the Soviet Union's collapse, ending the cold war, and the continued reorganization of the world economy, American unions were particularly ill-prepared to struggle against the removal of the social safety net by a new generation of multinational capitalists and conservative political leaders. For too long they had operated as self-reproducing mediators displacing basic desires for self-determination; for too long they had functioned to maintain workers "in the subordination to which they are fundamentally opposed" (AC 181), and when the day inevitably arrived that capital renewed its never-relinquished opposition to workers' collective representation, the workers' unions were slow to develop new and effective modes of response.

James knows that workers, like management, are vitally interested in production, but, he quickly adds, they are interested from their own point of view (AC 181). Thus the same logic that organizes the mediated relationship of the masses to their public entertainments is at work in the relationships of the people to their political structures. The masses of the working people and the corporate producers of mass media in fact share a large set of presuppositions about their society, but each looks at that society from a different socioeconomic locus, and each will evidence that difference powerfully in relation to immediate and local issues. What James perceives here is a phenomenon that has been observed often in subsequent years by political polling organizations: "over and over again, the same workers who express as far as general politics are concerned, conservative and even reactionary sentiments, will immediately turn around and express with regard to their daily work sentiments with the most revolutionary implications conceivable. To those who do not grasp this duality, the real relations and forces at work in the great mass of the people in the United States will remain a mystery" (AC 167).

In looking to the future from his vantage point in the America of 1949 James is frequently mistaken. He greatly overestimated the potential of the C.I.O. for effecting radical change in the United States, and he was certainly miscalculating when he argued that a split in the Democratic Party would release the southern masses for the first time to have a politics of their own and that "this politics would undoubtedly be the politics of the labor movement" (AC 232). On the other hand, few in 1949 were as prescient as James in his prediction of where the great social movements of the next two decades would form in America. He believed that a breaking point had been reached in human relations in the United States and that "never before in human history has the antagonism between the sexes, the antagonism between racial minorities and national minorities; antagonism between the 'educated' and the 'non-educated' been so great as it is today" (AC 200). James always argued that "the great mass of the intellectuals *go with the power*" (AC 230), a formulation that can explain both the violence of the split within the ranks of American intellectuals over the war against Viet Nam and the ferocity of the subsequent political reactions to that conflictual split. Even after President George Bush declared victory simultaneously over Saddam Hussein and over the "Viet Nam Syndrome," the power struggles among intellectuals dating to that epistemic break in the united front of the liberal security state continue to define much of American politics, as does the lingering resentment among many American citizens against both the intellectuals who formulated the war policies in Viet Nam and the intellectuals who vocally opposed those policies.

Whatever our final judgment may prove to be of James's many statements over the years regarding the lives of women, there is no doubt that in *American Civilization* he had seen the resurgence of women's self-organization for political and social emancipation as one of the tremendous developments to come in the next decades. Just as workers, male and female, felt the continuing opposition between the dream of freedom and the reality they faced in their everyday lives, American women in increasing numbers were coming to question the spurious equality America offered to them. Though American women as a group were better off materially than almost any other class of women in the world, they were, James found, "the most unhappy, the most torn, the most dissatisfied, the most antagonistic in their relations with men that it is possible to find in history" (AC 213), and this largely because they were so often forced to an impossible choice between home and active work in the world outside the home. They confronted daily a widening gap between "the theoretical concept of equality and its actuality" (AC 214). Though James had known and worked in close association with many extremely intelligent independent women, he needed to look no further than the surrounding rows of apartments and houses to see the increasing levels of frustration American women felt as they were forced into double and triple duty trying to overcome "the handicaps inherent in the whole structure" of the American family and its economic context. More and more American women were recognizing what so many conservative political leaders still refuse to acknowledge, that the very geography of America was being redesigned *not* to support the viability of the family unit but to create the most effective systems for developing workers and moving them through the newer modes of productive organization. America's history was such that "modern society has now reached a stage where it must either turn backwards or women must become free independent human beings, in every way, and the whole sexual relation recreated upon this basis. But nowhere in the world is there so powerful a subjective onslaught upon this conception as in the United States, the country where women have reached so far in the pursuit of equality" (AC 221).

Because James viewed this impossible contradiction as being the result of the present and past modes of social organization, he also believed that "the revolution in the home rests upon a revolution outside of it" (AC 215). This does not mean that James subordinated gender questions to a "larger" imperative toward proletarian revolution but that he recognized that a sweeping reordering of the social and economic would be required to effect permanent equality between the sexes in America. As he advised Trotsky many years previously to respect the autonomy of African-American political movements, so did James in 1949 foresee the rapid proliferation of autonomous women's movements as one of the exciting modes of self-organization and self-activity among the people that one day would lead to revolutionary changes.

James was also right that the coming decades would witness a massive growth in the black-led movements for full civil rights and social equality, and he had been agitating for this prospect for years. He was terrifyingly on target, though, in another of his 1949 assessments: "The Negro intelligentsia is being combed and groomed to play precisely the role of the labor bureaucracy in its relation to the fundamental problems of the labor process" (AC 206). Drawing parallels to his own earlier theses on the popular arts, James observes that "the mercurial movie-makers" (AC 204) responded promptly to shifting public interests in black life and struggle, but what Hollywood's response meant in practice was an exploitation of "the Negro question in their own limited fashion for profit and prestige" (AC 204), producing films that placed a few black characters and situations before more sympathetic white audiences without ever engaging the depth and seriousness of the problems of race in America. James goes so far as to suggest that this smattering of more liberal films had the effect of strengthening rather than subverting the political power of southern reaction.

The system of racial segregation itself served as a massive and sometimes seemingly intractable mode of political displacement. Under Jim Crow, "the mass of the white population . . . knows that it has the power of life or death over ten million" of their black neighbors (AC 202), while they have often less power over their own lives. James details how this oppressive system operates to protect the material interests of the few and ends by repeating his belief that "the whole mighty apparatus of government which has now governed the United States for nearly twenty years can be completely upset by the freedom of the popular masses in the South" (AC 204). One has only to think of the constitutional crises provoked between southern states and the federal government whenever large numbers of black American citizens worked together to agitate for an end to segregation to see the truth of what James says in this passage. Government, like the film industry, is responsive to such mass outpourings as the Civil Rights movement, but its first response is self-preservation: "Any legislation that is passed therefore as far as government is concerned, will result in merely adding organizational bureaux, investigators, fact-finders, commissions, etc. (with a liberal sprinkling of Negroes) who become inevitably part of the whole gigantic apparatus of government with all its strains and stresses, its major national and international problems. Its primary function is not to disrupt the economic and social foundations of the country but to perpetuate itself and govern" (AC 206). This, of course, is just how the American government responded in the 1960s and into the 1970s, and in the years following the election of Ronald Reagan we have seen just how quickly government is willing to snatch back even these modest measures of amelioration.

Again, James argues that the only real solution to the problem of race in America is revolution, for the masses of the people to rise up out of their daily experiences of indignity and to smash the reigning parties to bits. Believing as he does that black Americans are in fact an integral part of American life, James believes that black people in their autonomous organizing to end their own immiserization represent synechdochally the needs and ambitions of the nation as a whole: "The Negroes are Americans and in them, in their combined segregation and integration, can be seen indications of the national crisis, strains, capabilities, needs and hopes, as in no other section of the population" (AC 208). Through the centuries of its history, American culture had projected its most fundamental horrors and aspirations alike onto its black population; now James sees African Americans in their struggle for freedom and the pursuit of happiness as embodying the full significance of America's telos. While James no longer believes in vanguard parties, he does believe that the black struggles for freedom are in the vanguard of the American masses. He sees in the organizations that black people have created for themselves the very type of self-activity for freedom today. In the black church James perceives an incredibly significant symbolic expression of social power. That power's expression is for the time confined within its own environment, but James recognizes it as the expression of a people possessed of the spirit that made America, the spirit that has now been "frustrated in so many spheres of American life" (AC 209). Likewise, James views the Garvey movement, even given its founding figure's West Indian origins (perhaps even *because* of those origins), as a determinedly American movement in its deepest character, sharing in the traditions of Jacksonian democracy, Populism, and the Wobblies. For James, "the Negroes have their cause simply and clearly posed before them, and the nation, and their segregation forces them and facilitates easier mobilization. But the whole history of America shows that political activity of this kind on their part heralds, is an advance notice of the whole nation in movement" (AC 210).

Whether writing of the incipient powers of resurgent movements seeking full equality and freedom for African Americans and for women, or examining the popularity of the comic strip, James's focus remains constant. As a historian, as a political philosopher, as a theorist of popular culture, James invariably was studying the origins and directions of those deep currents among the masses that he had always felt the greatest artists sensed before they had become more widely acknowledged, those portents of the future in the present that he found embodied in the greatest literary works in the form of new types of human character. His own early fictions were concerned above all with just such examinations of character that showed the new forms of social organization emerging from the responses of the masses of the people to their daily life. At one point in his "Notes" on *American Civilization* James says to his small circle of critical readers, "the writer of this as all readers of this outline know, is a Negro, and if it is thought advisable, could give examples of his own direct, personal experiences" (AC 203). What James had not yet done was to engage in writing with himself as character, as a figure in whose life the changing course of world history could be typed. It is not the case, as Anna Grimshaw asserts in her introduction to James's letters to Constance Webb, that James was just now beginning "to explore, and to seek to integrate, aspects of his personality which were normally suppressed or kept separate—such as art and politics" (SD 2). Rather, James was only now preparing to publish himself to the world, to examine in his own life, as he had in the life of Toussaint L'Ouverture, those historical forces and personal experiences that had made it possible for him to make the history he was in the act of making. Before accomplishing that, he would be expelled from the United States, and he would return in his writing to Tunapuna and to the window of his parents' house.

II. THE ART AND PRACTIC PART

If this is not social history what is?

C. L. R. James, *Beyond a Boundary*

We are moving too fast for any label to stick.

C. L. R. James, *Beyond a Boundary*

I believe that, effective as we are in stripping the wrappings from the underdeveloped countries, we will be more effective if, maybe not directly, but certainly we are ready to strip or have already stripped the wrappings from Western civilization itself.

C. L. R. James, *Cricket*

Unfolding the symbolism of Pablo Picasso's *Guernica,* James pauses over a series of drawings that the artist executed, noting in particular a drawing made on April 19, 1937, that Picasso titled "Negro Sculpture before a

Window" (FP 231). This is a powerfully overdetermined moment in James's life. As he meditated upon Picasso's abstract representation of the materiality of African abstraction, James must have thought long about that window. Picasso's works are, as has been so often pointed out, one of the myriad of places in which James could locate Africanity at the very center of the modernist vision. Alain Locke, in his essay on "The Legacy of the Ancestral Arts," which he included in *The New Negro*, as early as 1925 pointed to the importance of African art forms in the works of Matisse, Picasso, Derain, Modigliani, Utrillo, Archipenko, Epstein, Lipschitz, Zadkine, and Faggi, and he remarked the existence of a coterie of artists in Paris, gathered around Paul Guillame, "profoundly influenced by an aesthetic developed largely from the idioms of African art" (261). Melvin Tolson was one of many African-American intellectuals who had studied closely the work of Van Luschan and who had recognized the powerful influence that the Benin art works Van Luschan had collected in Germany had exercised over European artists and intellectuals beginning in the late nineteenth century (container 9). At several points in his *Cantos*, Ezra Pound had spoken directly of those same Benin arts, and he had also drawn on the work of Leo Frobenius, from whom, as Pound would have it, "all modern Africanologues derived" (*Negro* 393). Pound also contributed a quirky note on the value of Frobenius's African studies to modern thought for Nancy Cunard's massive *Negro* anthology, a collection published in 1933 that James knew well and often showed to his students in later decades. Despite Gertrude Stein's frequent slighting remarks about African arts, photographs of her at work in her Paris studio show clearly a small African sculpture standing on her desk before her, looking on as she writes. James knew what Locke, Tolson, Du Bois, and other black intellectuals knew, that the arts of black people were crucial sources of Western aesthetic modernism, even as black people in the West had been material sources of historical modernity. James's invocation of Picasso's "Negro Sculpture before a Window" places that work at an intersection between the classical motifs of ancient Greece (themselves connected in intriguing ways to Africa) and the aesthetic forms that had become canonical instances of the modern. The window itself, though, was a reinscription of that panoramic sensibility that James had posited as characteristic of twentieth-century life, and James's noting of "Negro Sculpture before a Window" also forms an intersection between the modernist panoramic consciousness, the ancient multidimensionality of African arts, and James's own work as an artist and as a theorist of culture.

The year before Picasso executed that drawing, James had published in England the novel he had written in Trinidad, *Minty Alley,* a novel that closes on a polysemous scene of the colonial subject, Haynes, standing in the imperial path, Victoria Street, looking through a window to a domestic life he longs to share, the life of an everyday family going about their communal affairs. Though the opening chapter of James's *Beyond a Boundary* has received considerably more critical attention than many of his other works, few studies have taken note of the symmetrical relationship that scene holds to the conclusion of *Minty Alley.* For *Minty Alley*'s Haynes, the window draws the boundary of his own ideological constraints. He cannot allow himself to pass beyond that boundary to rewrite in his own life a version of that scene that so captivates him. For James, however, as he portrays his own childhood days at "The Window" of his parents' home in Tunapuna, "there was no fence between the front yard and the street" (BB 3); he had already breached the boundaries that hold Haynes to the end.

There are, as it happens, two panoramic vistas opened before James on the first page of *Beyond a Boundary*'s narrative of his youth, each of them intensely social. Standing on a chair pressed to that window, the six-year-old James was able to take in the broad expanse of the recreation ground's cricket field beyond. The James household was situated directly behind the wicket; "an umpire could have stood at the bedroom window" (BB 3), James writes, inserting himself as child into the critical space of judgment. From this chair too, the boy was able to climb *into* the window, to mount the sill and thus to reach a curious hand to the top of the wardrobe and the books his mother had left there. Thus was James early on perched in the most liminal of positions, and "thus early the pattern of [his] life was set" (BB 3), he tells us, going on to remark the absence of a barrier between his home and the traffic of the street.

Cricket and books, these were the parameters of that lifelong pattern. The young James devoted his considerable mental capacities to feats of statistical memory and to the narrative of *Vanity Fair.* He drove himself to research with equal fervor the cricket careers of Grace and Ranjitsinhji and the plethora of names and numbers of the *Bible.* He devoted himself to the study of the Gospel According to Saint Matthew, and to an equally assiduous study of the life and times of a remarkable batsman, his next-door neighbor, Matthew Bondman. "Somewhere along the way" (BB 17) he internalized "the basic rhythms of English prose," and at the same time he was attuning himself to the rhythms of work and play, of cricket and culture in his Caribbean. Introducing *Beyond a Boundary*, he draws our attention to the recurrence of that early pattern set at his window so long ago, for *Beyond a Boundary*, his cultural study of cricket and colonial culture, was preceded by a work of literary-political critique, *Mariners, Renegades and Castaways*, just as nearly forty years before his first two juvenile publications concerned "The Novel as an Instrument of Reform" and a historic cricket match between Oxford and Cambridge that had taken place in the previous century.

Though James remained capable of turning out astute analyses with great rapidity, it was often the case that his books after 1940 underwent extended periods of gestation, assembly, and reconfiguration. Like the prospectus for *American Civilization,* the manuscript that was eventually to appear as *Beyond a Boundary* was shown to many critical readers and was the frequent subject of James's correspondence. On March 21, 1957, he sent an outline of the volume, which was not published until 1963, to his American colleagues in the Correspondence Committees, those associates who had continued with James following his break with Raya Dunayevskaya. The rough outline offered here is nearly that of the completed text, though the book was not yet completed. At the close of the letter, referring in passing to another proposed book that would not actually appear in its entirety for two decades, James expresses his fear that he will not have an opportunity to bring his project to a satisfactory end: "I can't continue with it. I have it roughly written but many of the points needed research and discussion. On a scale which you can judge from this brief outline. Yet the book remains extremely simple. And, like the Ghana book, which introduces such things as Montgomery, Alabama, it knits into a unity a tremendously wide variety of historical and social topics" (C 88). James was still enough of a Victorian reader to want a book that presented itself to readers as a unity, and he remained the type of Marxist who believed that a metanarrative of a social totality was a possibility. We learn also from letters such as this that James aspired to continue working in the way that he had with such earlier texts as *Notes on Dialectics,* subjecting his provisional draft to intense critical discussion with his intimate circles of collaborators (though it must be added that he changed little as a result of these consultations). But it was becoming increasingly difficult for James to work in that manner as he moved from country to country, nearly always without an assured source of steady income, and his deteriorating physical condition, especially the ever-worsening shaking of his hands, made it a challenge to write at all.

When *Beyond a Boundary* finally did appear, published in England by Hutchinson of London and subsequently reprinted in editions throughout the English-speaking world, it was evident to many that this book stood with *The Black Jacobins* as among James's finest achievements. His publishers promised readers of the volume "a great nuggety gold-mine of a book" and spoke of their author's "immense learning, which he wields as lightly as Worrell wields a bat." That dust jacket copy concludes with the publishers' proposal that James has become convinced through his own experiences, many narrated in the text, "that it was through English literature and English cricket that he and his people have made their most fruitful and most enduring contact with the essence of English life." Such remarks were no doubt reassuring to Britain's browsing book buyers, perhaps even to the radicals among the cricket-loving public, but what James himself had actually written (how often we find this gap between jacket blurb and prose interior) carried a different sort of edge. James had told his American friends that the early part of the book took up the theme of his upbringing with English literature, cricket, and Puritanism. He proposed to demonstrate in his book that "precisely because they were not native to the West Indies, they assumed a reality for me that placed me in violent contrast with the people among whom I lived" (C 87). James states this yet more dramatically in *Beyond a Boundary*: "A British intellectual before I was ten, already an alien in my own environment among my own people" (BB 18). This much would probably not terribly trouble an Arnoldian critic of the old school (who might indeed think it a good thing for a young intellectual to experience alienation from the masses), but it sits oddly adjacent to another autobiographical observation. Of his graduation from school James writes, "I had educated myself into a member of the British middle class with literary gifts and I had done it in defiance of all authority" (BB 32). If British literature and cricket were to be the Caribbean's most fruitful contact with the essence of English life, it appeared to be a contact that placed one in defiance of all authority, a contact that in many ways alienated the Caribbean from itself (which could be seen as the intended essence of the colonial relationship), and ultimately a contact that alienated the colonial intellectual from the intellectual world of the metropole. James describes his first voyage to England in 1932 as a case of "the British intellectual . . . going to Britain." However interpellated within the colonial ideology of British imperial culture through his enduring contact with the essence of English life, James quickly discovered that contact with Britain itself had an additional estranging property. "People educated as I had been," he writes, "could move rapidly from uncritical admiration of abstractions to an equally uncritical hostility to the complex reality" (BB 111). James had stripped the wrappings from his colonial past of underdevelopment in the Caribbean, but his book also promises, despite the assurances of its formal jacket, its own wrapping, to strip the wrappings off of the essence of English life and off of Western civilization.

V. S. Naipaul found in *Beyond a Boundary* a book that was not only important, both to England and to the West Indies, but one that "gives a base and solidity to West Indian literary endeavour" (22). This book that Naipaul saw as in many ways foundational he also saw as brilliantly destabilizing. In his review of the volume, first published in *Encounter* in September 1963, Naipaul saw what the author of the book's promotional copy had seemingly missed. "*Beyond a Boundary* . . . is part of the cultural boomeranging from the former colonies, delayed and still imperfectly understood" (17). What Naipaul had understood, and what at least some among the book's initial readership apparently missed, was the full import of that rhetorical question James repeats in his study, "What do they know of cricket who only cricket know?" (BB 233; oddly enough, Grant Farred, in making the case that James's work has not yet become so popular as to have achieved quotability, misquotes this most familiar of Jamesian sentences [14]). For James's boomeranging book brings back home to Britain a deeper understanding of their own exported sport. James has come to school them.

When James was asked late in his life to contribute commentary to accompany a series of photographs depicting black British life for the journal *TEN: 8,* he offered his memories of coming to England in the 1930s, along with comparisons to his subsequent periods of British residency in the 1950s and 1980s. The pure product of West Indian colonial education, James professes to have found on his arrival that "what surprised me most was that I had read more and absorbed more of English literature and history than almost every English person I met. My knowledge astonished them and I was astonished too because I thought I had been reading what the average educated person in England read. I only realized the width of my reading and the range of my memory by coming to England and meeting educated people at the universities" (n.pag.). It would seem, then, that what had truly set James apart from the English people that he met in 1932 was that he had made fruitful and enduring contact with the essence of English life through the media of English sport and letters, and that the

English themselves had not benefited to nearly the same extent from such vital contact with the essence of Englishness. Again the astonishment that readers need to register here is at the doubleness of racial displacement caused by James's middle-class education. The knowledge he has acquired within the British colonial system, in defiance of all authority, sets him apart both from his fellow West Indians and from the middle-class English who designed his education. It has created a social distance from which he feels he is better able to comprehend the history and culture both of his own island home and of the British isle. The rhetorical question framing *Beyond a Boundary*—"What do they know of cricket who only cricket know?"—is one that the English middle classes have displaced from their own thought, and one that their colonial students, having mastered the game, return to play in the imperial center. It is not by any essential trait that James is able to answer this question that the British have not answered; it is a result of his specific location within colonial culture. He once wrote to Naipaul saying, "I believe that, originating as we are within the British structure, but living under such different social conditions, we have a lot to say about the British civilization itself which we see more sharply than they themselves" (C 117). What James describes is a colonial experience linking descendants of Africa and India within British civilization, a mode of critique akin to Du Bois's double-consciousness and Ellison's trope of invisibility, insight proceeding from the structural anomaly of the colonialist educational fold; instruction within a culture that simultaneously strives to inculcate you with sameness while continuing to define you as the absolute other to itself.

James, who only a few years before had debated a prominent British professor over the question of the innate intelligence of the Negro, professes astonishment upon finding in England just how broad his knowledge is. It is only when he trains his intellect upon the evolution of cricket within British culture that he comes to form an explanation for this radical difference. In reading through the writings of Thomas and Matthew Arnold, and then examining the history of the transmission and transformation of their theories and practices, James produces an audacious conclusion. Thomas Arnold, James holds, was deeply suspicious of proposals for universal suffrage and was doubtful as to the educability of the masses. James describes the elder Arnold as one fearful of social chaos, who lodged his hopes in the creation of a moral political body. Arnold believed that a properly cultured upper class would persevere against both the vulgarism of industrialization and the riotous impulses of the masses. But as the methods put into practice at Rugby School spread through the kingdom they underwent a crucial metamorphosis. According to James, "The English ruling classes accepted Arnold's aims and accepted also his methods in general. But with an unerring instinct they separated from it the cultivation of the intellect and substituted for it organized games, with cricket at the head of the curriculum" (BB 164). To demonstrate just how far-reaching the effects of this metamorphosis were, James quotes from the 1856 *Rugby School Book:* "We are not students in England. Great Englishmen (generally speaking) are great in some departments of practical life. . . . Their nature is abhorrent of the Study" (qtd. in BB 165). Parents and masters were unified in what they wanted, James tells us, and they did not want scholars. What they did want was expressed in the form of the elaborate behavioral codes surrounding school and sport. Cricket was able to serve this unifying function for so long in part because it "provided a meeting place for the moral outlook of the dissenting middle classes and the athletic instincts of the aristocracy" (BB 166). Victorians held organized games to be a compulsory part of any young man's education, for it was the mode by which their moral code, their class ideology, was to be conveyed from one generation to another. And this is why it so often transpired that they valued competence in cricket "more than they did intellectual accomplishment of any kind" (BB 166). Yet this is also why, though James speaks of the inerrancy of the instinct that led Victorian England to this mode of moral education, Britain in effect was blinding itself to the fuller significance of the game that became their symbol for the very essence of English life. "It isn't cricket" came to mean "It isn't English," and still so few among the English seemed well-equipped or willing to understand just what was cricket, for cricket was all that they knew. In James's analysis the Victorians lacked self-knowledge because they deemphasized the study while at the same time raising cricket to its exalted level. Because they did not "study," because they only knew cricket, they knew nothing of cricket.

West Indian cricket, like the West Indian intellectual, becomes a boomeranging instigation. Cricket was exported to the colonies not only so that colonial Englishmen could continue to play but also as a mode of moral discipline. James argues that "as so often in any deeply national movement, . . . it contained elements of universality that went beyond the bounds of the originating nation" (BB 166). By this time, though, cricket began to communicate an altered morality. With the rise to power of the bourgeoisie in Britain came the proliferation of the school code. The British bourgeoisie, according to James, "needed an ideology. They took over the game of cricket and in the public schools established the rigorous code as a means of uniting and disciplining their class. This they exported to all the British colonies" (C 88). Cricket, still, was played on a different ground in the Caribbean colonies, and thus of necessity came to embody differing sets of social relationships. It is as he begins to tease out the significance of those differences that James begins to recognize similar class-based differences expressed in the history of British cricket as well, and it is in that history that James finds the meeting place of race, class, colonialism, and art.

Cricket, among British Victorians and colonial subjects alike, was once more a mode of expressivity through displacement, but it was not an evasion, and this is the point in James's work on culture where he departs most forcefully from many of his contemporaries in Marxist philosophy. In *Beyond a Boundary*, James describes his own moment of realization, his own recognition of the fact that he no longer viewed cultural practices in quite the same light as most of his colleagues in the radical movement. "Trotsky had said that the workers were deflected from politics by sports," James recalls. "With my past I simply could not accept that" (BB 153). His study of political history converges with his study of the history of cricket in his discovery that the public that so eagerly wanted sports and games and the public that so eagerly sought after popular democracy "were stirred at the same time" (BB 153). Neil Lazarus contrasts James's realization to the positions taken by Marxist critics whose works have enjoyed more widespread circulation and critical acceptance. Both Marcuse and Adorno, for example, persisted in defining art as an autonomous sphere, and "sport is specifically listed by Adorno, along with film and mass music, as a wholly fetishistic cultural practice, disclosive only of regressive social values" (97). It is to a large extent because of the force with which James counters that position that Lazarus considers James to be of the stature of such cultural theorists as Georg Lukács, Mikhail Bakhtin, and Stuart Hall (93). James's experience has taught him that cricket does not deflect people *from* politics. Rather, cricket becomes a field for the expression of politics, particularly when other fields have been closed off. In the colonial Caribbean of his youth, "social and political passions, denied normal outlets, expressed themselves so fiercely in cricket (and other games) precisely because they were games" (BB 66). In fact, James believes, as he wrote in *New Society* in the year of *Beyond a Boundary*'s publication, that "from its beginning to this day cricket in the

West Indies has expressed with astonishing fidelity the social relations of the Islands" (C 119). If this is true of the West Indies, the suggestion is, it may also be true of Britain. But if British intellectuals remain "blind to the grandeur of a game which, in lands far from that which gave it birth, could encompass so much of social reality and still remain a game" (BB 91), then perhaps they were blind to social realities at home as well, and perhaps what blinded them was precisely their concentration upon cricket as the bearer of the national ideology.

James's readings of cricket and cricket crowds are a seemingly endless source for teasing out lessons of caste, race, class, and art, far too many to explore sufficiently in a critical introduction such as this. He does not believe himself alone in the drawing of such lessons. Though he expresses them in the form of narrative and critical analysis, the players and their publics express similar conclusions with their bodies and in the politics of their attendance, loyalties, and arguments over the game. West Indian audiences know far more than only cricket. James argues that "West Indians crowding to Tests bring with them the whole past history and future hopes of the islands" (BB 233). This is why James believes that cricket had already taught him much of politics and history before he ever began to follow politics formally or to become a writer of histories. The case for West Indian self-government was successfully argued every day on the playing fields of the islands, and the future politics of independence were visible there too for those who could read the portents. No less was it true that the regrouping of the British Empire was on display in the heated politics of international Test matches, and, James claims, the politics of the emergent welfare state were inscribed in the very batting of the players.

James presents his study of cricket in autobiographical form so that we can follow the processes of development that taught him to read the games. He was not born to such insight, nor did he simply inhale the skill as a part of the ideological atmosphere of Trinidad. He can say of cricket what he has said so often of his own early writings, that it was only following years of reflection that he truly understood the political implications of his own previous experiences. In the much-anthologized chapter of *Beyond a Boundary* titled "Old School Tie," James offers up one such cultural-political trajectory as an instance. In part because it functions so well as a self-contained essay, it has not always been evident to readers how the chapter's narrative of James's loss of sporting innocence relates to other episodes in the book.

James begins by bringing memories of cricket and of his Aunt Judith together under the light of his own early Puritanism. James writes that he learned the same lessons of personal restraint from the playing field, from his reading, and from his black elders in the colony. From the outset he associates this stern moral code with the dominance of the middle classes. Those who were of that class in Trinidad, and those who aspired to it, internalized the codes of class loyalty and personal restraint as thoroughly as had the colonial administrators sent out from England to govern over them. The lower classes had an understanding of the code's imperatives, but, and this may be the most essentialist moment in all of James's work, there was a persisting "clash between the native temperament and environment, and this doctrine from a sterner clime" (BB 41). James portrays himself as the "strange fruit" of that hybrid acculturation, but it was only after he had left Trinidad, only when he attended sporting events in the United States, that a form of cognitive dissonance caused him to recognize the implications of the hybridity.

In 1938, C. L. R. James saw baseball. It wasn't cricket. He was poorly prepared to discover that baseball fans did not at all conduct themselves as he expected they ought, nor was he truly prepared for the self-revelations that followed as the Americans revealed themselves to him. James was by now a Marxist and had put English Labour politics behind him. His attitude toward the middle-class codes of conduct was, "if anything, contemptuous" (BB 43). But American baseball taught him just how much of the young British intellectual survived at the core of his consciousness:

> I didn't know how deeply the early attitudes had been ingrained in me and how foreign they were to other people until I sat at baseball matches with friends, some of them university men, and saw and heard the howls of anger and rage and denunciation which they hurled at the players as a matter of course. I could not understand them and they could not understand me either—they asked anxiously if I were enjoying the game. . . . When I played in some friendly games, from the start the players shouted and yelled at one another, even at their own side. (BB 44)

In order to gauge the irony in James's report of his shock during his introduction to American baseball etiquette, however, we must place this passage alongside others in *Beyond a Boundary*. As it happens, and as James makes evident, he had witnessed and heard of such things before. His parable is not meant simply to communicate to readers what an old Puritan he remained at age fifty.

The fifth part of *Beyond a Boundary* is titled "W. G.: Pre-eminent Victorian," and is seemingly far removed from James's day at the baseball game in North America. Yet, in making the case that W. G. Grace killed the professional fast bowling of the 1860s, recreated cricket, and became the vehicle through which cricket, "the most complete expression of popular life in pre-industrial England, was incorporated into the life of the nation" (BB 171), James also carefully distinguishes Grace from the Victorians. In James's evaluation Grace was "in every respect that mattered a typical representative of the pre-Victorian age" (BB 174). But W. G. Grace and his brother, E. M. (in this portion of his text initials begin to proliferate madly and the signature of C. L. R. James seems at home among the autographs of the eminent cricketers), resembled American baseball players in one key aspect of their conduct: "To the end of their days E. M. and W. G. chattered on the field like magpies. Their talking at and even to the batsman was so notorious that young players were warned against them" (BB 175). Further, W. G. Grace was not above a certain strategic dishonesty, and "it would be idle to discount the reputation he gained for trying to diddle umpires, and even on occasions disputing with them" (BB 176).

James records strikingly similar "uncricket" behavior again in his memories of playing cricket in Trinidad. In "The Light and the Dark," *Beyond a Boundary*'s fourth chapter, James recalls an uneasy moment when he had to choose to align himself with one or another of the local teams, teams that were delineated by color and class more than by playing ability or geography. The Queen's Park club was composed primarily of wealthy white men. Shamrock, also predominantly white, was the team for Catholics. Neither of these was really a possibility, nor could James join the team composed entirely of black police officers (captained by a white inspector). On his own account James ruled out the club called Stingo, too plebeian for his tastes in those early, Haynes-like days. That left Shannon and Maple. The Maple club was the team of choice for the brown-skinned middle class. Shannon was lower-middle-class and black. James's pain when he looks back at his decision to go with Maple is still evident a half-century later: "Faced with the fundamental divisions in the island, I had gone to the right and, by cutting myself off from the popular side, delayed my political development for years" (BB 53).

This much of the story is well known and has received much comment. What we need to take greater cognizance of is the way in which the Shannon club, the club James feels he should have joined, has crucial affinities with the play of W. G. Grace and with the atmosphere at the American baseball game attended by James in 1938 (before "sky lounges" had more completely separated the rich from the rest of us at sporting events). As he recollects his subsequent friendship with cricket great Learie Constantine, the former Shannon player whose autobiography James helped to write, James tells the story of a casual game of cricket played when Constantine and he were living in England: "in a quite insignificant friendly match in Lancashire, I was standing at shortleg when some batsman played an uppish stroke in my direction. Not one country cricketer in three could possibly have got to it, and in any case friendly is friendly. So I thought, until I heard a savage shout from Constantine who had bowled the ball. 'Get to it!' I recognized the note. It was one Shannon player calling to another" (BB 57). The note that James recognized (which has the rhetorical effect of retroactively making of him a Shannon player) is the same note that E. M. and W. G. Grace sang to one another in the field, the sound of the American baseball players hollering to one another around the diamond, and, more significantly still, it was the chorus James had heard before from the West Indian cricket crowds. Of the old school tie and cricket's moral code, James says: "The West Indian masses did not care a damn about this. They shouted and stamped and yelled and expressed themselves fully in anger and joy then, as they do to this day, whether they are in Bridgetown or Birmingham" (BB 40).

Why, then, James's shock in the stands during his first American baseball game? If we return to the passage in which he reports his discomfort the reason now stands clear. James's surprise came when he attended a baseball game with friends, "some of whom were university men" (BB 43), and heard their howls at the umpires and players. The friends he plays baseball with in an American park shout imprecations to one another after the style of Shannon and Grace. This is not, as James thought it might be in 1938, a matter of national character. The American players and fans, like Constantine and Grace, did not live within the disciplinary code of the old school tie; they were evolving another moral order out of their daily interactions with each other. James was still learning the class politics of organized sport. He was beginning to recognize more clearly than he had before the role of the chorus. Grant Farred writes of James in "The Maple Man: How Cricket Made a Postcolonial Intellectual" that, "as a man who fielded, bowled, and batted against Shannon, he recognized that the interplay between their players and spectators was a fundamental dynamic which had to be accounted for if the game itself was to be comprehended anywhere, but especially in the colonial Caribbean" (182).

Here we come to what James terms "the Art and Practic Part." The code of the old school tie was a unifying practice for those who intended to rule society. Those they intended to rule over played the same game, but they put a different spin on everything. What cricket meant to the students at Rugby was not synonymous with what it meant to the players outside James's Tunapuna home. Still, all players practiced an art. James does not believe that the relationship of base and superstructure produces an art that is a purely symptomatic encoding of economic relationships. He does, nonetheless, believe that a transformation within our social existence must transform our art. For James, the creators of modern cricket were responding to an underlying motivation similar to that of the ancient bushmen who, with line, curve, and movement, created in a new medium "in the form they needed a vision of the life they lived" (BB 209). Both the fans of Shannon and the audience at Hambledon find forms to express their approbation of line, curve, and movement, of accomplishments that fit their vision of the life they lead, but they don't have identical visions any more than they lead the same lives. What James calls the popular democracy of ancient Greece gave birth to a form of ritual public drama, drama judged by its popular audience. He sees the crowd at a cricket match as an expression of today's desire for popular democracy, grasping "at a more complete human existence" (BB 211).

The cricket match is to James a dramatic spectacle in which the dialectical relationships between the one and the many are continually reenacted and continually assessed. This, then, is aesthetic life of the most demanding and rigorous sort. The play of the cricket field offers spectators the significant form that their minds crave, and it is offered in an arena of public opinion. As organized sport becomes ever more overtly a capital-producing business; the arena may shift, the audience may reconstitute itself around other sites of spectatorship, but the essential relationship will remain. "Thus the game is founded upon a dramatic, a human, relation which is universally recognized as the most objectively pervasive and psychologically stimulating in life and therefore in that artificial representation of it which is drama" (BB 197). It is drama without guidance from a prescribed text, however, drama that is infinitely recombinant. The age of mechanical reproducibility has made it possible for all classes of people to have access to versions of the aesthetic previously restricted strictly by wealth. Organized games bring a different form of aesthetic satisfaction to the masses. They find there an aesthetic relationship of the type available in live jazz performance, or in their own play. Deeply appreciative of and desiring significant form, the public can find here interactions of a type not available in the same way at a theater or museum: "What is to be emphasized is that whereas in the fine arts the image of tactile values and movement, however effective, however magnificent, is permanent, fixed, in cricket the spectator sees the image constantly recreated, and whether he is a cultivated spectator or not, has standards which he carries with him always" (BB 205). Not only does the audience witness and appraise both the aesthetic and utilitarian aspects of the performance of the players, they witness as well the influence of their active presence upon the play. This is social and aesthetic history in the making.

When black Trinidadians witnessed the triumphs of a Constantine or a St. Hill, they saw beauty of form and skill of execution, but they also witnessed people like themselves, in a sphere of creation and competition that was open, the proverbial leveled playing field. Along with the excellence of art and cricket practice there was, for those colonial spectators, a powerful political overlay to the experience. Logic and history should tell us that one would do well not to expect excellence in art and on the playing field to be followed by social equality. "Perhaps," James conjectures, "it is only we on the periphery who think this way" (BB 93), but there is no underestimating the social investment involved when oppressed peoples choose as a group to view a performer as their representative (as when they see James, one of their boys, telling the British a thing or two about cricket). "A national hero must have a nation" (BB 108), James cautions while listening to West Indians discuss the acts and decisions of St. Hill and Constantine, and there is a sense in which that incipient nation was already coming into being at the point of the people's political affiliation with the players on the field, that it was another episode in the history of the construction of a national self-consciousness that James traces to the revolution in San Domingo. The artistic success on the field against the opposition of Britain's best symbolized for many the freedom of self-actualization beyond the boundaries of colonial constraint. The constraints were still visible, like chalk lines on freshly cut grass, but the boundaries had been transgressed.

By 1963 James had learned to look to the people for direction rather than to tell them constantly, as vanguards are wont to do, how they should direct their desires and activities. He knew too that if one really wanted an answer to Tolstoy's question "What is art?" it was among the masses of the people that one should look, for in aesthetics, as in politics, "We shall know more what men want and what they live by when we begin from what they do" (BB 182). In the lines of the Olympic Apollo, James read an entire civilization and inferred from it the relationships of artists to society. James argued that the same reading could be accomplished among the moving images at the wicket. We will know what art is, James concludes, "only when we learn to integrate our vision of Walcott on the back foot through the covers with the outstretched arm of the Olympic Apollo" (BB 211). This was a new way of looking at cricket, but it was the kind of newness that was a tradition in the West Indies. In a letter written to John Arlott the year before publication of *Beyond a Boundary*, James repeated his contention that "West Indians are a modern people in an underdeveloped society" (C 110), a society whose modernity and early stage of development he saw as parallel to the audiences that first heard Shakespeare's plays in the Globe Theater. James, who so often brought an eccentric thesis forth from his own readings of Shakespeare, told Arlott that "the same newness that West Indians bring to cricket they bring to the classic writers" (C 110), and that same newness, as we can see in the careers of James, Lamming, Harris, and Brathwaite, brought a newness to English writing in the twilight of empire as startling and as revivifying as what the West Indian players brought to Britain's national game.

Those who abhorred the study would, in James's opinion, fail to learn the lessons of history that were written on the playing fields of England. Those who draw a sharp line dividing the lines of the Olympic Apollo from the lines formed in space by cricket's artists could never know more of art, knowing as they did only art, and could never understand how art satisfies the deepest sensibilities of a community of people. The tactile values and movements of the plastic arts do not exist in an autonomous space apart from the social, and the free play of consciousness will invariably draw them together. James traces the controversies over form and play in cricket to transformations in society, concluding that "The Welfare State of Mind" will be overcome with the return of the cricketer to the community "(as so many of our professional experts in so many different spheres of modern life need to be returned)" (BB 218), with the appearance of some young Romantic who "will extend the boundaries of cricket technique with a classical perfection" (BB 222).

James had never been content to compose a cricket memoir of the usual sort. "Though I read that sort of book," he says in his book, "I have no intention of writing one" (BB 152). In *Minty Alley* he had broken the boundaries of the English realist novel, bringing that form and its techniques to the colonial barrack-yards and, in the act, altering the form itself. In *Mariners, Renegades, and Castaways* he had transgressed the borders of academic literary criticism, creating a form of personal political testament joined to criticism rare in its day. With his last great book, he did indeed extend the boundaries of both sports writing and cultural criticism, extending as he had hoped our previously too limited conceptions of both history and the fine arts; he was a Caliban pioneering into regions Caesar never knew. *Beyond a Boundary* is perhaps the best example of what James meant to convey to the audience for his lectures on *Modern Politics* when he defined his conception of dialectical motion:

(a) All development takes place as a result of *self-movement, not* organization or direction by external forces.
(b) Self-movement springs from and is the overcoming of antagonisms *within* an organism, not the struggle against external foes.
(c) It is not the world of nature that confronts man as an alien power to be overcome. It is the alien power that he himself created. (MP 115)

In the end, it is that self-movement that James defines as life itself. Cricket was dying in England, he believed, because in the welfare state the dream of the free movement of the people had been replaced by the security of the capitalist bureaucracy, and the people who thought they knew cricket best did not know what to do about its decline.

Just as much at a loss were most English intellectuals. Reading Sir Kenneth Clark's *Civilization* James is struck by one of Clark's few confessions: "We have no idea where we are going." James quickly underscores the irony of this. He writes, "Now, friends, I am not making jokes. I am telling you the opinion of the people who rule the world" (RV 237). In James's way of thinking, study means historicizing dialectical movement precisely so that one can see where the people are going. Thinking back upon the history of his own thinking, James writes with equal irony of his own intellectual journey: "Time would pass, old empires would fall and new ones take their place, the relations of classes had to change, before I discovered that it is not the quality of goods and utility which matter, but movement; not where you are or what you have, but where you have come from, where you are going and the rate at which you are getting there" (BB 113). That creative movement, as James advised his listeners in Trinidad in 1960, was freedom, not utility. Self-realization based upon the incorporation into the individual of the previous development of all humanity, that was universality. And that, as a writer and as a student of culture, was freedom for C. L. R. James. Always in motion himself, James thought of the Caribbean as a region for which such panoramic boundary crossing was a defining principle. "We West Indians," he writes in *Beyond a Boundary*, "are a people on our way who have not reached a point of rest and consolidation" (BB 148).

At the conclusion of a pamphlet titled *Punching Out*, Martin Glaberman, who for many years did more than anybody else to keep the intellectual legacy of C. L. R. James available in print, repeats a lesson that James and his colleagues had learned from Marx and Hegel, a lesson that gave James his mission as a writer, "the new society appears within the old" (32). Across six decades of life James worked to discern the emerging social formations that would remake the world. In his early fiction and literary criticism he sought to find the lineaments of the new society in the outlines of new types of human character. In his last major writings he was still endeavoring to establish the relationships between new modes of social organization and the new modes of social expression devised by the masses of the people in their interactions with popular arts and in their attitudes toward sport. His major theoretical contributions are efforts to refine dialectical modes of thought for the purpose of comprehending where the new society will appear and what direction it shall take. As a historian his concern was to make available a still more usable past, to produce narratives of emancipation, rooted in solid scholarship. James meant not only to correct the falsehoods of the dominant and dominating views of history but to provide critical histories that would open up to their readers the reality of revolutionary possibility in the present.

From the beginning of his career to the end, James's activism was centered in the act of publication. One of his first undertakings after joining the Trotskyist movement in England was, in collaboration with like-minded activists, to write a comprehensive analysis of what was wrong with the organization's publications and what could be done to improve them. "In other words," James later recalled, "we expressed not only our political differences directly with the paper, but we brought it to a criticism and technique of improving it as a political paper" (LO 13). When James met with Trotsky in Mexico, a central part of the plan of action they developed was the authoring and dissemination of critical histories, theoretical documents, and popular publications. When James, Dunayevskaya, Lee, Paine, Glaberman, and the rest of the Johnson-Forest tendency made the final break from Trotsky's theories and organizations, their most effective form of work was through publication, a series of groundbreaking books, pamphlets, and the *Correspondence* newspaper. In later life, James associated nearly all of his major theoretical breakthroughs with particular publications. "Sometimes it is only after you write something that you fully understand what you are driving at," he wrote in 1962. "*Facing Reality* was an attempt to break out of the stranglehold" (LO 4). Near the end of his life, James's consistent advice to young radicals was that they should publish a statement of their understandings, and his own return to greater public view was in large part the result of new generations of radical thinkers rediscovering and reprinting his works. James and his organizations developed methods for the collaboration between working people and intellectual writers, methods that produced such still useful documents as Phil Singer and Grace Lee's *The American Worker,* which was to have such great importance to the *Socialisme ou Barbarie* group in Europe. This too marks a difference between James and other radical intellectuals. In his *Letters on Organization* he points to the difference in both attitude and working methods between his associates and those Marxists still committed to the dream of a vanguard party. "This, if you please," writes James: "is a clear example of the difference between . . . the Trotskyists and ourselves. They came to Detroit, and to the working class in general, in order to teach the working class and to make it realize that they were the vanguard party and the destined leaders. We came to Detroit, and we did the work, as the British prayer book has it, in that sphere of life in which it had pleased God to call us" (LO 46). James, in all the spheres of his life, was called to be a speaker and a writer. This never meant that he felt a divide between the sphere of the word and the spheres of human labor; he felt, rather, called to the labors of the most human of all acts, language, and he felt called to speak in the cause of human liberation from oppression and suffering.

In 1989, James did reach the point of final rest, but his work is in many ways still moving too rapidly for labels to stick. For James, rest and consolidation were always preparatory for further work, further dialectical movement, further emancipatory action. Perhaps my strongest memory of James in his classroom is still the animation in his figure, his hands waving in the air as if he were conducting a chorus, and the joy in his voice as he recited from long memory his favorite lines from a song that his friend Paul Robeson had often sung:

I went to the valley,
I didn't go to stay,
But my soul got happy
And I stayed all day.

WORKS CITED

Althusser, Louis. *For Marx.* Trans. Ben Brewster. London: Verso, 1975.
Anderson, Kevin. *Lenin, Hegel, and Western Marxism: A Critical Study.* Chicago: U of Chicago P, 1995.
Benjamin, Walter. "N [Re the Theory of Knowledge, Theory of Progress]." *Benjamin: Philosophy, Aesthetics, History.* Ed. Gary Smith. Chicago: U of Chicago P, 1989.
——. *Reflections: Essays, Aphorisms, Autobiographical Writings.* Ed. Peter Demetz. New York: Harcourt Brace Jovanovich, 1978.
Berman, Paul. "*Facing Reality.*" Buhle, *C. L. R. James: His Life and Work* 206–11.
Birbalsingh, F. M. "The Literary Achievement of C. L. R. James." *Journal of Commonwealth Literature* 19.1 (1984): 108–21.
Buhle, Paul. *C. L. R. James: The Artist as Revolutionary.* London: Verso, 1988.
——, ed. *C. L. R. James: His Life and Work.* London: Allison and Busby, 1986.
Buhle, Paul, and Paget Henry, eds. *C. L. R. James's Caribbean.* Durham: Duke UP, 1992.
Cain, William E. "The Triumph of the Will and the Failure of Resistance: C. L. R. James's Readings of *Moby-Dick* and *Othello.*" Cudjoe and Cain 260–73.
Callinicos, Alex. *Trotskyism.* Buckingham, Eng.: Open University Press, 1990.
Carby, Hazel V. "Proletarian or Revolutionary Literature: C. L. R. James and the Politics of the Trinidadian Renaissance." *South Atlantic Quarterly* 87.1 (1988): 39–52.
Césaire, Aimé. *Return to My Native Land.* Trans. John Berger and Anna Bostock. Baltimore: Penguin Books, 1969.
Cudjoe, Selwyn. "The Audacity of It All: C. L. R. James's Trinidadian Background." Buhle and Henry 39–55.
Cudjoe, Selwyn, and William E. Cain, eds. *C. L. R. James: His Intellectual Legacies.* Amherst: U of Massachusetts P, 1995.
Cumberbatch, Stephen. "Long Innings." *New Society* 4 Aug. 1977: 243.
Derrida, Jacques. *Specters of Marx: The State of the Debt, the Work of Mourning, and the New International.* Trans. Peggy Kamuf. London: Routledge, 1994.
Dhondy, Farrukh. "Reviews." *Race Today* 9.5 (1977): 116–18.
Du Bois, W. E. B. *Black Reconstruction in America, 1860–1880.* 1935. New York: Atheneum, 1977.
——. *Darkwater: Voices from within the Veil.* 1920. New York: AMS Press, 1969.
——. *John Brown.* 1909. New York: International Publishers, 1987.
——. *The Souls of Black Folk.* 1903. New York: Signet, 1969.
Dunayevskaya, Raya. *The Philosophic Moment of Marxist-Humanism.* Chicago: News and Letters, 1989.
Dunayevskaya, Raya, et al. *The Raya Dunayevskaya Collection.* Wayne State University Archives of Labor History and Urban Affairs. Microfilm Edition.
Dupuy, Alex. "Toussaint Louverture and the Haitian Revolution: A Reassessment of C. L. R. James's Interpretation." Cudjoe and Cain 106–17.
Everett, Anna. " 'Operation Restore Hope': Recolonizing Africa for the Twenty-first Century." *Ufahamu: Journal of the African Activist Association* 21.1 & 2 (1993): 3–13.
Farred, Grant, ed. *Rethinking C. L. R. James.* Oxford: Blackwell Publishers Ltd., 1996.
Gilkes, Michael. *The West Indian Novel.* Boston: Twayne Publishers, 1981.

Glaberman, Martin. "C. L. R. James: The Man and His Works." *Flambeau* No. 6. (Nov. 1966): 22–23.
———. "C. L. R. James—A Recollection." *New Politics* 2.2 (1990): 78–84.
———. *Punching Out.* 1952. Detroit: Bewick Editions, 1973.
———. "Review of *Notes on Dialectics.*" *Race and Class* 23.1 (1981): 97–99.
Gomes, P. I. *The Marxian Populism of C. L. R. James.* Working Papers on Caribbean Society Series A No. 1. Department of Sociology, University of the West Indies. n.d.
Grierson, Flora. "Man's Inhumanity to Man." *New Statesman and Nation* 16.398 (New Series) (8 Oct. 1938): 536.
Grimshaw, Anna. "C. L. R. James: A Revolutionary Vision." James, *The C. L. R. James Reader,* 1–22.
———. Introduction. James, *Special Delivery* 1–35.
Hamilton, Cynthia. "A Way of Seeing: Culture as Political Expression in the Works of C. L. R. James." *Journal of Black Studies* 22.3 (1992): 429–43.
Harland, Sidney C. "*Magna Est Veritas Et Praevalebit:* A Reply to Mr. C. L. R. James." *Beacon* 1.7 (1931): 18–20.
———. "Race Admixture." *Beacon* 1.4 (1931): 25–29.
Hill, Robert. "In England, 1932–1938." Buhle, *C. L. R. James: His Life and Work* 61–80.
———. "Literary Executor's Afterward." James, *American Civilization* 293–366.
Ivy, James W. "Book News and Reviews." *Crisis* 46.8 (1939): 250–51.
James, Cyril Lionel Robert. "Africans and Afro-Caribbeans: A Personal View." *TEN:8* 16 (1984): n.pag.
———. *American Civilization.* Ed. Anna Grimshaw and Keith Hart. Cambridge: Blackwell, 1993.
———. *At The Rendezvous of Victory: Selected Writings.* London: Allison and Busby, 1984.
———. *Balance Sheet: Trotskyism in the United States, 1940–1947.* With Raya Dunayevskaya and Martin Glaberman. New York: Johnson-Forest Tendency, 1947.
———. *Beyond a Boundary.* 1963. Durham: Duke UP, 1993.
———. *The Black Jacobins.* 1938. New York: Vintage Books, 1989.
———. "The *Black Scholar* Interviews: C. L. R. James." *Black Scholar* 2.1 (1970): 35–43.
———. "Capitalist Society and the War." *New International* 6.6 (1940): 114–28.
———. *C. L. R. James and Revolutionary Marxism: Selected Writings of C. L. R. James, 1939–1949.* Ed. Scott McLemee and Paul Le Blanc. Atlantic Highlands, N.J.: Humanities Press, 1994.
———. *C. L. R. James's Eightieth Birthday Lectures.* Ed. Margaret Busby and Darcus Howe. London: Race Today Publications, 1981.
———. *C. L. R. James on the "Negro Question."* Ed. Scott McLemee. Jackson: UP of Mississippi, 1996.
———. *The C. L. R. James Reader.* Ed. Anna Grimshaw. Oxford: Blackwell Publishers, 1992.
———. *Cricket.* Ed. Anna Grimshaw. London: Allison and Busby, 1986.
———. *Education, Propaganda, Agitation: Post-War America and Bolshevism.* Internal Bulletin, Workers Party [1943, 1944, 1945].
———. "The Elemental Urge to Socialism." *Militant* 11 Aug. 1947: 2.
———. *Every Cook Can Govern and What Is Happening Every Day.* Ed. Jan Hillegas. Jackson: New Mississippi, Inc., 1986.
———. *Facing Reality.* With Grace Lee and Cornelius Castoriadis. 1958. Detroit: Bewick Editions, 1974.
———. "From Jobs to the Struggle for Socialism." *Labor Action* 2 June 1941: 4.
———. *The Future in the Present: Selected Writings.* London: Allison and Busby, 1977.

———. "The Gathering Forces: Peasants and Workers; and The Way Out—World Revolution." (Excerpts.) With Martin Glaberman, William Gorman, and George Rawick. *Radical America* 5.6 (1971): 5–50 and 55–61.
———. "Germany and European Civilization." *New International* 10.11 (1944): 357–61.
———. "The Haitian Maroons." *Black World* 25.1 (1975): 64–68.
———. *A History of Negro Revolt.* 1938. London: Race Today Publications, 1985.
———. "The Intelligence of the Negro: A Few Words with Dr. Harland." *Beacon* 1.5 (1931): 6–10.
———. "An Interview: C. L. R. James and Pan-Africanism." With Patrick Griffith. *Black World* 21.1 (1971): 4–13.
———. "Interview with C. L. R. James." Munro and Sander 23–41.
———. "Introduction to the Original Edition of *Red Spanish Notebook* (1937)." *Arsenal: Surrealist Subversion* 4 (1989): 177.
———. *The Invading Socialist Society.* With Raya Dunayevskaya and Grace Lee. 1947. Detroit: Bewick Editions, 1972.
———. *Letters on Organization.* Detroit: Facing Reality Publishing Committee, 1963.
———. *The Life of Captain Cipriani.* Nelson, Eng.: Coulton and Company, 1932.
———. *Mariners, Renegades and Castaways: The Story of Herman Melville and the World We Live In.* 1953. London: Allison and Busby, 1985.
———. "Michel Maxwell Philip: 1829–1886: Sometime Solicitor-General of Trinidad: An Impression." *Beacon* 1.6 (1931): 16–23.
———. *Minty Alley.* 1936. London: New Beacon Books, 1971.
———. *Modern Politics.* 1960. Detroit: Bewick Editions, 1973.
———. "Negro History Week and the Workers." *Militant* 7 Feb. 1949: 3.
———. *The Negro's Fight. Labor Action* 27 May 1940: 1.
———. *Nkrumah and the Ghana Revolution.* London: Allison and Busby, 1977.
———. *Notes on Dialectics: Hegel, Marx, Lenin.* 1948. Westport: Lawrence Hill and Company, 1980.
———. *The Old World and the New: Shakespeare, Melville and Others.* Detroit: Friends of Facing Reality, 1970.
———. "One Tenth of the Nation. *Labor Action* 13 Jan. 1947: 2.
———. *Party Politics in the West Indies.* San Juan, Trinidad: C. L. R. James, 1962.
———. "Production for the Sake of Production." *Internal Bulletin,* Workers Party, Apr. 1943.
———. "Resolution on the International Situation: The Fourth International and the World Socialist Revolution." 27 April 1946. Ts. 27 pp. *Raya Dunayevskaya Collection.* 598–624.
———. "The Resolution of the Minority." *New International* 11.1 (1945): 13–20.
———. "Resolution on the Russian Question." *The Russian Question: Resolutions of the 1941 Convention on the Character of the Russian State. Workers Party Basic Documents.* Series No. 1 (1941): 16–30.
———. "The Social Ties in the Factory." *Militant* 13 Oct. 1947: 3.
———. *Special Delivery: The Letters of C. L. R. James to Constance Webb, 1939–1948.* Ed. Anna Grimshaw. Oxford: Blackwell Publishers, 1995.
———. "Speech on Our Negro Resolution." *Internal Bulletin of the Socialist Workers Party* 11.4 (1949).
———. *Spheres of Existence: Selected Writings.* London: Allison and Busby, 1980.
———. *State Capitalism and World Revolution.* With Raya Dunayevskaya and Grace Lee. 1950. Chicago: Walter H. Kerr Publishing Company, 1986.
———. *Walter Rodney and the Question of Power.* London: Race Today Publications, 1983.
———. "The West Indian Intellectual." Thomas 23–49.

———. *World Revolution, 1917–1936: The Rise and Fall of the Communist International.* 1937. Atlantic Highlands, N.J.: Humanities Press, 1993.
Kelley, Robin D. G. Introduction. *A History of Pan-African Revolt.* By C. L. R. James. Chicago: Charles H. Kerr Publishing Company, 1995. 1–33.
———. "The World the Diaspora Made: C. L. R. James and the Politics of History." Farred 103–30.
LaGuerre, John Gaffar. *The Social and Political Thought of the Colonial Intelligentsia.* Mona, Jamaica: Institute of Social and Economic Research, 1982.
Lamming, George. *The Pleasures of Exile.* 1960. London: Allison and Busby, 1984.
Larsen, Neil. "Negativities of the Popular: C. L. R. James and the Limits of 'Cultural Studies.'" Farred 85–102.
Lazarus, Neil. "Cricket and National Culture in the Writings of C. L. R. James." Henry and Buhle 92–110.
LeBlanc, Paul. "Introduction: C. L. R. James and Revolutionary Marxism." James, *C. L. R. James and Revolutionary Marxism* 1–37.
Lee, Grace. "Thinking and Acting Dialectically: C. L. R. James, The American Years." *Monthly Review* 45.5 (1993): 38–46.
Levi, Darrell E. "C. L. R. James: A Radical West Indian Vision of American Studies." *American Quarterly* 43.3 (1991): 486–501.
Locke, Alain. "The Legacy of the Ancestral Arts." *The New Negro.* Ed. Alain Locke. 1925. New York: Atheneum, 1983. 254–67.
Logan, Rayford. "New Books on the Bookshelf." *Opportunity* 17.2 (1939): 58–60.
Marx, Karl. *Capital: A Critique of Political Economy.* Trans. Samuel Moore and Edward Aveling. Ed. Frederick Engels. 1906. New York: Modern Library, n.d.
———. *Capital Vol. 2: The Process of Circulation of Capital.* Ed. Frederick Engels. 1919. New York: International Publishers, 1967.
———. *Capital Vol. 3: The Process of Capitalist Production as a Whole.* Ed. Frederick Engels. 1909. New York: International Publishers, 1967.
———. *The Economic and Philosophic Manuscripts of 1844.* Trans. Martin Milligan. Ed. Dirk J. Struik. New York: International Publishers, 1964.
———. *The Revolutions of 1848: Political Writings Volume I.* Ed. David Fernbach. New York: Vintage Books, 1974.
———. *Surveys from Exile: Political Writings Volume II.* Ed. David Fernbach. New York: Vintage Books, 1974.
McLemee, Scott. "Afterword: American Civilization and World Revolution: C. L. R. James in the United States, 1938–1953 and Beyond." James, *C. L. R. James and Revolutionary Marxism* 209–38.
Melville, Herman. *Pierre, or The Ambiguities.* Ed. Harrison Hayford, Hershel Parker, and G. Thomas Tanselle. Chicago: Northwestern UP, 1971.
Mendes, Alfred. "Is the Negro Inferior?" *Beacon* 1.6 (1931): 27.
Mentor, Ralph. "A Study of Mr. James's Political Biography." *Beacon* 2.6 (1932): 15–17.
Munro, Ian, and Reinhard Sander, eds. *Kas-Kas: Interviews with Three Caribbean Writers in Texas.* Austin: African and Afro-American Research Institute, University of Texas at Austin, 1972.
Murdoch, H. Adlai. "James's Literary Dialectic: Colonialism and Cultural Space in *Minty Alley.*" Cudjoe and Cain 61–71.
Naipaul, V. S. *The Overcrowded Barracoon and Other Articles.* London: Andre Deutsch, 1972.
Needham, Anuradha Dingwaney. "Inhabiting the Metropole: C. L. R. James and the Postcolonial Intellectual of the African Diaspora." *Diaspora* 2.3 (1993): 281–303.

Padmore, George. *Pan-Africanism or Communism.* Garden City, N.Y.: Anchor Books, 1972.
Parris, D. Elliott. "*Minty Alley.*" Buhle, *C. L. R. James: His Life and Work* 200–02.
Phillips, Wendell. *Wendell Phillips on Civil Rights and Freedom.* Ed. Louis Filler. New York: Hill and Wang, 1965.
Postgate, Raymond. "Du Côté De Chez Trotsky." *New Statesman and Nation* 12.324 (New Series) (8 May 1937): 776–78.
Pound, Ezra. "Leo Frobenius." *Negro: An Anthology.* Ed. Nancy Cunard. 1933. Abridged and Ed. Hugh Ford. New York: Frederick Ungar Publishing Company, 1970. 393–94.
Pyne-Timothy, Helen. "Identity, Society and Meaning: A Study of the Early Stories of C. L. R. James." Cudjoe and Cain 51–60.
Ramchand, Kenneth. Introduction. *Minty Alley.* By C. L. R. James. London: New Beacon Books Ltd, 1971. 5–15.
Richardson, Al. "Introduction to the Paperback Edition." James, *World Revolution* xi–xxiii.
Robinson, Cedric J. "C. L. R. James and the World-System." Cudjoe and Cain 244–59.
Robinson, Edwin Arlington. *Selected Poems of Edwin Arlington Robinson.* Ed. Morton Dauwen Zabel. New York: Collier, 1965.
Ross, Andrew. "Civilization in One Country? The American James." Farred 75–84.
Said, Edward. "Third World Intellectuals and Metropolitan Culture." *Raritan* 9.3 (1990): 27–50.
Salkey, Andrew. *Havana Journal.* Hammersmith, Middlesex, Eng.: Penguin Books Ltd., 1971.
Samaroo, Brinsley. Introduction. *The Beacon: Port of Spain, Trinidad: 1931–1939.* Millwood, N.Y.: Kraus Reprint Co., 1977. i–xiii.
Sander, Reinhard W. "Introduction: *The Beacon* and the Emergence of West Indian Literature." *The Beacon: Port of Spain, Trinidad: 1931–1939.* Millwood, N.Y.: Kraus Reprint Co., 1977. xv–xxv.
Singham, A. W. "C. L. R. James on the Black Jacobin Revolution in San Domingo—Notes toward a Theory of Black Politics." *Savacou* 1.1 (1970): 82–96.
Spanos, William V. *The Errant Art of Moby-Dick: The Canon, The Cold War, and the Struggle for American Studies.* Durham: Duke UP, 1995.
Stewart, John. "The Literary Work as Cultural Document: A Caribbean Case." *Literature and Anthropology.* Ed. Phillip A. Dennis and Wendell Aycock. Lubbock: Texas Tech UP, 1989. 97–112.
Surin, Kenneth. "The Future Anterior: C. L. R. James and Going *Beyond a Boundary.*" Farred 187–204.
"Swan Song." Unsigned review of *The Case for West Indian Self Government. Beacon* 2.2 (1933): 19.
Thomas, John Jacob. *Froudacity: West Indian Fables.* 1889. London: New Beacon Books Ltd., 1969.
Tolson, Melvin B. *The Melvin B. Tolson Papers.* Manuscript. Library of Congress. Washington, D.C.
Turner, Lou. "Epistemology, Absolutes, and the Party: A Critical Examination of Philosophic Divergences within the Johnson-Forest Tendency, 1948–1953." Cudjoe and Cain. 193–204.
Walker, John, ed. *Halliwell's Film Guide.* New York: HarperCollins Publishers, 1995.
Walker, Margaret. *Richard Wright: Daemonic Genius: A Portrait of the Man: A Critical Look at His Work.* New York: Warner Brothers, 1988.
Ward, Joshua. "One Negro to Another." *Beacon* 2.5 (1932): 16–18.
Webb, Constance. *Richard Wright: A Biography.* New York: G. P. Putnam's Sons, 1968.
Weir, Stanley. "Revolutionary Artist." Buhle, *C. L. R. James: His Life and Work* 180–84.
Whitlock, Gillian. "The Bush, The Barrack-Yard and the Clearing: 'Colonial Realism' in the

Sketches and Stories of Susanna Moodie, C. L. R. James and Henry Lawson." *Journal of Commonwealth Literature* 20.1 (1985): 36–48.
Wickham, John. "Book Review of *Minty Alley.*" *Bim* 14.54 (1972): 111–13.
Williams, Patricia J. *The Rooster's Egg: On the Persistence of Prejudice.* Cambridge: Harvard UP, 1995.
Williams, William Carlos. *The Embodiment of Knowledge.* Ed. Ron Loewinsohn. New York: New Directions, 1974.
Winter, Sylvia. "Beyond the Categories of the Master Conception: The Counterdoctrine of the Jamesian Poiesis." Buhle and Henry 63–91.
Worcester, Kent. *C. L. R. James: A Political Biography.* Albany: State University of New York Press, 1996.

INDEX

Adorno, Gretel, 146
Adorno, Theodor, 104, 144, 146, 177
Allen, James, 59
Althusser, Louis, 106
Anderson, Kevin, 117
Aptheker, Herbert, 47, 57, 58–60
Arbuckle, Roscoe "Fatty," 22
Archipenko, Alexander, 170
Aristotle, 43, 72–73, 151
Arlott, John, 184
Arnold, Matthew, 152, 173, 175–76
Arnold, Thomas, 175–76
Austin, J. L., 105

Bakhtin, Mikhail, 177
Baldwin, James, 143
Batista, Fulgencio, 85
Baudelaire, Charles, 152
Baudrillard, Jean, 103
Beckett, Samuel, 15, 38
Beethoven, Ludwig von, 143
Beneditti, Mario, 99
Benjamin, Walter, 116, 117, 144, 146–47, 151, 155–56
Bennett, Arnold, 6
Berman, Paul, 103
Birbalsingh, F. M., 26
Blake, William, 41
Boggs, Grace Lee, 101, 103, 104, 105, 107, 109, 110, 111, 112, 113, 114, 116, 117, 119, 186, 187
Bonaparte, Napoleon, xv–xvi, 73–74
Bondman, Matthew, 171
Borodin, Mikhail Markovich, 97
Boswell, James, 7
Bowser, Eileen, 159
Brathwaite, Kamau, 184
Broué, Pierre, 89
Brown, John, 48, 128
Brown, William Wells, 48
Buhle, Paul, 3, 4, 89, 104, 105, 114, 131
Bukharin, Nikolai, 96, 117
Bush, George, 165

Caesar, Julius, xx, 69
Cagney, James, 155
Cain, William, xxiv, 38–39, 41, 45
Callinicos, Alex, 114
Carby, Hazel, 52
Carlyle, Thomas, 5
Carpentier, Alejo, 20
Castoriadis, Cornelius, 101, 103, 104, 105, 122
Castro, Fidel, 76, 80, 85
Cayton, Horace, 36
Césiare, Aimé, 14, 38, 61, 78–79, 81, 143
Chaplin, Charles, 22, 144, 151, 152, 156, 158
Chaucer, Geoffrey, 42
Chevalier, Maurice, 22
Chilembwe, John, 83
Chopin, Frederic, 148
Christophe, Henri, 62, 74
Cipriani, Captain Arthur Andrew, 3, 4, 6–7
Clairveaux, General, 74
Clark, Kenneth, 185
Constantine, Learie, 3, 52, 181, 183
Cooper, James Fenimore, 3, 49–50
Cromwell, Oliver, 70
Cudjoe, Selwyn, xxiv, 4–5
Cumberbatch, Stephen, 140
Cunard, Nancy, 170

d'Auberteuil, Hilliard, xxi
Davis, Angela, 139
Davis, Bette, 150
de Boissiere, R. A. C., 5, 12
Debord, Guy, 103–04
Defoe, Daniel, 41
de Heredia, José Maria, 14
De Lisle, Leconte, 13
DeMille, Cecil B., 157
Derain, André, 170
Derrida, Jacques, 101–07
Dessalines, Jean-Jacques, 62, 74–75
Dhondy, Farrukh, 49
Dickens, Charles, 40
Dietrich, Marlene, 149
Douglass, Frederick, 47, 57, 60, 137

Dostoyevsky, Fyodor, 15, 46
Drake, St. Clair, 36
D'Souza, Dinesh, 11–12
Du Bois, W. E. B., 11, 13, 47, 52, 55–56, 59, 67, 81, 82, 126, 128, 130–31, 133, 134, 137, 141, 163, 170, 175
Dumas, Alexandre, 14
Dunayevskaya, Raya, 55, 104, 107, 109–12, 114, 115, 117, 139, 159–60, 172, 186
Dunning, William A., 56, 57
Dupuy, Alex, 74
Dutt, R. Palme, 88

Einstein, Albert, 11
Eisenstein, Sergei, 151, 158
Eliot, T. S., 14–15, 144
Ellison, Ralph, xviii, 36, 43, 163, 175
Emerson, Ralph Waldo, 48
Empson, William, 16
Engels, Friedrich, 55, 102, 108, 117, 118, 128, 129
Enmale, Richard, 59
Epstein, Jacob, 170
Evans, Frank, 26
Everett, Anna, 84

Fairbanks, Douglass, 22, 23
Farred, Grant, xxiv, 174, 181–82
Farrell, James T., 36
Faulkner, William, xiii, xvii, 68
Field, Marshall, 37
Flaubert, Gustave, 46
Florsheim, Clara, 37
Franco, Francisco, 65
Franklin, H. Bruce, xiv
Frazier, E. Franklin, 36
Frobenius, Leo, 170
Froude, James Anthony, 5, 13
Fukuyama, Francis, 103, 107

Galton, Francis, 9–10
Garrison, William Lloyd, 47, 48, 60
Garvey, Amy Ashwood, 131
Garvey, Marcus, 5, 76–77, 83, 134, 168
Ghandi, Mahatma, 6
Gilkes, Michael, 27
Gilroy, Paul, 106, 139
Glaberman, Martin, 37, 111, 115, 142, 186
Gomes, Albert, 5–6, 12, 26
Gomes, P. I., 140
Gorman, William, 111

Gould, Chester, 154
Grace, E. M., 180, 181
Grace, W. G., xxvi, 171, 180, 181
Gramsci, Antonio, 42, 144
Gray, Thomas, xviii
Gregoire, Abbé, 62
Grierson, Flora, 63
Griffith, D. W., xxvi, 144, 152
Griffith, Patrick, 139
Grimshaw, Anna, 52, 161, 169
Guillame, Paul, 170

Haley, Alex, 36
Hall, Stuart, 177
Hamilton, Cynthia, 16–17, 30
Harland, Sidney, 8–12
Harris, Wilson, xx, xxv, 15, 38, 42, 47, 49, 78, 139, 152, 184
Hawthorne, Nathaniel, xiv
Hayworth, Rita, 159
Hazlitt, William, 40
Hegel, G. W. F., xxv, xxvi, 16, 55, 103, 105–23, 142, 143, 151, 186
Heidegger, Martin, 103
Hemingway, Ernest, 152
Henry, O., 18
Henry, Paget, 105
Herrnstein, Richard, 9, 10
Higginson, Thomas Wentworth, 48
Hill, Robert, 52, 53, 88, 144–45, 151, 160, 161
Hitler, Adolph, 90, 97–98
Holloway, Marvin, 80
hooks, bell, 139
Howe, Irving, 108
Hume, David, 39
Hussein, Saddam, 165

Ibsen, Henrik, 18
Iturbi, José, 148
Ivy, James W., 64

Jackson, Andrew, 47, 168
Jackson, George, xiii, xiv
Jacobs, Harriet, xviii
Jakobson, Roman, 104
James, Cyril Lionel Robert, published works of: "Abyssinia and the Imperialists," 131–32; "Africans and Afro-Caribbeans: A Personal View," 174–75; *American Civilization*, 22–23, 45–50, 58, 148–69, 172; "The American People in

the World," 50; "The Artist in the Caribbean," 39; *At the Rendezvous of Victory*, 14–15, 16, 17, 22–23, 40, 134–36, 141, 185; *Balance Sheet*, 114, 120; *Beyond a Boundary*, xiv, xx, xxi, xxii, 4, 76, 145, 161, 169–86; *The Black Jacobins*, xv, xix, xxi, xxii, xxiii, 52, 55, 56, 59, 61–80, 81–82, 84, 86, 87, 88, 93, 98, 107, 114, 128, 132, 133, 136, 137, 140, 173; "Black Studies and the Contemporary Student," 56; "Capitalist Society and the War," 52; *The Case for West Indian Self-Government*, 7, 53, 127; *C. L. R. James and Revolutionary Marxism*, 47, 51, 56, 57, 59, 61, 90, 133; *C. L. R. James's Eightieth Birthday Lectures*, 75; *C. L. R. James on the "Negro Question,"* xxvii, 35–36, 136–37; *The C. L. R. James Reader*, xx, 3, 14, 18–20, 23–24, 39, 43, 45, 54, 56, 107, 127, 130, 132, 133, 146, 147, 151, 152, 153, 154; *Cricket*, 35, 169, 172, 173, 175, 177, 184; "Dialectical Materialism and the Fate of Humanity," 54, 107; "Discovering Literature in Trinidad," 5, 7; "Discussions with Trotsky," 134–36; *Education, Propaganda, Agitation*, xxvii, 131; "The Elemental Urge to Socialism," 137; *Every Cook Can Govern and What Is Happening Every Day*, 124; *Facing Reality*, 101, 102, 103, 104, 105, 109, 123, 124, 187; "From Jobs to the Struggle for Socialism," 125–26; *The Future in the Present*, 39, 49, 140, 145, 169–70; "The Gathering Forces," 111–12; "Germany and European Civilization," 105; "The Haitian Maroons," 51; *A History of Negro Revolt*, 47, 53, 77, 80–87, 131, 133, 135, 139–40; "The Intelligence of the Negro," 7–12; *The Invading Socialist Society*, 109, 117, 118, 123; "La Divina Pastora," 18–20, 24; *Letters on Organization*, xxiv, xxv, xxvi–xxvii, 186–87; *The Life of Captain Cipriani*, 3, 6–7, 53, 127; "The Making of the Caribbean People," 13, 14, 16, 50; *Mariners, Renegades and Castaways*, xiv, xvi, xix–xx, xxi–xxiii, 34, 37–38, 39, 44–46, 114, 159–60, 161–62, 171, 185; "Michel Maxwell Philip," 4, 5; *Minty Alley*, 3, 16, 17, 24, 25, 26–35, 53, 171, 185; *Modern Politics*, xv, 92–93, 124, 143, 144, 146, 148–49, 151, 185; "A National Purpose for Caribbean Peoples," 14–15; "Negro History Week and the Workers," 56–57; *The Negro's Fight*, 35–36; Nkrumah and the Ghana Revolution, 86, 93, 125, 126, 132, 137–38, 140, 172; *Notes on Dialectics*, xxiii, 95, 106–23, 142, 172; "Notes on Hamlet," 43; *The Old World and the New*, 40–43; "The Olympia Statues, Picasso's *Guernica* and the Frescoes of Michelangelo in the Capella Paolina," 145, 169–70; *One Tenth of the Nation*, 128; "On Federation," 17; "On Wilson Harris," 42, 49; *Party Politics in the West Indies*, 122, 134, 140; "The Philosophy of History and Necessity," 52; "Popular Art and the Cultural Tradition," 146–48; "Production for the Sake of Production," 108, 140–41, 142; "Resolution on the International Situation," 121; "The Resolution of the Minority," 136–37; "Resolution on the Russian Question," 118, 119; "Revolution," 17–18, 24; "Revolution and the Negro," 61, 133; "The Revolutionary Answer to the Negro Problem in the United States," 57, 130, 132–33; "The Social Ties in the Factory," 123; *Special Delivery*, 87, 143, 148, 149, 150, 160, 169; "Speech on Our Negro Resolution," 57–59; *Spheres of Existence*, 5, 13, 21, 42, 49, 51, 52; "The Star that Would Not Shine," 21, 22–23, 24, 150; "Stalinism and Negro History," 47, 55–56, 59–60; *State Capitalism and World Revolution*, 109, 117, 119, 120–21; "Triumph," 6, 23–25, 27; "Trotsky's Place in History," 52, 90; "Turner's Prosperity," 21; *Walter Rodney and the Question of Power*, 81; "The West Indian Intellectual," 5, 13; "Whitman and Melville," 43; *World Revolution*, 52, 87–99, 102, 107, 113, 121

Johnson, James Weldon, 9, 11, 48
Joyce, James, 15, 152
Juarès, H., 71

Kadalie, Clements, 83
Kaiser, E., 58
Kamenev, Lev, 92
Kant, Immanuel, 11
Kelley, Robin D. G., 67, 83, 86

Kenyatta, Jomo, 77, 131
Kimbangu, Simon, 83
King, Martin Luther, 139
Kojéve, Alexandre, 103

La Guerre, John Gaffar, 131, 133
Lake, Veronica, 159
Lamming, George, xx, 12, 13, 15, 47, 184
La Rose, John, 144
Larsen, Neil, 152
Lazarus, Neil, 177
Leclerc, General, 74
Lee, Grace. *See* Boggs, Grace Lee
Lefebvre, M. Georges, 32
Leibnitz, Gottfried Wilhelm, 112
Lenin, V. I., 54–55, 86, 87, 90–99, 102–23, 125, 126, 128
Levi, Darrell E., 37
Lévi-Strauss, Claude, 56
Libertas, Bayou de, 68
Lincoln, Abraham, 57–58
Lipchitz, Jacques, 170
Lloyd, Harold, 22, 155
Locke, Alain, 170
Logan, Rayford, 36, 64
Lopez, Consuelo, xxvi
L'Ouverture, Toussaint, xiii, xv–xxii, xxvi, 9–10, 49, 61–80, 81–82, 92, 94, 122, 125, 169
Lukács, Georg, 144, 177
Luxemburg, Rosa, 55
Lyotard, Jean-François, 103, 106, 107

McLemee, Scott, 113, 114
Makonnen, Ras, 131
Mandela, Nelson, 138
Marcuse, Herbert, 104, 177
Marx, Karl, xx, 14, 39, 40, 41, 44–55, 56, 65–66, 95, 101–23, 125, 126, 128–30, 131, 137, 146, 149, 186
Matisse, Henri, 170
Mays, Willie, 144
Melville, Herman, xiii, xiv, xv, xvi, xix–xx, xxi, xv, xxvi, 18, 34, 37–38, 41, 43–47, 48, 49, 50, 159–60
Mendes, Alfred, 5, 8, 11–12, 19, 23, 26
Mentor, E. V., 62
Mentor, Ralph, 7
Michelangelo, Buonarroti, 145
Milton, John, 14
Modigliani, Amedeo, 170
Morehead, Agnes, 153

Morrison, Toni, 38, 47
Munroe, Ian, 23
Murdoch, H. Adlai, 21, 28
Murray, Charles, 9, 10
Myrdal, Gunnar, 57

Naipaul, V. S., 16, 78, 174, 175
Needham, Anuradha Dingwaney, 62–63, 132
Newton, Huey P., 139
Newton, Isaac, 11
Nietzsche, Friedrich, 103
Nixon, Richard, 162
Nkrumah, Kwame, 77–78, 85, 86, 125, 126, 132, 137–38
Nyerere, Julius, 84, 86, 92

O'Brien, E. J., 18
Olson, Charles, 37
O'Neill, Eugene, xviii
Orwell, George, 61
Oxaal, Ivar, 114

Padmore, George, 76–78, 79, 81, 131
Paine, Freddy, 186
Paine, Lyman, 186
Parris, D. Elliott, 16, 23, 28
Perse, Saint-John, 14
Philip, Michel Maxwell, 4
Phillips, Wendell, 48–50, 57, 69–70, 71–72
Picasso, Pablo, 144, 145, 148–49, 169–71
Pickford, Mary, 22, 23
Pitt, William, 71
Plekhanov, Georgi Valentinovich, 117
Pliny, 12
Poe, Edgar Allan, xiv
Postgate, Raymond, 88–89
Pound, Ezra, 14–15, 144, 170
Pyne-Timothy, Helen, 16, 19

Ramchand, Kenneth, 24, 26
Ranjitsinhji, Kumar Shri, 171
Rawick, George, 111
Raynal, Abbé, xxii, 65, 66, 69
Reagan, Ronald, 21, 167
Redding, Saunders, 36
Reid, Vic, 78
Ricardo, David, 143
Richardson, Al, 89, 90
Rimbaud, Arthur, 46, 152
Robeson, Paul, 187
Robespierre, Maximilien, 74

Robinson, Cedric, 65, 67, 114, 131
Robinson, Edwin Arlington, xiii, xvi, xviii, xix
Rodney, Walter, 81, 84, 132
Roosevelt, Franklin Delano, 109, 163
Ross, Andrew, 152, 162
Rukeyser, Muriel, xx
Russell, Bertrand, 146

Said, Edward, 104
St. Hill, Wilton, 183
Saint John, 143
Saint Matthew, 171
Salkey, Andrew, 144–45
Samaroo, Brinsley, 6, 7
Sander, Reinhard, 7, 23
Sartre, Jean Paul, xxv, 152
Saussure, Ferdinand de, 106
Shakespeare, William, xv, xix, 11, 14, 38, 39, 40, 41–43, 184
Shange, Ntozake, xx, 38
Shelley, Percy Bysshe, 143
Shostakovitch, Dmitri, 98
Silone, Ignazio, 146
Singer, Phil, 187
Singham, A. W., 54–55
Sitwell, Edith, 38
Socrates, xiii
Souvarine, Boris, 53
Spanos, William, 37–38, 44
Spengler, Oswald, 53
Spivak, Gayatri, 106, 108
Stalin, Josef, 51, 54, 65, 89–99, 102, 118–23
Stanwyck, Barbara, 153
Stein, Gertrude, 170
Stevens, Thaddeus, 57
Stewart, John, 23, 24, 33–34
Stollmeyer, Hugh, 5, 12
Sturges, Preston, 158–59
Styron, William, xviii
Surin, Kenneth, xxiv-xxv
Swanson, Gloria, 22
Swift, Jonathan, 15

Thackeray, William Makepeace, xx, 12, 13, 38, 40, 41, 171
Thelwell, Michael, 38
Thomas, Jacob, 4, 13
Thoreau, Henry David, 48
Tolson, Melvin B., xiv, 16, 36, 170
Tolstoy, Leo, 184

Trotsky, Leon, xxiv, 52, 55, 88, 89–99, 103, 109, 113–23, 125, 128, 134–36, 166, 177, 186, 187
Tubman, Harriet, 57
Turner, Lou, 110–12
Turner, Nat, xvii, xviii, xix, xx, 47, 83
Twain, Mark, xiv

Utrillo, Maurice, 170

Van Luschan, Felix, 170
Vesey, Denmark, 47

Walcott, Clyde, 184
Walcott, Derek, 38
Walker, Alice, xiv, 38
Walker, David, 47
Walker, Margaret, 35
Wallace, Henry, 58
Warburg, Frederick, 88
Ward, Joshua E., 6–7
Webb, Constance, 3, 4, 14, 36–37, 39, 60, 87, 148, 149, 150, 160, 169
Webber, A. R. F., 4–5
Weber, Samuel, 116–17
Weir, Stanley, 4
West, Cornel, 139
Whitlock, Gillian, 12, 24, 27–28
Whitman, Walt, xx, xxv, 6, 38, 43–44, 46, 48, 160
Wickham, John, 26, 27, 35
Wideman, John Edgar, xviii
Wilberforce, Wilber, 71
Williams, Eric, xv, xxi, 52, 56, 71, 122, 124
Williams, Patricia J., 55
Williams, Sherley Anne, xviii
Williams, William Carlos, xxvii, 14, 42
Winter, Sylvia, 19, 25, 28
Wittgenstein, Ludwig, 105
Woolf, Leonard, 7, 127
Woolf, Virginia, 7, 127
Worcester, Kent, xxv–xxvi
Wordsworth, William, 14, 144
Worrell, Frank, 173
Wright, Richard, xiii, xviii, 35–36, 160

Yerkes, Robert M., 10–11

Zhdanov, Andre Aleksandrovich, 122
Zinoviev, Grigori Yeyseyevich, 92, 96, 117

www.ingramcontent.com/pod-product-compliance
Lightning Source LLC
Chambersburg PA
CBHW030621230426
43661CB00053B/2099